THE RE-CREATION OF LANDSCAPE

JAMES A. W. HEFFERNAN

THE RE-CREATION
OF LANDSCAPE

A Study of Wordsworth, Coleridge,

Constable, and Turner

**PUBLISHED FOR DARTMOUTH COLLEGE
BY UNIVERSITY PRESS OF NEW ENGLAND**
Hanover and London, 1984

UNIVERSITY PRESS OF NEW ENGLAND

BRANDEIS UNIVERSITY

BROWN UNIVERSITY

CLARK UNIVERSITY

UNIVERSITY OF CONNECTICUT

DARTMOUTH COLLEGE

UNIVERSITY OF NEW HAMPSHIRE

UNIVERSITY OF RHODE ISLAND

TUFTS UNIVERSITY

UNIVERSITY OF VERMONT

Printed in the United States of America

LIBRARY OF CONGRESS CATALOGING IN PUBLICATION DATA

Heffernan, James A. W.
   The re-creation of landscape.

   Bibliography: p.
   Includes index.
   1. Romanticism—Great Britain.   2. English poetry—
19th century—History and criticism.   3. Landscape in
literature.   4. Landscape painting—19th century—Great
Britain.   5. Wordsworth, William, 1770–1850—Criticism
and interpretation.   6. Coleridge, Samuel Taylor, 1772–
1834—Criticism and interpretation.   7. Constable, John,
1776–1837.   8. Turner, J. M. W. (Joseph Mallord William),
1775–1851.   9. Literature and art—Great Britain.

I. Dartmouth College.   II. Title.
PR575.L27H4   1985   821′.7′09145   84-40302
ISBN 0-87451-312-X

For Nancy

Painting and Poetry, flowing from the same fount mutually by vision, constantly comparing Poetic allusions by natural forms in one and applying forms found in nature to the other, meandering into streams by application, which reciprocally improve, reflect, and heighten each other's beauties like . . . mirrors.

—J. M. W. TURNER

Could the histories of all the fine arts be compared, we should find in them many striking analogies.

—JOHN CONSTABLE

CONTENTS

LIST OF ILLUSTRATIONS

All illustrations follow page 138

1. J.M.W. Turner, *Buttermere Lake* (1798).
   Tate Gallery, London.

2. William Kent-N. Tardieu, *Spring* (1730).
   Engraving. Houghton Library, Harvard University.

3. Claude Lorrain, *Landscape: Hagar and the Angel* (1646).
   National Gallery, London.

4. John Constable, *Dedham Vale* (1802).
   Victoria and Albert Museum, London.

5. John Constable, *Dedham Vale* (1828).
   National Gallery of Scotland, Edinburgh.

6. John Constable, *The Hay Wain* (1821).
   National Gallery, London.

7. John Constable, *Full-scale Study for "The Leaping Horse"*
   (1824–25).
   Victoria and Albert Museum, London.

8. Jacques-Louis David, *Napoleon Crossing the Alps* (1799).
   Musée Nationale du Chateau de Malmaison.

9. John Constable, *Salisbury Cathedral from the Meadows* (1831).
   Lord Ashton of Hyde.

10. David Lucas (after John Constable), *Old Sarum: First Plate, 1830*
    (from *English Landscape Scenery*, London, 1830).
    Engraving. Yale Center for British Art, New Haven.

11. John Constable, *Landscape Sketch: Hadleigh Castle* (?1828–29).
    Tate Gallery, London.

12. John Constable, *The Cenotaph at Coleorton* (1823).
    Victoria and Albert Museum, London.

13. John Constable, *The Cenotaph at Coleorton* (1836).
    National Gallery, London.

14. J.M.W. Turner, *The Fifth Plague of Egypt* (1800).
    Indianapolis Museum of Art.

ACKNOWLEDGMENTS

 THE IDEA of writing this book was long ago suggested to me by the Turner exhibition which Lawrence Gowing and Monroe Wheeler mounted at New York's Museum of Modern Art in 1966. Since that time, I have incurred debts to many others: to Graham Reynolds, Keeper of the Department of Prints & Drawings and Paintings at the Victoria and Albert Museum; to Sir John Rothenstein; to Leslie Parris of the Tate Gallery and Ian Fleming-Williams, who have both generously shared with me their expert knowledge of Constable; to the courteous and efficient staffs of the British Library, the Department of Manuscripts, and the Department of Prints and Drawings at the British Museum. For many personal kindnesses during my periods of research in London I am also grateful to David and Mary Walton, to Sally and Jeremy Roberts, and especially to David Lea.

A Dartmouth College Faculty Fellowship enabled me to begin work on this book, and two Dartmouth college Humanities Development Grants helped me to complete it. In addition, the Dartmouth Research Committee kindly underwrote the cost of typing and of reproducing pictures.

It is a pleasure to thank those who have read parts or all of this manuscript at various stages of its development and who have graciously offered encouragement as well as detailed and specific advice. They include Ronald Paulson, Morris Eaves, George Landow, John Dixon Hunt, E. D. H. Johnson, Karl Kroeber, Jean Hagstrum, W. J. T. Mitchell, Louis Cornell, Sally Cornell, and my Dartmouth colleagues Louis Renza and James Cox. I have also profited from questions raised and suggestions made by various individuals at institutions where I have lectured on the material in this book: at Princeton, Rutgers, University of California at Berkeley, University of Chicago, University College (London), University of Pennsylvania, Northwestern University, UCLA, and—on two occasions—at the Wordsworth Summer School in Grasmere. Among those whose comments proved particularly useful are Peter Thorslev, Paul Sheats, and Fred Burwick.

Portions of this book have been previously published elsewhere in different form. Yale University Press has kindly allowed me to use material from "The English Romantic Perception of Color," which appeared as a chapter in *Images of Romanticism*, ed. Karl Kroeber and William Walling (1978), 133–48. Also, the Associated University Presses has allowed me to base two chapters of this book on essays that have appeared in *Bucknell Review*: "Reflections on Reflections in English Romantic Poetry and Painting" (Fall 1978, 15–37) and "Wordsworth, Coleridge, and Turner: The Geometry of the Infinite" (1984).

The manuscript of this book was expertly typed by Barbara Cunningham and Deborah Hodges, and Nancy Herington helped me to compile the index. To all three I am grateful.

My greatest debt is to my wife Nancy, who has helped to make this book possible in more ways than I can name, and who richly deserves the dedication.

Hanover, N.H., May 1984

PREFACE

THIS STUDY originates from the fact that during the last quarter of the eighteenth century in England, two major poets of landscape appeared at the same time as two major landscape painters. Wordsworth, Coleridge, Turner, and Constable were all born between 1770 and 1776, and each of them grew up to practice the art of landscape: to recreate the life of natural objects in pictures or in words. The differences among them are at least as sharp and striking, of course, as the differences between the arts in which they worked. Precisely because each of them was original, each formulated a style that is decisively his own. The naturalistic, understated way in which Wordsworth tells the story of Michael is hardly the way in which Coleridge's ancient mariner tells his supernatural "Rime," and the visionary fire of a picture like Turner's *Slavers* is a world away (in every sense) from the dewy glitter of Constable's naturalistic *Hay Wain*.[1] We can nevertheless identify the points at which these four figures converge, just as we can say what makes six different major poets "romantic," what Wordsworth's "Michael" has in common with his "Intimations" ode, or what Turner's *Buttermere* has in common with his *Slavers*. The tie that binds the sometimes very different works of a single poet or a single painter invites us to consider the more complicated ties that bind the works of different poets, of different painters, or of men who work in different arts. These four men are bound by ties of place, time, and inclination. All British, all coming of age about 1800, they all also wrought significant changes in our perception of landscape. I believe we can learn something of value from comparing the ways in which they re-created it.

Previous studies of English romantic poetry and painting have focused on one or two major figures.[2] This one takes in four, but it does not pre-

1. "The one all heat, the other humidity" is what a contemporary said of Turner and Constable; see Constable *JCC* 3: 39.
2. Notable examples are Russell Noyes, *Wordsworth and the Art of Landscape* (1968), Karl Kroeber, *Romantic Landscape Vision: Constable and Wordsworth* (1975), and Ronald Paulson, *Literary Landscape: Turner and Constable* (1982). I feel bound to say a special word here about Paulson's fine book, which aims chiefly to show how the elements of

tend to encompass many others. In examining the work of Wordsworth,
Coleridge, Constable, and Turner, I have made some effort to indicate
what came before them in their respective arts, what attitudes toward
landscape they inherited and challenged, what distinguishes the verbal
landscapes of Wordsworth and Coleridge from those of Dyer and Thomson and the graphic landscapes of Turner and Constable from those of
Wilson and Gainsborough. I have also touched on the poetry and painting of their contemporaries—on the poetry of Blake, Shelley, and Byron,
and on the painting of figures such as Girtin and de Loutherbourg. But I
have made no effort to survey all the poetry and painting of landscape in
this period; I have concentrated instead on just four major figures.

In re-creating landscape, these four figures could not simply express
an unmediated response to a primordial "nature," however much any one
of them might have wished to believe that he was her first-born birth. By
the end of the eighteenth century, landscape was not a natural phenomenon but a cultural one, something jointly created by the triangulated arts
of painting, poetry, and landscape gardening. To re-create landscape,
therefore, poets and painters had to re-create the arts of landscape, and
inevitably to challenge and redefine the traditional "sisterhood" of the
arts. Chapter 1 explains how this sisterhood was strained: how romantic
poets repudiated the notion that poetry should make pictures with words
and insisted on its intellectual freedom from visible form; how romantic
painters came to resent the expectation that they should illustrate poetry,
should represent the "pregnant moment" of a poetic or historical narrative that literature alone could explain in full. Yet a crucial part of my
argument in chapter 1—and in the book as a whole—is that in the very
act of declaring their independence of each other, the romantic poets and
painters reveal a deeper and more subtle relation between their respective arts.

The remaining chapters explore aspects of this relation. Chapter 2
treats the displacement of history in works such as Wordsworth's "Tin-

history painting and iconography—of traditionally "literary," emblematic, or allegorical
painting—subtly survive even when transformed or suppressed in landscapes that may
seem purely visual. Declining to seek or draw analogies between painting and poetry
(though he touches occasionally on romantic poetry), Paulson connects Turner and Constable not so much with romantic literature as with the history of literary landscape painting, which he now believes can be extended beyond the point at which "emblem" gives
way to "expression." By contrast, the present book directly compares romantic poetry
and painting.

tern Abbey" and Constable's *Hay Wain*, where the weight and grandeur of public history is at once invoked and set aside by the private history of an individual's relation to landscape or by the "natural history" of a rural day. Study of this concern with private history then leads to one of the major theoretical questions prompted by any comparison of literature and the visual arts: to what extent can pictures represent time? To answer this question, I compare the "spots of time" in Wordsworth's *Prelude* with what I call the temporalized space of Constable's *Cornfield*, which subtly juxtaposes the painter's past and present selves. This autobiographical reading of Constable's picture leads in turn to the central question of chapter 3: How far does romantic painting share with romantic poetry the capacity to internalize a prospect, to make a landscape represent the mind?

Chapters 4 to 6 explore three distinct elements that powerfully inform romantic poetry and painting alike: their self-referential concern with the language and processes of transformation; their pursuit of what I call the geometry of the infinite; and their preoccupation with reflections in water, which serve not only to integrate earth and sky in a harmonious totality but also to symbolize the very act of artistic re-creation. More specifically, chapter 4 shows how the languages of romantic poetry and painting transformed the natural world even as they reenacted the transformations naturally wrought by atmosphere. Yet for all the atmospheric indistinctness that we commonly associate with romanticism, chapter 5 goes on to show that linearity was crucial to the romantic vision of landscape: that poets and painters had to establish boundaries in order to cross them, that they caught from evanescent phenomena the permanence of implied geometrical forms, and that paradoxically, they used such forms to represent both serene transcendence and vital interaction, pure rationality and passionate subjectivity, finitude and infinitude. Finally, chapter 6 shows how the romantic poets and painters revalued the significance of reflections in water, which they regarded no longer as insubstantial copies of real things but rather as embodiments of brilliance, symbols of tranquillity, agents of elemental integration, and representatives of representation itself.

For the most part, the method of this book is synoptic rather than contrapuntal. Though I sometimes compare a particular painting with a particular poem or passage, I do not try to establish a point-for-point series of comparisons. Nor do I try to prove that particular poems influenced particular pictures, or vice versa.[3] Instead, I approach the painting and poetry through gradually unfolding categories of comparison, through conceptual frameworks largely created by analysis of what the painters and poets themselves say about their respective arts. In the process, I aim to show how the synoptic study of English romantic poetry and painting can lead to a new understanding of English romanticism as a whole.

A final word on documentation. To keep footnotes to a minimum, I use the new MLA style of citation, with page references given parenthetically in the text. The author's name is given in parentheses only if it has not already been mentioned in connection with the material cited or if it is needed for clarification. Titles are given—in short or abbreviated form—only when I have used more than one work by the same author. Complete information on all references, including abbreviations, will be found after each author's name in the Reference List at the end of the book.

3. The whole question of influence is treated in the Appendix, where I reach negative conclusions.

THE RE-CREATION OF LANDSCAPE

CHAPTER 1

LANDSCAPE AND THE TRIANGULATION OF THE ARTS

 IN WORDSWORTH'S "Expostulation and Reply," which first appeared in the *Lyrical Ballads* of 1798, an anxious promoter of book learning accuses the poet of looking at landscape with utterly uninstructed eyes:

> You look round on your Mother Earth
> As if she for no purpose bore you;
> As if you were her first-born birth
> And none had lived before you.

The irony of this accusation becomes clear when the speaker goes on to recommend the light of books—"the light bequeathed / To beings else forlorn and blind" and to urge that the poet "drink the spirit breathed / From dead men to their kind." Figuratively, of course, the speaker is urging the poet to read texts that have survived their authors; but literally and unwittingly, he is asking the poet to inhale the vaporous stench that passes from one corpse to another—from dead men to their kind. The bibliophile's attack on the poet's ignorance thus becomes an unwitting tribute to the Adamic freshness of his vision. When we move from "Expostulation and Reply" to its companion piece, "The Tables Turned," the metaphorical light of books gives way to the actual, visible light of the setting sun shedding its yellow luster through all the long green fields, and the barren leaves of ancient texts are displaced by the green and living leaves of the vernal wood. The poet expresses an original relation to nature in words that have recovered their original, prefigurative relation to things. Re-created in such language, nature becomes—momentarily at least—the paradise that Wordsworth later promised to unveil in the *Recluse*:

> Paradise, and groves
> Elysian, Fortunate Fields—like those of old
> Sought in the Atlantic Main—why should they be

> A history only of departed things,
> Or a mere fiction of what never was?
> For the discerning intellect of Man,
> When wedded to this goodly universe
> In love and holy passion, shall find these
> A simple produce of the common day.
>
> (*PW* 5: 4)

This desire to recover and more especially to represent an original or Adamic relation to nature was just as strong in Constable as it was in Wordsworth. "When I sit down to make a sketch from nature," said Constable on one occasion, "the first thing I try to do is, *to forget that I have ever seen a picture*" (Leslie 279). What Constable sought to express not only in his pencil sketches but in his oil sketches and in the large-scale oil studies of his later years was the intensity of a direct, unmediated apprehension of landscape. In the very last of the lectures on landscape painting which he gave during the final year of his life, he said:

We are all of us no doubt placed in a paradise here if we choose to make it such. All of us must have felt ourselves in the same place and situation as that of our first parent, when on opening his eyes the beauty and magnificence of external nature broke on his astonished sight intensely. (*JCD* 72–73)

Constable then quotes Milton's description of what Adam saw and felt when he first awakened in paradise (*Paradise Lost* 8. 257–77). Yet in quoting Milton, Constable not only illustrates the impact of an original revelation; he also situates himself within the history of landscape as a cultural phenomenon. Horace Walpole believed that Milton's account of paradise inspired the whole development of English landscape gardening in the eighteenth century (Malins 1). Departing from the geometrical formality of a typical seventeenth-century garden, Milton's paradise is "a happy rural seat of various view," a place of natural freedom and contrast, of bright open fields and shaded bowers, of flowers planted not "in Beds and curious Knots" but in wild profusion (*Paradise Lost* 4. 132–42, 242–8). These are the features Walpole found in the celebrated mid-century gardens of Henry Hoare at Stourhead and George Lyttleton at Hagley. And whether or not Walpole is right, however tenuous the links between Milton's Eden and the landscapes fashioned by Hoare and Lyttleton, we can hardly begin to understand how the romantic poets and painters re-created landscape without first considering just what kind of landscape they inherited.

This was not simply the ground on which they walked and worked but a complex phenomenon jointly created in the eighteenth century by the arts of poetry, painting, and landscape gardening. Because each of these three arts was distinguished by its own point of departure and yet power-fully drawn to the other two, I speak of them as triangulated. My first aim in this chapter is to show briefly how these three arts together defined landscape in the eighteenth century, and particularly how they collabo-rated in the genesis of the picturesque. I shall then consider some of the ways in which the arts of landscape were re-created in the romantic pe-riod, and how the sisterhood of the arts was reconceived.

THE ARTS OF LANDSCAPE IN THE EIGHTEENTH CENTURY

The history of landscape as a cultural phenomenon in England be-gins with painting. Elizabeth Manwaring exaggerates when she says that landscape was "fully established . . . as a separate and important branch of painting" by 1640 (v), but by the first decade of the eigh-teenth century, the educated English public had definitely begun to de-velop a taste for certain kinds of landscape painting: in particular for the delicately harmonized classical vistas of Claude Lorrain (1600–1682), for the wild and stormy scenes of Salvator Rosa (1615–1673), and for the erudite and austerely executed works of Nicolas Poussin (1594?–1665). The widespread dissemination of prints in the eigh-teenth century made these three names virtually synonymous with land-scape. The word *landscape* itself—originally spelled *landskip*—was at first used as a technical term for a picture representing natural inland scenery; then it was also used to mean a particular tract of land that could be seen from one point of view, *as if* it were a picture; and finally it came to mean the whole of natural scenery.[1] For much of the eigh-teenth century, landscape was not so much a natural object as a way of looking at natural objects, or just as often a way of representing them in pictures or words. In 1705, for instance, Addison could speak of comparing "the Natural Face of the Country with the Landskips that the Poets have given us of it" (preface to *Italy*, quoted in *OED*).

By the end of the eighteenth century, however, the clear distinction Addison saw between nature and the landscapes of art—whether ver-bal or pictorial—had begun to melt in the heat of widespread enthusi-

1. See the *OED* and Barrell, *Idea of Landscape* 1–2.

asm for the picturesque, which gave travellers something culturally respectable to look for in natural scenery. The picturesque parts of nature, wrote Payne Knight, are

those which nature has formed in the style and manner appropriate to painting; and the eye, that has been accustomed to see these happily displayed and embellished by art, will relish them more in nature. . . . The spectator, having his mind enriched with the embellishments of the painter . . . applies them, by the spontaneous association of ideas, to the natural objects presented to his eye, which thus acquire ideal and imaginary beauties; that is, beauties, which are not felt by the organic sense of vision; but by the intellect and imagination through that sense. (154)

The picturesque, therefore, was something created by the observer out of elements presented to the eye; something initiated by nature, which forms objects "in the style and manner appropriate to painting," and completed by the viewer, who creates a picture by associating what he sees in nature with what he has seen on canvas.

Because the picturesque gave travellers a way of looking, it aesthetically legitimized not just scenery in general but a class of objects that might otherwise be considered ugly or even morally objectionable, such as ruins and unkempt farms. William Gilpin, the peripatetic painter and clergyman who from 1782 to 1804 published seven works on the picturesque features of British scenery, said that the picturesque eye looks "with disgust" at cultivated fields and seeks instead a nature "untamed by art, and bursting wildly into all its irregular forms."[2] The picturesque was therefore closely allied to the sublime, the aesthetic category that Edmund Burke had specifically contrasted to the beautiful in his *Philosophical Enquiry* of 1757. Insofar as sublimity and beauty could be predicated of natural objects, the word *beautiful* for Burke meant smooth, polished, light, delicate, gracefully curved, comparatively small, and pleasurable; *sublime* meant vast, gloomy, rugged, jagged, and terrifying.[3] But since objects too small to be terrifying and too rough to be beautiful could fit neither of these categories, the word *pic-*

---

2. Gilpin, *Cumberland and Westmoreland* 2: 44. "Moral, and picturesque ideas," says Gilpin, "do not always coincide" (2: 44).

3. Burke 124. Though I am concerned for the moment with the external features of the sublime, Samuel H. Monk rightly notes that Burke's theory of the sublime depends not so much on the qualities of objects as on their psychological effect (98). I discuss the internality of the sublime in chapter 4.

turesque was specifically applied to them: to small-scale scenery marked by roughness, intricacy, and irregularity, full of sharp contrasts and a variety of tints (Price 82, 98–99).

This restricted meaning of the picturesque, however, coexisted with the much broader meaning articulated by Gilpin in 1768, when he defined the picturesque simply as "that peculiar kind of beauty, which is agreeable in a picture" (*Essay upon Prints* x). Given all that had been done in landscape painting by the middle of the eighteenth century, this definition encompassed a good deal. Even if we set aside the rich and various achievements of Breughel, Ruysdael, Rubens, and Rembrandt, the long-standing popularity of Rosa on the one hand and Lorrain on the other showed that what was "agreeable in a picture" could range from gracefulness to ruggedness, from gentle sunlit plains to dark and rocky steeps. In the familiar words of Thomson, then, the picturesque might well include "Whate'er Lorrain light-touched with softening hue, / Or savage Rosa dash'd, or learned Poussin drew."[4] In any case, *picturesque* was a verbal chameleon. Though Gilpin distinguished it from the beautiful (*Three Essays* 8), and though its association with roughness and irregularity gave it the coloration of the sublime, Gilpin himself insisted that the rules of the picturesque were rules of beauty. In his *Observations . . . on . . . Cumberland and Westmoreland* (1786), he says that he does not think satisfactory pictures can be made of any vast object—such as a huge lake or mountain—which is disproportionate to the scenery around it:

The mountains of Sweden, Norway, and other northern regions, are probably rather masses of hideous rudeness, than scenes of grandeur and proportion. Proportion, indeed, in all scenery is indisputably necessary; and unless the lake, and its correspondent mountains have this just relation to each other, they want the first principle of beauty.[5]

It might have been this very statement that led Coleridge to ask whether there was "a real Difference between the Picturesque & the Beautiful,"

4. Thomson, *Castle of Indolence* (1748) 1.38. "Savage Rosa" epitomized the sublime for eighteenth-century aestheticians, but it is symptomatic of the confusion surrounding the words *sublime, picturesque,* and *beautiful* that all three terms were applied to Rosa's *Landscape with Figures* in the early nineteenth century. "This sublime landscape," said a critic, "represents in part a wild forest, which is depicted with grandeur, and at the same time with a beautiful picturesque effect" (*Annals* 2: 235–36).

5. Gilpin, *Cumberland and Westmoreland* 1:3. On the aesthetic significance of mountains in the eighteenth century as a whole, see Nicolson, *Mountain Gloom.*

and to define the picturesque as a condition in which "the parts by their harmony produce an effect of a whole."[6]

Unfixed in its meaning, ubiquitously applied, and hovering somewhere in the space between pictures and natural scenery, the picturesque was just one manifestation of the extent to which nature and art became entangled in the eighteenth century, and specifically of the extent to which the experience of landscape—in the sense of natural scenery—was dominated by painting. But just as strong in its impact on the experience of landscape was the art of landscape gardening, where the commingling of art and nature sometimes approached the point of identity.

The line between nature and the art of gardening was clear enough at the beginning of the eighteenth century, when Shaftesbury voiced an irresistible urge to experience "all the horrid Graces of the *Wilderness* itself, as representing NATURE more, . . . and appear[ing] with the Magnificence beyond the formal Mockery of princely Gardens" (*Moralists* 2: 393–94). Even later in the century, the artificiality of gardening was perfectly clear to Joshua Reynolds, who firmly stated that "Gardening, as far as Gardening is an Art . . . is a deviation from nature," and therefore no fit subject for landscape painters, "who love to have recourse to Nature herself" (*D* 240). But as recent commentators have shown, the art of landscape gardening in eighteenth-century England was not so much one of deviation from nature as of accommodation to it: to its irregularity, its fluid life, its unpredictable twists and turns. In a sense, English landscapists sought to inscribe in the earth itself the Longinian principle that to achieve perfection, art must be disguised as nature.[7] At the beginning of the eighteenth century, art was only too apparent in the rigid geometrical regularity of French landscape gardening, paradigmatically exemplified by what André Lenôtre did at Versailles. In place of such "formal Mockery," as Shaftesbury called it, English landscapists beginning with William Kent (1684–1748) brought variety and flexibility to gardening: in short, made gardens more natural.

The kind of "nature" produced by any art is of course never identical

6. Coleridge, *NC* 1: 1755, and 2: 2012, f. 41ᵛ; *BL* 2: 309. Coleridge mentions Gilpin in a notebook entry of 1800 (*NC* 1: 760), well before either of the other notebook entries quoted here, and since Wordsworth owned the volume in which Gilpin made his pronouncement about proportion (Wordsworth, *LW* 1: 170, 227), Coleridge may have seen it.

7. I take the liberty of paraphrasing Boileau's translation of Longinus, which has itself been Englished thus: "Art is perfect just when it seems to be nature, and nature successful when the art underlies it unnoticed" (quoted in Malins viii).

with nature per se, the capitalized NATURE enshrined in Shaftesbury's rhapsodic prose. In the discourse from which I have just quoted, Reynolds rightly insists that a garden shorn of "every appearance of Art, or any traces of the footsteps of man . . . would be no longer a Garden" (*D* 240). By this criterion, the gardens of Kent stopped well short of capitulation to nature. Kent not only created vistas bordered by woods serving as Claudian coulisses or wing-screens; he also set temples and statuary in various places to guide the viewer along a route meant to be "readable"—that is, emblematic and hence intellectually significant.[8] But just as important, Kent broke up the straight lines of traditional formality in gardening. He replaced them with winding paths, and by means of the sunk fence, he literally removed the barrier that traditionally separated the garden from the surrounding countryside. "He leaped the fence," said Horace Walpole, "and saw that all nature was a garden."[9]

What kept the garden from turning wholly into nature was not only the ubiquitous appearance of temples and statuary but also the pervasive influence of landscape painting. Walpole was oversimplifying when he wrote that "the pencil of [Kent's] imagination bestowed all the arts of landscape on the scenes he handled" (4: 138). But the word "bestowed" calls to mind Cobham's estate at Stowe, where beginning in the 1730s Kent created a series of pictorially organized compositions (Malins 114). Significantly, it was while visiting Stowe in the 1740s that Gilpin conceived the picturesque method of looking at landscape as a sequence of changing vistas (Wilton, *TS* 31; Barbier 21–23). In its genesis, then, the picturesque was doubly artificial: a way of looking at scenery as if it were a landscape garden designed to resemble a picture.

We might say it was Gilpin rather than Kent who saw all nature as a garden. Yet to see it this way is of course to reverse the originating goal of eighteenth-century English landscaping, which was to make the garden more like nature. The conflict between the Shaftesburian lust for the wildness of a genuinely primitive nature and the connoisseur's love of a well-composed picture is in fact nowhere more evident than in the work of Gilpin himself. On the one hand, Gilpin says that the picturesque eye

8. See Paulson, *Emblem* 26, and J. R. Watson 30. John Dixon Hunt writes of "gardenist structure" and of "the covert design that the garden has upon those who explore it" (*Figure* 116, 118).

9. Quoted in Watson 16. The sunk fence, or "ha ha," was first used at Stowe by Charles Bridgeman, Kent's predecessor, but Bridgeman's designs were otherwise formal and symmetrical; see Malins 28–29.

seeks a nature "untamed by art, and bursting wildly into all its irregular forms." Yet on the other hand, Gilpin announced in the very first book of his *Observations* that he would examine nature "*by the rules of picturesque beauty* (*River Wye*, 1–2), and in applying these rules, Gilpin clearly seeks a nature tamed by art, a nature whose irregular forms have been carefully regulated by the principles of pictorial composition. What Gilpin typically sees in nature is not a ready-made picture but a picture that could *be* made—mentally or manually—from the raw materials offered to the eye. In the very book that contains the tribute to a nature "untamed by art," Gilpin says of northern England:

it cannot be supposed that every scene, which these countries present, is *correctly picturesque*. In such immense bodies of rough-hewn matter, many irregularities, many deformities, must exist, which a practised eye would wish to correct. Mountains are sometimes crowded—their sides are often bare, when contrast requires them to be wooded—promontories form the water boundary into acute angles—and bays are contracted into narrow points, instead of swelling into ample basins.

In all these cases, the imagination is apt to whisper, What glorious scenes might here be made, if these stubborn materials could yield to the judicious hand of art.[10]

Here Gilpin sounds like no one so much as "Capability" Brown (1715–83), who made no pretense of suppressing art for nature. According to one contemporary, Brown's "sole aim" was "to form scenes for the poet and the painter."[11] To this end, he cleared ground ruthlessly. Enlarging the relatively narrow vistas of Kent, he created wide open spaces: sweeping expanses of turf flanked with serpentine belts of wood; ground sloping gently to a river or lake; clumps of trees as wing-screens used to define a receding perspective; ground sloping gently to a river or lake reflecting the trees; and on the far side, ground rising to a distant hori-

10. Gilpin, *Cumberland and Westmoreland* 1: 3. Note also his comment on a voyage up the Thames: "All is beautiful, sylvan, and highly pleasing; . . . the whole is amusing, but not picturesque; it is not sufficiently divided into portions adapted to the pencil" (*Western Parts* 237). Gilpin reportedly said to William Mason, "I am so attached to my picturesque rules that if nature gets wrong, I cannot help putting her right" (quoted in Lindsay 233).

11. Pott 63–64. Brown himself actually stopped short of calling this his "sole aim." Gardening, he said, should "supply all the elegance and all the comforts which Mankind wants in the Country and (I will add) if right, be exactly fit for the owner, the Poet and the Painter" (quoted in Hunt, *Figure* 218).

zon. The result was called "many beautiful and picturesque scenes" (Malins 99; Pott 63–64).

Yet even as gardens were made to look like pictures, they also offered an alternative to pictorial structure. While a painting typically shows a large, extended scene from one fixed point of view, and while the traditional garden typically offered just one dominant prospect, John Dixon Hunt usefully notes that eighteenth-century gardens were often meant to be seen at close range and from many points of view, so that the experience of a garden was essentially one of submission to a process. Such an experience gave poets an alternative to painting as a model for the representation of landscape. "Poetry that is organized after the pattern of landscape gardens," says Hunt, "is characterized by its concern with movement through scenery, the 'kinema' not the prospect picture, the mysterious process of discovering what comes next to eye and mind rather than an apprehension of landscape at a distance" (*Figure* 228).

Though Hunt supports his thesis by pointing to the poetry that followed Thomson's *The Seasons*, the difference between pictorial and "gardenist" structure can actually be seen in *The Seasons* itself, the most important poem on landscape written in the eighteenth century. Introduced by "Winter" in 1726 and first published as a whole in 1730, *The Seasons* was a major treatment of the life and rhythm of the external world. At once and continuingly successful, it went through over two hundred editions by 1800 (Cohen, *Art of Discrimination* 173–85). Its descriptions of landscape were vivid enough to win the special admiration of both Turner and Constable, and it probably did more than any other poem of its time to create a public taste for the poetry of landscape. Significantly, it did so largely by representing landscape as if it were a series of pictures. Thomson himself referred to one section of "Spring" as a "landskip," meaning of course a verbalized landscape painting, and as Jean Hagstrum has shown, Thomson frequently took details for his descriptions not only from the naturalistic works of Lorraine and Rosa but also from the heroic landscape paintings of the High Renaissance and seventeenth-century baroque (257ff.). What he typically offers, therefore, is a spreading prospect dominated by a grand or triumphant personification, as in this description of a sunrise:

> But yonder comes the powerful king of day
> Rejoicing in the east. The lessening cloud,

> The kindling azure, and the mountain's brow
> Illumed with fluid gold, his near approach
> Betoken glad. Lo! now, apparent all,
> Aslant the dew-bright earth and coloured air,
> He looks in boundless majesty abroad,
> And sheds the shining day, that burnished plays
> On rocks, and hills, and towers, and wandering streams
> High-gleaming from afar.
>
> ("Summer," lines 81–90)

The alternative to this poetry of grand pictorial prospect is—as Hunt suggests—the poetry of exploration and investigation, of movement through a landscape of changing scenes. Occasionally Thomson offers such movement. In the revised version of "Spring," which he wrote during a visit to George Lyttleton's estate at Hagley in 1743, he imagines Lyttleton taking a meditative walk through Hagley Park. This imaginary or projected walk provides a succession of sights, sounds, and opportunities for reflection. Lyttleton silently steals through a dale of overhanging woods and shaggy rocks; he sees waters gush at close range "or gleam in lengthened vista through the trees"; he sits beneath shady oaks listening to "the herds, the flocks, the birds, / The hollow-whispering breeze, the plaint of rills"; he wanders philosophically to somber thoughts of Britain's past, present, and future; if his young wife Lucy is with him, he sees nature joyously in the light of their love; and finally he, or they, who are in any case addressed as "you,"

> gain the height, from whose fair brow
> The bursting prospect spreads immense around;
> And snatched o'er hill and dale, and wood and lawn,
> And verdant field, and darkening heath between,
> And villages embosomed soft in trees,
> And spiry towns by surging columns marked
> Of household smoke, your eye excursive roams—
> Wide-stretching from the Hall in whose kind haunt
> The hospitable Genius lingers still,
> To where the broken landscape, by degrees
> Ascending, roughens into rigid hills
> O'er which the Cambrian mountains, like far clouds
> That skirt the blue horizon, dusky rise.
>
> ("Spring," lines 950–62)

Thomson's account of a walk through Hagley thus concludes with a description of a supremely harmonious prospect.[12] But the prospect—grand as it is—is just one of the scenes that Thomson gives us. Insofar as he guides us through a succession of scenes in the park, he invites the inference that landscape gardening may have spurred the evolution of poetry from loco-descriptive pictorialism to romanticism, which—as Jay Appleton says—"summoned rational man back to the role of a participant in the events and processes of nature" (40). Certainly Thomson points in this direction. His imaginary account of what Lyttleton sees, hears, and feels in his progress through the park looks forward not only to Wordsworth's early *Evening Walk* but more importantly to Coleridge's "Lime-Tree Bower My Prison," where the temporarily crippled poet imagines an excursion taken by his friends through a shadowy "o'er-wooded" dell to a wide open promontory from which they can view "the many-steepled tract magnificent / Of hilly fields and meadows, and the sea" (lines 10, 20–21). Thomson bequeathed to the romantic poets not just the glory of a prospect per se, but the glory of a prospect discovered by a traveller emerging from shadowy depths. Indeed, Thomson's vision of the distant Cambrian Mountains might be read as a prevision of what Wordsworth would see from the summit of Snowdon—the highest of the Cambrians—when he climbed up through the mist one night and saw the moon shining on the "dusky backs" of a hundred hills (*Prelude* 14. 40–43).

Yet to say so much is immediately to realize how far we have travelled—both figuratively and literally—from the world of landscape gardening. If the art of landscaping did indeed help to turn poetry from pictorialism toward a romantic engagement with nature, the assistance was limited. Lyttleton's journey through Hagley Park significantly culminates in what no landscaped park can contain: villages, towns, and mountains. Indeed, for all the psychic attractions of eighteenth-century landscaping, poets felt a persistent urge to leave it behind. Thomson saluted "the wide extended walks, / The fair majestic paradise of Stowe!" ("Autumn," lines 1041–2), but he also admired

12. Thomson's lines, says Ralph Cohen, suggest "the harmoniously ordered view that the landed aristocrat provides from his retreat. As space extends the 'broken Landskip' . . . ascends by degrees and becomes part of that infinity of space which belongs to the ideal—so that the mountains (earth) rise like 'far Clouds' (airy moisture) and Hagley Park becomes a unifying outlook from which the elements blend into one another" (*Unfolding* 72).

> The negligence of nature wide and wild,
> Where, undisguised by mimic art, she spreads
> Unbounded beauty to the roving eye.
>
> ("Spring," lines 505–7)

Likewise, though Hunt shows that Thomas Gray appreciated gardens
and sometimes used a "gardenist vocabulary" to describe natural scenery, Gray had to abandon both the garden and its vocabulary to experience the sublimity of the Alps, where—in the familiar words of his 1739
letter to Richard West—"not a precipice, not a torrent, not a cliff, but is
pregnant with religion and poetry." Gardens could offer surprise, intricacy, a variety of views, and occasions for introspection, but not the intense stimulation Gray found in a natural valley "with prospects that
change every ten steps." And as for sublimity, gardens could offer no
more than what Joseph Warton called "Art's vain Pomps"—such as the
replica of Stonehenge installed by William Danby at Swinton Park in
North Yorkshire (Hunt, *Figure* 150–55).

The connection between landscape gardens and the romantic response
to nature becomes still more complicated when we consider what happened to the emblematic or "readable" garden. Ronald Paulson has argued that eighteenth-century landscaping moved from emblem to expression, from the intellectually significant temples and statuary of Kent
to the purely emotive spaces created by Brown, who cleared his landscapes of emblematic artifacts so that they could simply elicit moods
such as melancholy, excitement, and calm (*Emblem* 26–27). This development seems to point toward romanticism. When gardens discarded
their emblematic signposts, they could teach poets to interpret nature
subjectively, to say how it feels as well as how it looks. But did later
eighteenth-century landscaping actually have such an effect? Insofar as
it is epitomized by the work of Brown, I do not think it did. Brown's landscapes put too much distance between the viewer and the viewed. Unlike
the small-scale grottoes and winding paths of Kent, his vast and belted
expanses kept nature at bay, and in their grandiose assertiveness they
uncomfortably recalled the ostentation—if not the sterility—of Timon's
villa, the fictional estate satirically described in Pope's "Epistle to Burlington" (lines 99–132). Brown did not create "monotony and baldness,"
as Price contended; his wide open spaces had variety and grace, a paradoxically decorous sublimity. Yet by another paradox, the very grandeur
of this spaciousness limited its value for the romantic imagination,

which—in Wordsworth's words—could "build up greatest things / From least suggestions."[13]

The line between eighteenth-century landscape gardening and the romantic response to nature is therefore an interrupted one. Wordsworth's conception of landscape gardening itself resembles not so much the theories of the later as of the earlier eighteenth century. In 1731, Pope told Burlington that his own landscaping at Twickenham was guided chiefly by "*Sense*," and in his "Epistle to Burlington," he urged variety, respect for "the Genius of the Place," and concealment of the bounds: "He gains all points, who pleasingly confounds / Surprizes, varies, and conceals the Bounds" (lines 55–56). Similar advice passed from Wordsworth to his friend and patron George Beaumont when Beaumont was beginning alterations on the house and grounds at Coleorton Hall, his estate in Leicestershire. "Laying out grounds," wrote Wordsworth, ". . . may be considered a liberal art, in some sort like Poetry and Painting; and its object, like that of all the liberal arts, is, or ought to be, to move the affections under the controul of good sense; that is . . . to assist Nature in moving the affections" (*LW* 1: 627). Pope's fascination with pictorial intricacy gives way here to the characteristically Wordsworthian concern with emotional effect, but both insist upon a delicate respect for nature and condemn the pompous display of appropriation. As Pope satirized the Brobdignagian barrenness of Timon's villa, Wordsworth attacked the ruthless clearing of grounds. He told Beaumont that his house "should belong to the Country and not the Country be an appendage to [the] House" (*LW* 1: 623), and in a later letter he deplored the "impoverishing and *monotonizing* [of] Landscapes" (*LW* 2: 506). Wordsworth also shared Pope's love of suppressed boundaries. Years after he designed and supervised the installation of the Winter Garden at Coleorton, he was happy to see that the boundary plantings had lost their edges:

> We see not nor suspect a bound,
> No more than in some forest wild,
> The sight is free as air—or crost
> Only by art in nature lost.[14]

---

13. *Prelude* 14: 101–2. Though Wordsworth (to my knowledge) nowhere mentions Brown, he disapproved of the wholesale clearing that was Brown's trademark (see Noyes 95).

14. "A Flower Garden," lines 27–30. For this point I am indebted to Noyes, who also

Wordsworth clearly relished this effect. The suppression or disruption of boundaries is a distinctive feature of the landscape presented in the opening lines of "Tintern Abbey," where Wordsworth pleasurably notices "hedge rows, hardly hedge-rows, little lines / Of sportive wood run wild" (lines 15–16). Nevertheless, examples such as this can hardly justify the inference that eighteenth-century landscape gardening significantly influenced Wordsworth's treatment of landscape in his poetry. For Pope and Kent, the purpose of suppressing boundaries was to open up an uninterrupted prospect or vista, to give the viewer an unwalled, unobstructed sense of lateral expansion. But the landscape presented in "Tintern Abbey" is profoundly vertical. It is monumentally walled by "steep and lofty cliffs / That on a wild secluded scene impress / Thoughts of more deep seclusion" (5–7). The hedge rows that are hardly hedge rows—the borderlines erased or broken up even as we look at them—serve not so much to enhance the sense of outward prospect as to symbolize the instability of the borderline that lies within: the borderline between the speaker's past and present self.

To enter this interior territory is to see how Wordsworth has transformed the terms of eighteenth-century landscape gardening. More precisely, it is to see just one example of what I will consider at length in chapter 3: the internalization of prospect. Where are the "paradise, and groves / Elysian" that Wordsworth promised to deliver in *The Recluse*? We know that what Thomson called "the fair majestic paradise of Stowe" included a glade called the Elysian Fields (Malins 114), and thus that well before Wordsworth tried to re-create paradise in his poetry, Kent and "Capability" Brown had tried to recreate it in the earth.[15] But Wordsworth's aim was something quite different: not to reconstruct the earth, but to reconceive man's vision of the earth, which was now to become an essential part of his inner life. Emotionally revitalized, rediscovered by an intellect wedded to it "in love and holy passion," the universe would appear *as* paradise and groves Elysian; these would be discovered as "a simple produce of the common day."

Yet Wordsworth's first problem as a poet was precisely to discover them for himself, to establish an original relation to nature. When the very word *landscape* almost inevitably denoted something composed by

---

notes that Wordsworth got his idea for the Winter Garden from Addison's *Spectator* 477 (Noyes 120, 113).

15. On this point see also Prest.

the painter, the poet, or the landscapist, what did an unmediated experience of landscape mean? Walking through the Lake District one day in
1800, Coleridge wryly observed: "Ladies reading Gilpin's &c while passing by the places instead of looking at the places" (*NC* 1: 760). Wordsworth and Coleridge did look at the places, of course, but by the end of
the eighteenth century, the pervasive influence of the picturesque had
made it difficult for any educated traveller even to see scenery without
thinking of pictures, much less describe it without doing so. Hence the
relatively simple irony of Wordsworth's "Expostulation and Reply" becomes teasingly complex in "The Tables Turned." When Wordsworth
urges his bibliophilic antagonist to give up the metaphorical light of
books for the putatively literal light of the setting sun, for the "first sweet
evening yellow" spread through all the long green fields, is he articulat-
ing his own direct perception or is he deliberately using what William
Gilpin called "picturesque description"?[16] Whatever the answer to this
question, Wordsworth's desire to communicate an unmediated apprehension of nature is inevitably qualified by his dependence on the medium
of language. Whether or not Wordsworth sees a physical landscape, we
as readers do not; we see only a verbal one. And if the opening words of
"The Tables Turned" are implicitly meant for us as well as for the bibliophile, then the command to quit our books is clearly not meant to include the one in which we are reading this poem. Wordsworth's words at
once beckon us to nature and keep us from it.

To escape literature within literature is of course impossible, though
literature can pretend to offer an escape from itself. In an early poem
called "To the Nightingale" (1795), Coleridge quotes Milton's description of the bird in "Il Penseroso": "Most musical, most melancholy" (line
17). Three years later, in "The Nightingale," he quotes the same line and
then immediately rejects it as a literary conceit: "Oh! idle thought! / In
Nature there is nothing melancholy" (lines 14–15). Yet if Coleridge seems
to reject a literary conceit in favor of his own experience, he nevertheless retains the distinctly literary language of synaesthesia and personification to describe that experience, and as Fred Randel has recently
shown, he uses Miltonic elements in "The Nightingale" even after pro-
fessing to leave Milton behind.[17]

16. In Gilpin, *Cumberland and Westmoreland*, a book Wordsworth owned (see above,
note 6), Gilpin says that "picturesque description" demands a kind of vividness that he
calls "high-colouring" (1: xix).
17. Randel 37–50. For examples of synaesthesia and personification in "The Night-

Coleridge could hardly reject all literature. Still less could he or Wordsworth or the two major painters of this study reject the arts of landscape: the whole phenomenon of landscape as a cultural artifact defined and framed by the triangulation of the arts. It is one thing for a poet to reckon with the influence of another poet; it is something else for a poet or painter to reckon with influences at once verbal and pictorial, influences so subtle and pervasive that they may come to seem inseparable from the direct experience of nature. Though Shaftesbury at the beginning of the eighteenth century and Wordsworth at the end of it each expressed the urge to experience a nature innocent of art, where was this nature? Where was the nature freed—in Reynolds's words—from "every appearance of Art, or any traces of the footsteps of man"? And where was the art undistracted from this nature by any other art? When "Capability" Brown sets out to form scenes for the poet and the painter, he is at once imitating painting and seeking to influence it, as well as to influence poetry. Likewise, when Thomson describes vistas and prospects in *The Seasons*, he is at once imitating landscape paintings and creating what were called "sublime pictures" by Solomon Gessner (102), the Swiss poet and painter who recommended such pictures to painters in a "Letter" on landscape painting that profoundly impressed the young Constable (*JCC* 2: 9).

THE RE-CREATIVE IMITATION OF ART

To understand, then, the ways in which English romantic poets and painters re-created landscape, we must grasp the complexity of their relation to influences which could neither be ignored nor submissively accepted, which by turns they received and sought to resist.[18] The romantic preoccupation with natural landscape—the longing for an unmediated experience of it—fosters the belief that romanticism is the struggle to escape from art into nature; but it is really the struggle to move from one kind of art to another, to find new ways of representing

---

ingale," see lines 43–48, where the bird precipitates "his delicious notes" in his eagerness to "disburthen his full soul / Of all its music!"

18. My language perhaps suggests Harold Bloom's theory of literary influence, wherein each new poet must contend with and swerve from the influence of a great precursor, who assumes the authority of a father figure (see *The Anxiety of Influence*). Here, however, I refer not to particular precursors but to a convergence of various influences, both verbal and pictorial.

man's relation to nature. In seeking to define just what is genuinely original about the vision of landscape represented in romantic poetry and painting, we sometimes find ourselves reenacting the strategies with which the poets and painters sought to define their own originality—especially when we take at face value their often overstated assertions about the extent to which they are repudiating or transcending the past. But our real task is analogous to theirs. Instead of indulging the illusion that the romantics could somehow manage to abandon art for nature— that they could quit their books or forget all pictures, as Constable tried to do—we must rather try to understand just how they re-created their respective arts in the very act of re-creating nature.

I shall therefore consider three illustrative examples of the romantic response to the triangulation of the arts. In each of these cases, the re-creative imitation of nature goes hand in hand with the re-creative imitation of art: with an intense consciousness that art itself is an integral part of what is to be at once imitated and transformed.

I begin with something to which I have already alluded—Wordsworth's response to the picturesque. The point usually made on this subject is that after a brief affair with the picturesque in the early 1790s, Wordsworth decisively broke the habit of seeing and describing nature in picturesque terms, and thus overthrew what he called the "tyranny" of the eye (*Prelude* A 11. 171–80). In *The Prelude* he chides himself for once judging nature "by rules of mimic art transferr'd / To things above all art," for superficially comparing scene with scene instead of feeling and expressing "the spirit of the place" (A 11. 154–64). He then goes on to say that he

> shook the habit off
> Entirely and for ever, and again
> In Nature's presence stood, as I stand now,
> A sensitive, and a creative soul.
>
> (A 12. 254–57)

Wordsworth wrote this passage in 1804. Yet in 1810, in the first published version of what later became his *Guide through the District of the Lakes*, he criticized Alpine scenery in explicitly pictorial terms, citing the harshness of its coloring and the jaggedness of its forms to show that the Alps were not as well suited to painting as the Lake District, whose richly harmonious coloring he describes at length (*PW* 2: 176–77, 234). The irony of his so conspicuously doing what he triumphantly claimed to have stopped doing becomes still more evident when we realize that in the very act of seeming to repudiate "the rules of mimic art," he mimics Thomson, who praised the beauty of a nature "undisguised by mimic art" ("Spring," line 506) and yet repeatedly expressed his admiration for that beauty in pictorial terms.

In saying so much, I do not mean to argue that Wordsworth was inescapably bound by the influence of Thomson or the picturesque but rather that his desire to experience and express an unmediated relation to nature sometimes led him to ignore or deny the picturesque features of his own work. Consider his description of an oak tree at sunset in *An Evening Walk* (written ca. 1787–89):

> And, fronting the bright west in stronger lines,
> The oak its dark'ning boughs and foliage twines.
>
> (Lines 193–94)

In his seventies, Wordsworth told Isabella Fenwick that he had noticed this effect when he was a boy of fourteen or less. "The moment," he said, "was important in my poetical history; for I date from it my consciousness of the infinite variety of natural appearances which had been unnoticed by the poets of any age or country so far as I was acquainted with them; and I made a resolution to supply, in some degree, the deficiency" (*PW* 1: 319). This statement has led critics to commend Wordsworth for his originality.[19] But it tells something less than the whole truth. Specifically, it conceals the fact that by the time he wrote *An Evening Walk*—if not by age fourteen—Wordsworth *was* acquainted with the picturesque accounts of sunsets, especially in the poetry of Thomson. He may have discovered the darkening boughs for himself, but in writing about them in this poem, I believe that he was consciously applying a well-established method of picturesque description.[20]

The influence of Thomson and of picturesque methods of description is less obvious in *Descriptive Sketches*, which Wordsworth wrote for the most part in 1791–92 and published in 1793 along with *An Evening Walk*. While *An Evening Walk* describes the scenery of the Lake District, *Descriptive Sketches* represents the Alps—something Gilpin had implicitly classified as unpaintable in a book Wordsworth owned (see above,

19. J. R. Watson, for instance, finds in the quoted lines a "directness of response, overriding all picturesque considerations" (Hunt, *Encounters* 112).

20. For specific evidence on this point, see Heffernan, *WTP* 20–21.

pp. 5 and 6n). In a note on a passage describing an Alpine sunset, Wordsworth at once echoes Gilpin and anticipates the comment he would later
make in his *Guide through the District of the Lakes:*

I had once given to these sketches the title of Picturesque; but the Alps are
insulted in applying to them that term. Whoever, in attempting to describe their
sublime features, should confine himself to the cold rules of painting would give
his reader but a very imperfect idea of those emotions which they have the irresistible power of communicating to the most impassive imaginations. The fact
is, that controuling influence, which distinguishes the Alps from all other scenery, is derived from images which disdain the pencil. Had I wished to make a
picture of this scene I had thrown much less light into it. But I consulted nature
and my feelings. The ideas excited by the stormy sunset I am here describing
owed their sublimity to that deluge of light, or rather of fire, in which nature
had wrapped the immense forms around me; any intrusion of shade, by destroy-
ing the unity of the impression, had necessarily diminished it's grandeur. (*PW*
1: 62)

This long note can easily be read as a declaration of poetic independence, an act of rebellion against the picturesque.[21] Though Wordsworth
in a sense anticipates his complaint about the Alps in the *Guide*, he does
so in positive rather than negative terms. Instead of faulting the Alps for
their failure to meet pictorial criteria, he acclaims the fiery sublimity
with which they transcend "the cold rules of painting." He thus plainly
implies that in representing this sublimity, he himself has transcended
the rules of picturesque description.

But in fact he has not quite left pictorialism behind. The first clue to
its survival is the fact that while *picturesque* gave way to *descriptive* in the
title of the poem, the word *sketches* remained. And even if we dismiss
this word as a dead metaphor for descriptions of all kinds, we must still
acknowledge that the essence of what Wordsworth represents is something unmistakably visible if not by all criteria picturable: light. According to Wordsworth, the "cold rules of painting" require in all pictures a
certain amount of shade. But do all pictures obey such rules? In 1793,
Wordsworth could not have known that Turner would produce a "deluge
of light" in his *Morning after the Deluge* (1843), or that all shade would
be consumed in the fiery sunset of his *Slavers* (1840). But indirectly at
least, Wordsworth could have known that the heroic landscapes of the

21. Martin Price infers from this note that "for Wordsworth the picturesque moment
had already passed" (Hilles and Bloom 289).

High Renaissance and the baroque were often bathed in a dominant, pervasive glow of light, if not an absolute deluge of it. His own personification of the setting sun as a warrior shaking his flashing shield against a storm recalls Thomson's personification of the rising sun as "the powerful king of day / Rejoicing in the east"; in turn, as Jean Hagstrum has noted, Thomson's personification recalls the grand and glowing figures of such pictorial allegories as Guido Reni's fresco, "Aurora" (260–63). Wordsworth does not seem to have known this picture, but he certainly knew Thomson's description of the sunrise, which makes no reference to shade and which is studded with references to light ("kindling," "Illumed," "gold," "dew-bright," "coloured," "shining," "burnished," "high-gleaming"). The radiance of Thomson's language and the style of heroic personification which he draws from pictorial allegory are both reflected in Wordsworth's description of the Alpine sunset:

> 'Tis storm; and hid in mist from hour to hour,
> All day the floods a deeper murmur pour;
> And mournful sounds, as of a spirit lost,
> Pipe wild along the hollow-blustering coast,
> 'Till the sun walking on his western field
> Shakes from behind the clouds his flashing shield.
> Triumphant on the bosom of the storm,
> Glances the fire-clad eagle's wheeling form;
> Eastward, in long perspective glittering, shine
> The wood-crown'd cliffs that o'er the lake recline;
> Wide o'er the Alps a hundred streams unfold,
> At once to pillars turn'd that flame with gold;
> Behind his sail the peasant strives to shun
> The west that burns like one dilated sun,
> Where in a mighty crucible expire
> The mountains, glowing hot, like coals of fire.
>
> (*PW* 1: 62, lines 332–47)

Wordsworth's language at once recalls the radiant personification of Thomson and anticipates the apocalyptic fire of Turner's late work. Indeed, if it can be read—in Coleridge's words—as an emblem of Wordsworth's emerging genius (*BL* 1: 56–57), it might also be read as a prophecy of things to come in Turner's art. But whatever this passage signifies, it can hardly be read as a repudiation of pictorialism. After the opening lines on the sounds of the storm, the passage offers a series of pictorial images: the flashing shield of the sun, the fire-clad eagle, the cliffs glittering "in long perspective," the streams turned to flaming pillars, the peasant behind his sail, and the mountains glowing like fiery coals. This last image, in fact, may well have been suggested to Wordsworth by the critic John Scott, who cited a passage about a "prospect all on fire" to show how a contemporary poet had rendered "the picturesque effect of [the] sun's radiance on the clouds of the horizon."[22] Once again, therefore, in spite of his claim to the contrary, Wordsworth uses a vocabulary that is picturesque at least in part and represents nature in demonstrably pictorial terms.

I stress this point because Wordsworth's strictures on the picturesque can too easily lead us to believe that he wished to renounce picture-making altogether, to subvert the tyranny of the eye by simply exploiting

> whate'er there is of power in sound
> To breathe an elevated mood, by form
> Or image unprofaned.
>
> *(Prelude* 2. 304–6)

Certainly Wordsworth aimed to take poetry beyond the limits of the purely visible, and he used a variety of means—including sound—to help him to do so. In *The Prelude*, the sight of a blind beggar wearing a sign on his chest makes Wordsworth see what the superficially dazzling "sights" of London have thus far failed to show him: an emblem of man's quest for origin and identity, "the utmost we can know / Both of ourselves and of the universe" (7. 645–46). Yet Wordsworth's own quest for his origin and identity culminates in the experience of a spectacle offered sumptuously to the eye: an ocean of moonlit mist engulfing the hills around Mount Snowdon. To recognize that this spectacle is auditory and profoundly emblematic as well as visual is to see that Wordsworth has not so much renounced the art of picturesque description as he has intensified and transformed it.

We can see this clearly in his first decisively original response to the pictorialist tradition: "Tintern Abbey." To fully appreciate what Wordsworth does in this poem, we must realize that by 1798, when he wrote it, the abbey itself had become an object of pictorial distinction. Gilpin had

22. Scott 349–51. In *An Evening Walk*, Wordsworth uses the phrase "prospect all on fire" to describe a Lake District sunset, and in a note on the Thomsonian couplet that includes the description, he cites Scott (*PW* 1: 18–20).

illustrated it in his *Observations on the River Wye* (1782), where he wrote that the "splendid ruin," the woods, the glades, the winding river, and the "elegant line" of the surrounding hills made "all together a very enchanting piece of scenery" (48). Tintern Abbey also fascinated Turner, who made at least seven watercolors of it in the 1790s, including one that he exhibited in 1794 and that fully exploits the picturesque appeal of broken walls, mottled stone, Gothic arches wreathed in foliage, and fragments of ruin.[23] Yet it is precisely the picturesque appeal of the abbey that Wordsworth deliberately excludes from his poem. As its full title tells us, he focuses instead on a landscape a few miles above the abbey: a landscape seen for a second time after a five-year separation from it.

It is in this second viewing or second sight of a landscape profoundly personalized over years of recollection that Wordsworth strikingly transforms the picturesque tradition. In the picturesque response to a natural scene, the observer sees it in the light of a remembered picture; as Payne Knight says, he associates it either with a specific painting or with features characteristic of pictures in general. Wordsworth seeks a relation to nature unmediated by either literary or pictorial tradition. Yet in "Tintern Abbey" the relation *is* mediated by his own memory of what was originally unmediated. The remembered picture which informs his response to the scene is not a painting but a mental landscape directly experienced: an image preserved in memory and now used to mediate between the poet and the landscape stretching before him in time present:

> And now, with gleams of half-extinguished thought,
> With many recognitions dim and faint,
> And somewhat of a sad perplexity,
> The picture of the mind revives again:
> While here I stand, not only with the sense
> Of present pleasure, but with pleasing thoughts
> That in this moment there is life and food
> For future years.
>
> (Lines 57–64)

---

23. Reproduced in Wilkinson, *TES* 28. When Gilpin visited the abbey in 1770, he was amusingly disappointed with its tidiness. "More *picturesque* it would certainly have been," he wrote, "if the area, unadorned, had been left with all its rough fragments of ruin scattered around" (*River Wye* 49–50). Unless the ruins were actually there when Turner visited the abbey—some twenty-two years after Gilpin saw it—I am tempted to believe that he put them in for picturesque effect. But in any case, Tintern Abbey had a

Significantly, Wordsworth calls the remembered landscape a "picture of the mind."[24] The key term in the vocabulary of picturesque response is thus made to generate two meanings that take us far beyond the picturesque. The picture of the mind is first of all the mind's possession, an image painted not on any canvas but only in the poet's memory, where the poet alone can see, study, and interpret it. Yet as a picture of the mind, it is also a picture representing the mind—or more precisely what Nelson Goodman might call a "landscape-picture representing the mind."[25] Insofar as the scene in the memory can be called a picture, it can be classified as a landscape picture. But just as a unicorn picture can represent Christ or virginity, so the landscape picture in the poet's memory represents his mind: what he thought and felt when he first visited the Wye. Wordsworth says pointedly, "I cannot paint / What then I was" (75–76). He cannot depict the complex state of love and dread and rapture with which nature once filled him. But having learned how to depict landscape in words, he can use a verbal picture of landscape seen in time present to revive dimly and faintly a mental picture of landscape seen in time past: a picture that is now to be not so much seen as seen through.

To perceive this penetrative movement of the poem is to see what Wordsworth does with the pictorialist tradition he inherits. Consider the opening lines:

---

well-established connection with the picturesque by the time Wordsworth wrote his poem; J. R. Watson says that he mentions it in the title "to direct the reader's attention toward the picturesque" (83).

24. Wordsworth here may be echoing Cowper, who in *The Task* (1785) describes the poet's continuing efforts

> T' arrest the fleeting images that fill
> The mirror of the mind, and hold them fast,
> And force them sit till he has pencil'd off
> A faithful likeness of the forms he views.
> (2: 290–93)

Cowper's "mirror of the mind" obviously resembles Wordsworth's "picture of the mind," but the two phrases are used differently. Cowper treats the mirror as simply the metaphorical property of a mind which reflects the "fleeting images" of the external world; Wordsworth's "picture" is the mind's representative as well as its possession. For more on this point, see L. J. Swingle, "Wordsworth's 'Picture of the Mind'" (Kroeber and Walling 81–90).

25. Goodman distinguishes between the classification of a picture and what it represents or denotes. Thus an "infant-picture" (what is normally called "picture of an infant") may represent Churchill, or we can alternatively say that such a picture represents Churchill *as* an infant (21–32).

Five years have past; five summers, with the length
Of five long winters! and again I hear
These waters, rolling from their mountain-springs
With a soft inland murmur.—Once again
Do I behold these steep and lofty cliffs,
That on a wild secluded scene impress
Thoughts of more deep seclusion; and connect
The landscape with the quiet of the sky.

(1–8)

The kind of picture-making embodied here is so peculiarly Wordsworthian that we may not recognize it as picture-making at all. What seems at first to make the passage unpictorial is the reference to auditory effect—to the sound of rolling waters. Yet Thomson's verbal pictures include such things as "the hollow-whispering breeze, the plaint of rills" ("Spring," line 921), and it is worth noting that when Wordsworth refers to "the sugh of swallow flocks" in *An Evening Walk*, he cites Gilpin's definition of *sugh* as a word denoting the sound of moving air (*PW* 1: 30). Before Wordsworth, picturesque description was sufficiently elastic to include auditory effects; what it did not include were pictures layered by time, pictures leading to and through other pictures into the depths of the mind. It is this penetrative movement that the language of the opening lines subtly but unmistakably signals. The opening reference to the passage of time suggests that behind the verbal picture offered us in time present ("I hear," "I behold") is another picture, a kind of pentimento or undersketch or "impress"—to nominalize Wordsworth's suggestive verb—of time past. Wordsworth's words define a space that in turn defines a remembered time. The cliffs impress upon a wild secluded scene "Thoughts of more deep seclusion." The thoughts cannot be depicted, but we are drawn to see our way to them through a picture of visible seclusion pointing to invisible seclusion, a picture both in and of the mind.

What we find in "Tintern Abbey," then, is not the renunciation of verbal picture-making but the penetrative exploitation of its possibilities. In Wordsworth's hands, the verbal picture becomes a means of representing time as well as space, a way of opening the eye to second sight as well as ordinary sight. During his five years away from it, the scene Wordsworth remembers from his first visit has not been "as is a landscape to a blind man's eye" (line 24); he can look both at it and through it to his own past self. A landscape seen in time present revives the sight of a landscape seen in time past, and this in turn leads to the kind of vision in which "we see into the life of things."

I have used *pentimento* as a metaphor for the way in which a remembered landscape underlies the landscape of putatively present experience, a landscape depicted in the present tense. Painters themselves, however, do not normally use actual pentimenti in this way; when they wish to "remember" one picture in another, they imitate its composition. This is precisely what Constable does in his *Dedham Vale* of 1828 (plate 5), a picture that recalls not only one of his own earlier works but also a celebrated landscape by Claude. Yet paradoxically, this doubly derivative picture triumphantly exemplifies the mature style of a man commonly called "the natural painter." For this reason, the 1828 *Dedham Vale* may help us to understand how Constable—like Wordsworth— could achieve and represent an original relation to nature even as he was deliberately imitating art.

The phrase "natural painter" comes—by a misreading—from one of Constable's letters. It was written on 29 May 1802, in London, where Constable had spent the better part of the previous two years learning to draw at the Royal Academy, studying the fine collection of masterworks at the Grovesnor Square house of George Beaumont, and copying landscapes by Claude, Jacob Ruysdael, and Richard Wilson. By the end of May 1802 he was weary of the work, and he poured out his heart to a friend named John Dunthorne, an amateur artist who had remained behind in Constable's native village of East Bergholt. Constable's letter to Dunthorne is a kind of manifesto, the equivalent of Wordsworth's preface to the *Lyrical Ballads* of 1800. In the preface, Wordsworth says that he has tried in his own work to use "the very language of men" and to avoid anything that is not a "natural part of that language" (*PrW* 1: 130). Constable takes a comparable stand in his letter to Dunthorne. He scolds himself for "running after pictures and seeking the truth at second hand"; he dismisses the paintings in the current Royal Academy exhibition as so much fashionable extravagance ("an attempt at something beyond the truth"); he says he will spend the summer in Bergholt making "laborious studies from nature" and endeavoring "to get a pure and unaffected representation" of scenery; and in the sentence that is often misquoted, he says, "there is room enough for a natural painture" (*JCC* 2: 32).

Constable writes with a Wordsworthian fervor, but the all-too-easily misread "painture" is what complicates if not compromises his apparent determination to forswear art for nature, to stop running after pictures and return to the study of his native ground. The word *painture* means a *style of painting*, which is to say a certain kind of art. Like all styles, this one has its history and precedents, and in spite of his desire to forget his knowledge of pictures when he sat down to make a sketch from nature, Constable could scarcely help but remember what earlier painters had done to make their landscapes look "natural." Late in his life, he told C. R. Leslie, his memoirist, that he hoped "I may yet make some impression with my 'light'—my 'dews'—my 'breezes'—my *bloom* and my *freshness*—no one of which qualities has yet been perfected on the canvas of any painter in this world" (*JCC* 2: 96). Yet just a few months after making this statement, he spoke in a public lecture of what Rubens did with these qualities: "dewy light and freshness, the departing shower, with the exhilaration of the returning sun, effects which Rubens, more than any other painter, has perfected on canvas" (*JCD* 61). And in 1834, just three years before his death, the painter who yearned to express what no one else had perfected could write to Leslie about a "truly sublime Cuyp" in which "lightning descends to the earth . . . with a *glide* that is so much like nature, that I wish I had seen it before I sent my Salisbury away."[26]

It is startling to hear this from a man who had spent his life laboriously developing a style of his own. Yet the statement is finely balanced; Constable judges art by the standard of nature, and is willing to learn from any art in which he can recognize the nature he knows. When he left London for East Bergholt in the summer of 1802, he did not leave art behind; he took with him, among many other things, a profound and intimate knowledge of Claude's *Landscape: Hagar and the Angel* (plate 3). This was one of the pictures he had copied at Beaumont's house, and Leslie tells us that he regarded his first sight of it as an important epoch in his life (5). So it is unsurprising if also somewhat ironic that at the end of the summer of 1802—the summer given to laborious study of nature on his own native ground—he produced a picture demonstrably modelled after Claude's *Hagar*: his first version of *Dedham Vale* (plate 4).

26. Constable, *JCC* 3: 118–19; the picture by Cuyp is *Dordrecht in a Storm*. The complexity of Constable's attitude toward the relation between nature and landscape painting may be illustrated by two other remarks made at widely different times. While spending the summer of 1799 in Suffolk, he found it "a most delightful country for a painter. I fancy I see Gainsborough in every hedge and hollow tree" (Leslie 9). On the other hand, travelling from Suffolk to London in July of 1831, he wrote to Leslie: "Nothing can exceed the beauty of the country—it makes pictures seem sad trumpery" (*JCC* 3: 41).

In some obvious ways the two pictures differ. Claude's biblical figures in the left foreground have given way to a low bush; the broad river in the middle distance has been replaced by a narrow winding stream; and the arched bridge with the rocky hillside overlooking it in the distance has become a level horizon barely broken by the spires of a church tower. But the composition of Constable's picture is essentially the same as that of Claude's. In both pictures the foreground is defined by a tall group of trees at right and some slightly protruding branches at left—the dark wing-screens with which Claude characteristically established a vista of receding planes leading to infinite light.

To study Constable's trees, however, is to see evidence of something more than Claudian influence. Claude's trees undulate slightly; Constable's have exaggerated bends, and the two nearest the foreground form an hourglass of perfect symmetry. This is not natural painture; it is Claude redrawn with Hogarth's "line of beauty." In *The Analysis of Beauty* (1753), a book recommended to Constable in 1796 and at some time bought for his library (Constable, *JC: FDC* 32, 200), Hogarth had said that beauty springs from undulation: a line of tempered variety free of any fixed geometrical form and uninterrupted by sharp turns (54–55). This is the line that unmistakably informs the shapes of the large trees in Constable's picture. Accentuated by contrast with the vertical spires of the distant church, the undulating line of the trees reappears in the winding stream behind them—a stream that recalls not only Hogarth but also the serpentine line of eighteenth-century landscape gardening.

The *Dedham Vale* of 1802 (plate 4), then, strikingly reveals the almost tyrannical power of convention. Though Constable produced this picture after several months of studying nature at first hand, he could neither forget nor escape the compositional patterns of traditional landscape painting or of beauty in the abstract; he could hardly think of producing a "beautiful" landscape without them.[27] Only the declining row of weeds in the left foreground gives a hint of the sharp particularity with which he will later create the density of his great canvases—including the *Dedham Vale* he painted in 1828 (plate 5). To look at this imitation of an imitation of Claude is paradoxically to see that by 1828, Constable had unquestionably achieved what he himself called "an original style" (*JCC* 6: 191). His originality asserts itself within and against pictorial tradi-

27. He was bound by what E. H. Gombrich calls "a developed system of schemata" (*AI* 87). In art, says David Summers, "a formulation once arrived at may have almost perfect authority simply because it is identified with the thing it is" (119).

tion. Just as Wordsworth's verbal landscape in "Tintern Abbey" penti-
mentally discloses a "picture of the mind" and thus transforms the tradition of picturing landscape in words, Constable transforms inherited
patterns of pictorial beauty. Essentially, what we find in the later *Dedham Vale* is an angularity that vitally offsets the curves of the earlier one,
and a richness of detail that literally fills up its empty or textureless
spaces.

The later *Dedham Vale* clearly repeats the composition of the earlier
one. Once again a foreground framed by a tall group of trees at right and
shrubbery at left defines a vista looking down the length of a valley with a
river running through it to a distant view of Dedham church. But the
geometry of the later picture differs sharply from that of the earlier one.
The group of trees at right retains some curvature, but they have been
strikingly energized by the introduction of straight lines and angles. The
trees no longer undulate to form an hourglass; they bend and cross to
make a decisive triangle, and in the branches soaring above this powerful base, curves become oblique angles, turn into semicircular hooks, or
intersect with straighter lines to form more triangles. The result is a dynamic reconciliation of opposites. Where the serpentine via media of
Hogarth eschews both circles and straight lines alike, Constable sets
both of these forms before us in order to make them interact. In the
middle distance, the river no longer winds through the valley but rather
crosses diagonally from left to right in a mirror image of the cumulus
clouds above it, which in a roughly scalloped line descend from upper
left to the edge of the trees at right. The treetops themselves are at once
rounded and angled downward so as to present a contrasting diagonal
against the line of the clouds, and thus to create a rich blue triangle
in the sky. The later *Dedham Vale*, then, moves far beyond the placid
curvature of the earlier one. By integrating curves with straight lines,
by suggesting both circles and triangles while binding objects absolutely
to neither, Constable captures the irreducible complexity of natural
forms.

This geometrical complexity of the later work separates it not only
from the earlier one but also from the tradition of the picturesque. Constable certainly felt the influence of this tradition. He owned several of
Gilpin's books on picturesque beauty; he expresses admiration for Gilpin's style in a letter of 1796 (*JCC* 2: 7); and as late as 1834, he could
write: "I have too much preferred the picturesque to the beautiful—

which will I hope account for the *broken ruggedness of my style*" (*JCC* 3: 111). It is in this broken ruggedness that Constable owes most to the picturesque tradition, which made roughness desirable because it produced chromatic density—a surface of broken colors and contrasting lights. But formal density is something conspicuously lacking in most picturesque landscapes, where space is often filled by the simple and ultimately monotonous repetition of bumps or ripples. Picturesque roughness was actually a way of ornamenting traditional patterns of beauty. A direct descendant of rococo intricacy, it turned lines into nervous wriggles, and its studied avoidance of straight lines left the undulating lines of traditional beauty essentially unchallenged and unchanged.[28]

Constable does challenge them. Straightening the trunks of his trees, setting the line of the horizon against the descending line of the clouds and the rising line of the stream, he subtly builds triangles into the very center of his picture. Furthermore, because straight lines and sharp angles also permeate the foliage in this picture, its texture is formally as well as chromatically dense. In the left foreground of the picture, where Claude had put Hagar and the angel, Constable has a mixture of spiky and bending weeds growing up around a leaning stump from which sharply angulated branches protrude over them. Like Hagar stirred by the touch of the angel, the old stump is stirred to a life of sharp and vivid particularity by the complexity of forms that are made to emanate from it. Constable thus re-creates art and nature at once. Transforming the picturesque even as he reflects it and profoundly revising an imitation of Claude, he shows us what a truly original artist could do with the undeniably inherited art of landscape.

From this example of the way Constable imitated painting we may usefully turn to an example of the way Turner imitated poetry. Turner's interest in poetry is doubtless partly attributable to the influence of Joshua Reynolds, who fervently believed that a knowledge of literature was essential to any painter seeking to raise his art from "mere mechanick" copying to "intellectual dignity" (*D* 43). Throughout the discourses

28. See, for instance, Gilpin's pen and wash *Forest Scene* (1771; reproduced in Barbier, plate 5), his watercolor *Ideal Landscape* (ca. 1780; reproduced in Wilton, *BW*, plate 47), and the two plates illustrating picturesque and nonpicturesque treatments of a landscape in Gilpin's *Three Essays* (reproduced in Parris 59). *The Sketcher's Manual*, a guide to picturesque technique published in 1837, stipulated that straight lines were to be strictly avoided (Gowing 27).

he gave as president of the Royal Academy from 1768 to 1790, Reynolds stressed this point, and in the very last of them, he frankly disclosed that he had emphasized the kinship of painting and poetry in order to promote the prestige of painting. "That approbation which the world has uniformly given [to painting]," he said, "I have endeavoured to justify by such proofs as questions of this kind will admit; by the analogy which Painting holds with the sister Arts, and consequently by the common congeniality which they all bear to our nature" (*D* 269).

The audience for these words almost certainly included J. M. W. Turner, who had become a student at the Royal Academy in December 1789—just one year before Reynolds delivered his valedictory discourse—and who ever after spoke of him and his teachings with the highest respect.[29] Turner clearly inherited or at the very least shared Reynolds's belief in the value of literature to painting. Good painters, he said once, cannot be made "without some aid from Poesy" (TMS BB, 22ᵛ), and there is abundant evidence of Turner's debts to English poetry as well as to the classical and biblical sources on which he drew for so many of his pictures.[30] In particular, Jack Lindsay argues that Turner was powerfully influenced by the poetry of Thomson, that in works such as *Dunstanburgh Castle* (1798) and *Warkworth Castle* (1799) he sought to incorporate the "dynamic symmetries" expressed by the passages from Thomson's "Summer," which he himself quoted beneath the titles of these pictures in the exhibition catalogues (Lindsay 58–59). But Turner's relation to Thomson's poetry—as well as to poetry in general—is not at all one of simple dependence. As a case in point, we may consider the way Turner uses Thomson in *Buttermere Lake* (plate 1), exhibited 1798.

Buttermere Lake is the work of an artist who had already studied and imitated a wide variety of English and Continental masters, and the crepuscular atmosphere of this work specifically reveals the influence of Rembrandt. But Turner himself connected *Buttermere Lake* with a literary landscape. Under the title *Buttermere* in the exhibition catalogue of 1798 he quoted the phrases I have italicized in the following passage from Thomson's "Spring":

29. See Lindsay 25. In the series of lectures that he gave at the Royal Academy beginning in 1811, Turner described Reynolds as "the Father of the English School" and the Royal Academy as "an Institution, to which I owe every thing" (TMS K, f. 2–2ᵛ). He later changed the "every thing" to "much" (TMS BB, 50ᵛ).

30. See Lindsay 57–69; Finberg 334, 353, 391; and Gage, *CT* 145–47.

Thus all day long the full-distended clouds
Indulge their genial stores, and well-showered earth
Is deep enriched with vegetable life;
Till, in the western sky, the downward sun
Looks out effulgent from amid the flush
Of broken clouds, gay-shifting to his beam.
The rapid radiance instantaneous strikes
The illumined mountain, through the forest streams,
Shakes on the floods, and *in a yellow mist*,
Far smoking o'er the interminable plain,
In twinkling myriads lights the dewy gems.
Moist, bright, and green, the landscape laughs around.
Full swell the woods; their every music wakes,
Mixed in wild concert, with the warbling brooks
Increased, the distant bleatings of the hills,
The hollow lows responsive from the vales,
Whence, blending all, the sweetened zephyr springs.
Meantime, refracted from yon eastern cloud,
Bestriding earth, the grand ethereal bow
Shoots up immense; and every hue unfolds,
In a fair proportion running from the red
To where the violet fades into the sky.
Here, awful Newton, the dissolving clouds
Form, fronting on the sun, thy showery prison;
And to the sage-instructed eye unfold
The various twine of light, by thee disclosed
From the white mingling maze. Not so the swain;
He wondering views the bright enchantment bend
Delightful o'er the radiant fields, and runs
To catch the falling glory; but amazed
Beholds the amusive arch before him fly,
Then vanish quite away.

(Lines 186–217)

The first part of this passage could well have influenced Turner's *Buttermere*. The lines about the sun striking the mountain are part of what he quotes, and we certainly have a sun-struck mountain in Turner's picture, along with broken clouds, a sun-struck valley, and brightening if not yellow mist. But the most striking element in Thomson's passage—

his description of the rainbow—is the one that bears least resemblance to what we find in Turner's picture.[31]

Thomson's rainbow is explicitly Newtonian. As a true product of the Enlightenment, it no longer bears the meaning it was given in the Book of Genesis; it no longer signifies the Covenant in which God promised never again to flood the earth (Gen. 9:12–17). Though this typological meaning of the rainbow is pointedly recalled in *Paradise Lost*, one of Thomson's sources,[32] and though Thomson himself describes the deluge later on ("Spring," lines 309–16), he treats the rainbow as a purely scientific phenomenon. The rainbow has become the property of Newton— "*thy* showery prism," as Thomson apostrophizingly says—because Newton has explained in his *Opticks* (1704) the principle of refraction and has thus shown how the white light of the sun is broken up into various colors as it passes through moisture. To "the sage-instructed eye," the rainbow is no longer an object of wonder, a "white mingling maze." It is rather a demonstration of Newton's analytical power. Unfolding "every hue," it is neatly divided into the seven colors of the spectrum from red to violet.[33] Significantly, Thomson's eighteenth-century illustrators took pains to emphasize the Newtonian character of the rainbow by representing it as a broad ribbon made up of narrow, well-defined stripes—stripes represented in black and white engravings as alternating bands of light and dark. This is the way the rainbow appears, for instance, in William Kent's illustration *Spring*, engraved by N. Tardieu (plate 2). Kent stops short of placing Newton over the rainbow; he puts over it instead a baroque circle of winged heavenly beings strewing flowers on the earth. But Kent's carefully banded rainbow is nonetheless an apt illustration of the way Thomson presents it—as a sign of Newton's scientific genius.

The rainbow of Turner's *Buttermere Lake* is altogether different. Though Turner quotes the phrase "every hue unfolds," what he gives us is an arc of delicate, evanescent, and ultimately indivisible light.[34] In so doing he implicitly takes the side of Thomson's "wondering" swain and rejects the

31. Gage notes the disparity in passing (*CT* 135), but does not comment on its significance.

32. See Cohen, *Unfolding* 92, and Milton, *Paradise Lost* 11. 879–98.

33. Commenting on this passage, Marjorie Nicolson writes that the "awe" felt by Thomson and other eighteenth-century poets "was less for a miracle of God than for the thinking mind of man which had come to comprehend the laws of nature, whether in the rainbow or the 'law of love' of the planets" (*Newton* 32).

34. Many years later, in his notes on Goethe's *Theory of Colours* (trans. Eastlake, 1840), Turner objected to Goethe's identification of the rainbow and the prismatic spectrum as comparable "phenomena of nature"; see Gage, *CT* 174.

vision of the "sage-instructed eye." To compare Turner's rainbow with those of Kent and Thomson, in fact, is to see exactly what Wordsworth means when he says: "our meddling intellect / Mis-shapes the beauteous forms of things:— / We murder to dissect." Those lines come from "The Tables Turned," published the same year in which *Buttermere* was exhibited, and though we have no evidence that Turner knew the *Lyrical Ballads*, Wordsworth's lines help us to see how Turner leaves Thomson behind. Wordsworth tells his biblophilic friend to quit his books, and Turner gives the same advice to us. Though he salutes Thomson and the sagacity of Newton in the exhibition catalogue, he turns his back on both in the painting, which at last compels us to relinquish all of our books: the *Opticks*, *The Seasons*, and even the exhibition catalogue.

There remains, however, the Book of Genesis. Turner's picture subtly evokes the biblical typology that Thomson discards. Floating on the lake in the center foreground of *Buttermere* are two figures in a small fishing boat. Because the arc of the rainbow is extended by its reflection in the water just beside them, they are caught in an uncompleted circle of light—an almost supernatural embrace. Coleridge said of Wordsworth that he aimed in his poetry "to give the charm of novelty to things of every day, and to excite a feeling analogous to the supernatural, by awakening the mind's attention from the loveliness and the wonders of the world before us" (*BL* 2: 6). Turner's *Buttermere* has a comparable effect. Without representing anything supernatural, it reveals—as Lawrence Gowing says—"the unearthly majesty of light" (7). Subtly but powerfully, its depiction of an "every day" rainbow hovering over a fishing boat recalls the primordial rainbow that hovered over Noah's ark.[35]

Turner would return to this theme much later in his explicitly biblical *Light and Colour (Goethe's Theory)—The Morning after the Deluge* (1843), for which the caption pessimistically describes the rainbow as a mass of "humid bubbles" reflecting earth's lost forms and offering an illusory vision of hope after the flood.[36] But in *Buttermere* the rainbow is an unequivocal sign of transcendence. Interrupted by the promontory that cuts it off from its reflection, partially obscured by the very light and mist from which it emerges, it nonetheless signifies the transcendent

35. Turner's picture is thus the antithesis of Atkinson Grimshaw's undated (but Victorian) picture, *The Seal of the Covenant* (City Art Gallery, Leeds), which shows a rainbow arching over a rocky hillside. Grimshaw, says George Landow, claims "a religious significance for the scene that it does not seem to warrant" ("The Rainbow" 342). By contrast, I think, Turner's picture expresses a good deal more than its title claims.

36. The caption is vexingly obscure, and may mean "refracting" earth's lost forms.

perfection of the circle. In the words Turner quoted from Akenside at the end of his first Academy lecture on perspective, *Buttermere* shows how the artist draws from "matter's mouldering structures, the pure forms / Of Triangle, or Circle, Cube, or Cone."[37]

The decisive circularity of Turner's bow also shows that he had begun to free himself from the rules of the picturesque, which he had virtually grown up with. Two of his first drawings, done about 1787, are copies of topographical engravings in Gilpin's *Observations on . . . Cumberland and Westmoreland* (Finberg 15), and the influence of Gilpin's nervously irregular line is clearly discernible in Turner's work of the early 1790s.[38] Other signs or at least suggestions of picturesque influence linger on in *Buttermere* itself. The somewhat unruly branches in the lower left foreground answer Gilpin's demand for "roughness," and the partial obscuring of the mountains by mist is fully consistent with Gilpin's admiration for the harmonizing and beautifying effect of atmosphere upon natural objects.[39] But as Lawrence Gowing says, the essence of the picturesque was asymmetry, a persistent deviation from straight lines and simple curves. What Turner began to do in *Buttermere* was—in Gowing's words—"To give radiance its natural symmetry" (27). Turner saw that just as Newtonian science could misshape the beauteous forms of things, so could the nervous irregularity demanded by the picturesque. Paradoxically, then, for all the freedom with which it expresses the dissolution of solid forms in mist, *Buttermere* triumphantly reveals the pure and imperturbable circularity of an aerial form.

THE STRAINED SISTERHOOD

We have seen that Wordsworth, Constable, and Turner each responded to the well-established arts of landscape with a combination of acquiescence and resistance, of imitation and independence. In part their re-

37. Turner, TMS K, f. 23. The quoted lines come from Akenside, lines 137–38. Turner was made Professor of Perspective at the Royal Academy in 1807, and almost every year from 1811 to 1828 he gave a series of lectures there.

38. For example, the wiggly branches on the left in Turner's *Rising Squall*, a watercolor of ca. 1791–92, closely resemble the branches in Gilpin's *Ideal Landscape*, cited above in note 28. John Gage finds many of Turner's pictures from the 1790s—particularly his sketches of the Isle of Wight in 1795—highly consistent with Gilpin's conception of the picturesque (Gage, "Turner and the Picturesque" 21–23). For more evidence of Gilpin's possible influence on Turner, see Matteson 389–98.

39. See passages cited from Gilpin's works in Fink 45–47, 58–59, 124–25.

sponses exemplify the way in which every original artist transforms what he inherits from predecessors within his own art. Wordsworth turns descriptive verse into a poetry of retrospective self-exploration; Constable turns the delicate serenity of Claude's *Hagar* into the electric vitality of his later *Dedham Vale*; Turner turns the wriggling lines of the picturesque into the transcendently graceful curve of *Buttermere*. But in two of these cases, the transformation of inherited models within one art has involved a transformation of the relation between one art and another. The "picture of the mind" created in "Tintern Abbey" cannot be seen as the verbal equivalent of a landscape painting, and the rainbow in what Andrew Wilton ingenuously calls Turner's "homage to Thomson" (*TS* 36) cannot be explained as an illustration of Thomson's poem. Wordsworth's poem and Turner's picture each demonstrate a resistance to the very thing they invoke: the long-established sisterhood of the arts.

Initially, the sisterhood of the arts was the critical principle that painting and poetry resembled or should be made to resemble each other.[40] Popularized in England by Dryden's translation of Alphonse du Fresnoy's Latin poem "De Arte Graphica" in 1695, the concept of the sisterhood permeated the criticism of the century that followed, and even in his somewhat revolutionary preface to the *Lyrical Ballads* of 1800, Wordsworth seems to accept it as a thoroughly established fact. "We are fond of tracing the resemblance between Poetry and Painting," he writes, "and accordingly, we call them Sisters" (*PrW* 2: 134). M. H. Abrams has said that romantic poets and critics reconceived poetry as an art of music-making rather than of picture-making (*Mirror* 50–51). But these two things were not mutually exclusive—as I have already begun to show.[41] What we actually find in romantic poets and painters is a profound ambivalence toward one another's art, a yearning for independence coupled with a recognition of lingering dependence. In the romantic period, each art constituted for the other a model to be imitated and radically transformed.

The relation between poetry and painting in the romantic period can therefore be understood in terms of a triangulation somewhat different from the one described in the first part of this chapter. In the eighteenth century, the arts of painting, poetry, and landscape gardening together

40. For comprehensive discussion of this principle as it developed in the eighteenth century, see Hagstrum and Lipking.

41. On the perseverance of pictorialism in romantic critical theory, see especially Park, "'Ut Pictura Poesis.'"

compose a triangle of harmony, all cooperating to define the cultural phenomenon of landscape. In the romantic period, landscape gardening becomes less important as a model for painting or poetry, and the emphasis
on cooperation and harmony between the other two arts gives way to an
emphasis on rivalry, independence, and antagonism. The result is a triangle of opposition. Though poets and painters continue to acknowledge
the sisterhood of the arts and in some ways to imitate each other, they are
each inclined to claim a special relation to their putatively common subject: to nature, to the human imagination, or both.[42]

To understand the complex set of pressures operating on the sisterhood of the arts in the romantic period, we must recognize that romantic
poets and painters inherited three incompatible doctrines: (1) that painting should be "poetical" in its subject matter and intellectual dignity; (2)
that poetry should be pictorial in the vividness and concrete particularity
of its descriptions; and (3) that poetry should distinguish itself from
painting by exploiting the auditory or purely emotive power of language.
I shall consider the romantic response to each of these doctrines in turn.

The belief that painting should be poetic—what might be called the
doctrine of *ut poesis pictura*—derives from the humanistic theory of
painting which can be traced from the art treatises of the Italian Renaissance to the *Discourses* of Joshua Reynolds.[43] The chief aim of the *Discourses* was to show that by taking its subjects from poetry or history and
by endowing them with "nobleness of conception" and "intellectual
grandeur," painting achieves its "true dignity, which entitles it to the
name of a Liberal Art, and ranks it as a sister of poetry" (*D* 50, 57).
Reynolds's desire to make painting the sister of poetry clearly springs
from his desire to make it culturally respectable, to raise it above the
level of "minute discriminations" (*D* 50) and mechanical reproduction.[44]

---

42. In *Deceit, Desire, and the Novel*, René Girard formulates a theory of sexual rivalry that could—with appropriate adjustments—be applied to the relation between English romantic poets and painters. In Girard's theory, the lover is led to desire the be-
loved by the example of someone else who already desires her, and who thereby becomes
at once a model to be imitated and a rival—an obstacle to be overcome. In the romantic
period, as I shall try to show, poets and painters seeking to represent an object—nature
or the human imagination—were sometimes led to imitate each other's art, to take it as
a model, and at the same time to regard it as a rival or obstacle to the development of
their own.

43. The classic study of this development is Lee, *Ut Pictura Poesis*.

44. The artist guided by "nobleness of conception," says Joshua Reynolds, "will disdain the humbler walks of painting. . . . He will leave the meaner artist servilely to sup-

Hence he stresses the "poetic" powers of painting. Though it cannot excite suspense by representing events in succession, it can equal poetry in its capacity to satisfy "our love of novelty, variety, and contrast" (*D* 146), and like poetry, it can rise above common nature and "servile imitation" to gratify by artificial beauties "all the natural propensities and inclinations of the mind" (*D* 234).

While Reynolds was thus seeking to elevate painting to a "poetic" realm above the mere depiction of minute particulars, a succession of eighteenth-century literary critics was seeking to redefine poetry as an art of representing particular visible objects in a vividly pictorial way. As Jean Hagstrum has suggested, they were prompted not only by the traditional practice of describing poetry in pictorial terms but also by the new empiricism of Newton and Locke. Since the object of poetry was a universe newly rejudged by the evidence of the senses, and since Locke particularly stressed the importance of sight, painting was held up as a model of poetry, a paradigmatic way of representing the visible world (Hagstrum 136). In his highly influential *Spectator* series entitled "Pleasures of the Imagination" (1712), Addison argued that poetry should strive to imitate the visual impact of painting (cited in Hagstrum 136–37), and the point was repeated with gathering force to the very end of the century. "A true poet," wrote Hugh Blair in 1790, renders an object so vividly "that a Painter could copy after him" (quoted in Hagstrum 138). The following year, in a dialogue that appeared in part 2 of Erasmus Darwin's *The Botanic Garden*, the "Poet" censures a line of Pope's because it "does not present the idea of a visible object to the mind, and is thence prosaic" (47–48).

Though Darwin's equation of the poetic with the pictorial hardly anticipates or defines the romantic conception of poetry, romantic critics recognized that poets and readers alike had something to learn from the kind of particularity that painting often presented to the eye. As Roy Park has noted, Hazlitt drew a connection between the rise of interest in painting and the taste for a poetry of descriptive particularity, for "the force and precision of individual details" (Hazlitt 11: 166; Park "'ut Pictura Poesis'" 158). Like Blake, Hazlitt detested the generalizing bias of Reynolds's *Discourses*, which urged the painter to "get above" all par-

---

pose that those are the best pictures, which are most likely to deceive the spectator" (*D* 50).

ticularities. He saw painting as an art of particulars, and as such, he believed that it had helped to restore "our eye for nature"—an eye enfeebled and perverted by "book-learning, the accumulation of wordy common-places, [and] the gaudy pretensions of poetical fiction."[45]

A more passionate and poignant tribute to the exemplary vividness of painting emerges from the notebooks of Coleridge, whose fascination with the shapes and colors of landscape made him periodically yearn for the visually expressive power of graphic art. Trying one September day in 1803 to describe the appearance of birch trees, he writes: "O Christ, it maddens me that I am not a painter or that Painters are not I!" (*NC* 1: 1495 f. 65ᵛ). And shortly afterwards he wrote: "Without Drawing I feel myself but half invested with Language" (*NC* 1: 1554). The notebooks he used from 1802 to 1804 actually show him struggling to speak the other half, crudely and compulsively sketching what he was unable to capture in words alone.[46] The sketches hardly prove that he was an artist, but they do reveal the intensity of his desire to make pictures, or somehow to make pictures spring out of his words.

A vestigial if not always conscious and lively respect for the value of pictorial vividness in language is also evident in the frequency with which romantic poets and critics used words such as *painting* to praise literary works. In the advertisement to the *Lyrical Ballads* of 1798, Wordsworth mentions writers who have distinguished themselves "in painting manners and passions" (*PrW* 1: 116). In the *Biographia Literaria*, Coleridge warmly commends the pictorial richness of Shakespeare's *Venus and Adonis*, wherein the "chain of imagery, always vivid and . . . often minute," reveals "the highest effort of the picturesque in words of

45. Hazlitt 11: 166; see also Park, *Hazlitt* 206. In discourse 3, Joshua Reynolds says that "the whole beauty and grandeur of the art consists . . . in being able to get above all singular forms, local customs, particularities, and details of every kind" (*D* 44; see also 131). Prompted by statements such as this, Hazlitt reduced "Sir Joshua's system" to the axiom that "*the great style in painting consists in avoiding the details, and peculiarities of natural objects*" (18: 70). But Reynolds could in fact appreciate the interplay of the general and the particular. Commenting in 1783 or later on Titian's painting of a bunch of grapes, he said that Titian achieves "breadth" even though "each individual grape . . . has its light, and shadow, and reflection" (*Literary Works* 3: 150; I have been unable to identify the painting to which Reynolds refers.) For Blake's defense of minute particulars against Reynolds's disparagement of them, see Blake 630, 632, 637.

46. See, for instance, Coleridge, *NC* 1: 1213, f. 11–f. 11ᵛ; 2: 1489, f. 59; 1899, f. 90–f. 97ᵛ. Two fairly competent sketches of a crag appear in a notebook Coleridge used during the summer of 1803 (*NC* 1: 1419–20), but it is not known who did them.

which words are capable" (*BL* 2: 15). Other examples abound. Coleridge commended Poole for his talent in "the *painting* of Poetry" (*LC* 3: 235); Shelley called one of his own characters "a painting from nature" (*Letters* 2: 108); at various times Crabb Robinson praised the "painting" of Southey, Wordsworth, and Scott (*CRB* 1: 25, 224, 277); and Hazlitt, after seeing a painting based on *Tam O'Shanter*, tersely declared: "Let no man paint after Burns. He held the pencil in his own hands" (18: 169).

Nevertheless, this respect for pictorial vividness in poetry was sharply qualified by the characteristically romantic conviction that poetry had to be more than a mirror or picture of the external world—even more than the neoclassical mirror that reflects the general nature of that world, abstracting ideal forms from particular manifestations.[47] To some extent, romanticism drives both poetry and painting back to the particular forms that neoclassical theory sought to "get above." Yet while painting could embody that intensification of individual form which profoundly appealed to the romantic imagination, it could also embody—and signify—a mindless submission to the details of a purely material world, a mirroring of externality rather than internality.

For this reason, romantic poets and critics strongly opposed the Darwinian idea that poetry should be nothing but picture-making, and especially the idea that its pictures should be minutely detailed. Hazlitt thought that Crabbe's attempt to do in his descriptive verse what Teniers and Hobbema had done in landscape painting led not to poetry but simply to "microscopic minuteness" of transcription.[48] Likewise, one of the several defects that Coleridge identified in the poetry of Wordsworth was precisely its pictorial elaboration, its "minute accuracy in the painting of local imagery" (*BL* 2: 102). And as for Darwin, who wished to equate the poetic with the pictorial, Coleridge thought he had succeeded only too

47. On the neoclassical mirror see Hagstrum 135–43, and Abrams, *Mirror* 32–36.
48. Hazlitt 19: 52–54. Byron likewise noted the "petty minutiae" in Cowper's "Dutch delineation of a wood" (*Letters and Journals* 5: 556–57), and Coleridge used the same terms to comment generally on the descriptive poetry of the late eighteenth and early nineteenth centuries: "All is so dutchified . . . by the most minute touches, that the reader naturally asks why words, and not painting are used?" *Coleridge's Shakespearean Criticism* 2: 174). Morris Eaves has noted that even Blake disparaged what he called "Niggling" in painting and poetry alike. Though he prized the minute particular as (in Eaves's words) "the inevitable technical emanation of precise visions of imagination," he distinguished this from niggling, which was simply an external system of ornamentation (159).

well. In Darwin's own poetry Coleridge found "a successon of Landscapes or Paintings—it arrests the attention too often, and so prevents the
rapidity necessary to pathos.—it . . . makes the great little" (*NC* 1: 132).

The terms in which Coleridge couches his criticism of Darwin partly
recall Lessing's classic distinction between painting as an art of space
and poetry as an art of time or movement.[49] But when Coleridge complains that Darwin's pictorialism forestalls "pathos," he points to a still
more important reason for which romantic poets and critics resisted pictorialism: its interference with what they saw as the essentially emotive
effect of poetry. Romantic theory on this point derives from Edmund
Burke, who believed that the emotive effect of any representation varies
inversely with its clarity. Precisely because words are—in Burke's opinion—more obscure than pictures, description will always "raise a
stronger *emotion*" than depiction, and "poetry with all its obscurity, has
a more general as well as more powerful dominion over the passions than
the other art" (60–61). For this reason, Burke sees picture-making as
nothing less than a threat to the emotional life of poetry. "So little does
poetry depend for its effect on the power of raising sensible images," he
says, "that I am convinced it would lose a very considerable part of its
energy, if this were the necessary result of all descriptions."[50]

Burke's position was challenged in his own time and remains open to
challenge now.[51] It is simply not true that obscurity is always more mov-

49. "Succession in time is the sphere of the poet, as space is that of the painter"
(Lessing 64–65). *Laocoön* was first published in Germany in 1766. Though not translated into English until De Quincey's version of 1826, it was probably known to Coleridge
by 1799, when he told Wedgewood that he intended to write a biography of Lessing—one
of his many unrealized projects (*LC* 1: 519). In any case, the Swiss-born painter Henry
Fuseli hailed Lessing's book in the *Analytical Review* of 1794 (cited in Hunt, *Encounters*
7), and in a Royal Academy lecture of 1801 he plainly echoed Lessing's dictum—without
acknowledging his source. "Successive action communicated by sounds, and time," he
said, "are the medium of poetry; form displayed in *space*, and momentaneous energy, are
the elements of painting" (1: 103–4). The *Laocoön* is further discussed in chapter 2.

50. Burke 170. Hagstrum suggests that Burke's theory of the sublime reflects the influence of Addison, who "makes it clear that the aesthetic value of the sublime object is
not exclusively visual but also psychological" (137). But Burke does not share Addison's
admiration for pictorial vividness; on the contrary, he seems to regard visual effect and
psychological effect as antithetical.

51. For objections to Burke's position on obscurity in contemporary reviews of his
book, see Burke 63n. Reynolds's observation that "obscurity . . . is one source of the
sublime"—something he might well have acquired from Burke—was sharply attacked
by Blake, who wrote that "obscurity is neither the source of the sublime nor of any thing
else" (647). See also Essick 150.

ing than clarity, or that description is always less clear than depiction. Turner's relatively distinct *Cottage Destroyed by an Avalanche* (1810) is surely more emotive than his almost indistinguishable *Sunrise with a Boat Between Headlands* (ca. 1835–40), and this depiction of a seascape is in turn less clear than the description of landscape that opens "Tintern Abbey." Nevertheless, Burke's assumptions about painting and poetry were for the most part shared by romantic poets and critics. Hazlitt thought the evocative power of words far transcended that of pictures. Criticizing Benjamin West's attempt to embody "terrible sublimity" in his *Death on a Pale Horse*, he wrote: "The moral impression of Death is essentially visionary; its reality is in the mind's eye. Words are here the only things; and things, the physical forms, the mere mockeries of the understanding."[52] Coleridge was likewise inclined to think of language as metavisual. "I could half suspect," he wrote, "that what are deemed fine descriptions, produce their effects almost purely by a charm of words, with which and with whose combinations, we associate *feelings* indeed, but no distinct Images."[53] And De Quincey, who translated Lessing's *Laocoön*, directly attacked Erasmus Darwin's equation of the poetic with the pictorial. "The fact is," he wrote, "that no mere description, however visual and picturesque, is in any sense poetic *per se*, or except in and through the passion which presides" (*CW* 11: 206n).

This insistence on the difference between the sister arts was in large part motivated by the urge to rank poetry above painting, or more precisely to reassert a superiority that the long tradition of pictorialism had threatened to undermine. Here too the literary men of the romantic period inherited the convictions—one might say the biases—of eighteenth-century theorists on the sister arts. Lessing, for instance, had set out to define the limits of poetry and painting alike, but he made no secret of his belief that poetry is "the more comprehensive art, that beauties are at her command which Painting can never attain."[54] The same belief in-

52. Hazlitt 18: 136. Hazlitt makes similar points elsewhere: "Painting gives the object itself; poetry what it implies" (5: 10); poetry "is but the language of feeling," while "in the language of painting, words become *things*" (10: 129). But Hazlitt did grant some emotive power to painting; see below, pp. 44–45.

53. Coleridge, *LC* 1: 511. Elsewhere Coleridge says, "By deep feelings we make our *Ideas dim*" (*NC* 1: 921). See also his comment on "feelings of dimness" and "yearnings & strivings of obscurity" (*NC* 2: 2509).

54. Lessing 36; see also 50–51. E. H. Gombrich says that Lessing wrote *Laocoön* not so much to show that painting should confine itself to a single moment—a point already

forms James Harris's important but generally underestimated discussion of the sister arts in the second of the *Three Treatises* which he first published in 1744. Harris carefully and often incisively analyzes the differences between poetry, painting, and music, but his ultimate aim is to show that poetry is far superior to the other two.[55]

Among romantic poets and theorists, claims for the superiority of poetry become still more pronounced. De Quincey called it "the most majestic of the Fine Arts" (10: 136). Crabb Robinson reported of Wordsworth that "in general, he will not allow the plastic artist of any kind to place himself by the side of the poet. And in this," adds Robinson, "he is beyond all doubt *right*."[56] Coleridge put poetry below music, but "infinitely" above painting in its emotive movement, "in passion & its transitions" (*NC* 2: 1963). Most importantly, what raised poetry above painting was language, which, said Shelley,

is a more direct representation of the actions and passions of our internal being, and is susceptible of more various and delicate combinations, than colour, form, or motion, and is more plastic and obedient to the control of that faculty of which it is the creation. For language is arbitrarily produced by the Imagination, and has relation to thoughts alone, but all other materials, instruments and conditions of art, have relations among each other, which limit and interpose between conception and expression. The former is as a mirror which reflects, the latter as a cloud which enfeebles, the light of which both are mediums of communication.[57]

Shelley's designation of language as a mirror superficially recalls the neoclassical doctrine that poetry and painting should hold a mirror to nature.[58] But nothing could be further from the doctrine than the way in

established by his predecessors—as to combat "the idea that poetry or drama should ever conform to the limitations of the visual arts" ("Moment and Movement" 294–95).

55. After comparing poetry with music and painting, Harris concludes: "POETRY IS THEREFORE, ON THE WHOLE MUCH SUPERIOR TO EITHER OF THE OTHER MIMETIC ARTS; *it having been shewn to be equally excellent* IN THE ACCURACY OF ITS IMITATION; *and to imitate* SUBJECTS, WHICH FAR SURPASS, AS WELL IN UTILITY, AS IN DIGNITY" (94). On the importance of Harris's work in eighteenth-century theorizing about the arts, see Malek 144–45 and Lipking 86–93. Among many other eighteenth-century theorists who contended for the superiority of poetry was Samuel Johnson, who said that compared with painting, poetry "is capable of conveying far more ideas; for men have thought and spoken of many things which they do not see" (2: 106).

56. Quoted in Field, f. 41.

57. "A Defense of Poetry" (1821) in *Shelley's Literary and Philosophical Criticism* 125.

58. On this doctrine see Abrams, *Mirror* 31–34, and Hagstrum 139–40.

which Shelley's mirror works. No longer reflecting the external world, the mirror of language reflects instead 'the actions and passions of our internal being," and "has relation to thoughts alone." For Shelley as for Burke, therefore, the privileged position of language is based on its special relation to the essentially immaterial world of the mind. Shelley does not follow Burke altogether; in contrasting the lucidity of language with the relative obscurity of the visual arts (a "cloud which enfeebles" the light of imagination), he suggestively reverses the terms in which Burke distinguished description from depiction. But the grounds for Shelley's elevation of poetry over painting remain essentially Burkean. Because it is made with language, poetry can better represent and express what Shelley presumes to be far superior to the external world—namely, our internal being.

Paradoxically, however, the clearest sign that poetry had regained or simply reasserted its superiority in the romantic period was the fact that "poetry" could sometimes embrace all means of expression. "Language, colour, [and] form," wrote Shelley, ". . . are all the instruments and materials of poetry."[59] Ostensibly magnanimous, such a statement actually preserves for the poetry of language much more than it gives away. For while *painting* ceased to be a word of unequivocal praise for poetry, *poetry* and its affiliates always carried honorific force when applied to painting. Significantly, poets and painters alike bestowed them on painting like so many medals—in phrases which themselves demonstrated the authority of words over pictures. Coleridge thought Wilson's *Niobe* first-rate "in poetic Conception" and said of Veronese's *St. Helena*: "That is a POEM indeed!" (*LC* 2: 1110); Wordsworth said that Haydon's etching of Wellington was "both poetically and pictorially conceived" (*LY* 2: 1033); Haydon said of himself that he "painted poetry" (*AMH* 1: 362); Joseph Severn, the artist who attended the dying Keats, thought that Turner's paintings in Rome "were like the doings of a poet who had taken to the brush" (Finberg 312); Constable described the drawings of J. R. Cozens as "all poetry" (*JCC* 6: 72); and Turner called Francis Danby "a poetical painter" (Finberg 290n).

What did it mean to call a painting or a painter "poetical"? Neither poets nor painters had any one simple definition. But they clearly saw that besides taking its subject matter from poetry, painting could mediate

59. *Complete Works* 5: 31; see also *Shelley's Literary and Philosophical Criticism* 125, 132.

between spirit and matter, and could thus transcend the mere copying of natural objects.

Coleridge defined painting as "the intermediate something between a thought and a thing."[60] For him the painted object was "a divine something corresponding to [something] within, which no image can exhaust."[61] To painting as well as to poetry he applied his distinction between imitation and copy, insisting that painting should not be a copy of nature—a deceptive simulation of it—but rather an imitation, a discernibly different and heightened re-presentation of the original.[62] This conviction was shared by both Turner and Constable. Turner ranked the Dutch school "lowermost" because it "takes its likeness by means of mere fidelity of imitation . . . sacrificing the independence of practice, and originality of invention for transcripts of nature, or servile imitation" (TMS S, f. 5). Likewise, Constable believed that art "pleases by *reminding*, not by *deceiving*," that great works of art must be far more than "mere copies of the productions of Nature," and that the artist's aim must be to "*unite imagination with nature*."[63]

Whether or not these statements adequately explain just what is meant by the application of "poetic" to a work of art, they suggest a remarkable degree of correspondence between the ways in which poetry and painting were conceived in the romantic period. Sometimes, in fact, the two were defined in virtually identical terms. Wordsworth wrote that "Poetry is passion" (*PW* 2: 513); Constable said that "Painting is but another word for feeling" (*JCC* 6: 78); and what Hazlitt called the "poetry of painting"

60. *TT* 57; see also *BL* 2: 253–55, where he makes the same point about music and the visual arts in general.

61. Coleridge, *Philosophical Lectures*, quoted in Park, "'Ut Pictura Poesis'" 161. Hazlitt described a picture gallery as "like a palace of thought. . . . The material is in some sense embodied in the immaterial" (10: 19; see also 17: 9, 11). Compare too Byron's account of the Venus de Medici as the moulding of a soul in stone (*Childe Harold's Pilgrimage* 4: 433–41) and Samuel Palmer's comment on one of Leonardo's skies: "the colour of the soul, not vulgar paint" (15).

62. See *BL* 2: 30, 256, and *LC* 3: 501, where he illustrates *copy* by the example of a marble peach and *imitation* by the example of Van Huysum's painting of fruit. Joshua Reynolds had likewise distinguished the aims of painting from the act of deceptive simulation, from what he calls the "imitation of external nature." But because *imitation* means *simulation* in Reynolds's vocabulary, he has no particular word for creative representation, for the complex act of representing nature *and* deviating from it to "gratify the mind" (*D* 232–44).

63. Leslie 106; Constable, *JCD* 110; Leslie 177. The last statement was actually made by Constable's friend and fellow artist John Jackson, and quoted by Constable with warm approval.

was precisely its expression of feeling, such as the "desolation" conveyed by Poussin's *Deluge* (10: 109, 136). Yet the terms applied to painting in the romantic period clearly work to the advantage of poetry, which
in effect supplies the criteria by which painting is to be judged and thus
forestalls the further imposition of distinctively pictorial criteria on poetry. If poetry was once expected to be *ut pictura* in empirical vividness
and fidelity to natural appearances, painting was now asked to be *ut
poesis* in its evocation of spirit. With painting itself thus redefined, or
rather with the old humanistic theory of painting thus revived and revised, poetry could use pictorial elements without—so to speak—sell-
ing its soul.

Romantic poetry is therefore powerfully depictive even as it resists
what Wordsworth calls the "tyranny" of the eye (*Prelude* 12.128–35) and
what Coleridge calls "dutchified" minuteness in description (see above,
note 48). Indeed, Coleridge's criticism of the pictorialism in certain
poems of Wordsworth does not spring from his opposition to all picture-
making in poetry but only to the laborious succession of minute pictorial
details. As an alternative, he warmly commends the "poetic painting"
exemplified by Milton's description of the fig tree, whose long and bending branches take root around the mother tree and grow to form

> a pillared shade
> High overarched, and echoing walks between;
> There oft the Indian herdsman shunning heat
> Shelters in cool, and tends his pasturing herds
> At loop-holes cut through thickest shade.
>> (*Paradise Lost* 9.1106–10)

"This," says Coleridge, "is *creation* rather than *painting*, or if painting,
yet such, and with so co-presence of the whole picture flash'd at once
upon the eye, as the sun paints in a camera obscura" (*BL* 2: 103). It is
striking to see that in the very act of illustrating and defining what he
calls "poetic painting," Coleridge invokes as a model for poetry the instantaneous impact of a picture—which is precisely one of the points on
which earlier theorists had distinguished painting from poetry.[64] What
Coleridge saw—as Lessing had before him—is that a fully detailed ver-

64. Painting is confined to a "single movement," said Lessing, while "succession of
time is the domain of the poet" (14, 64–65). Joshua Reynolds likewise said that poetry
engages the mind "by degrees" while painting strikes "at one blow" (*D* 146).

bal equivalent of a picture is not instantaneous but rather tediously successive.[65] To imitate the instantaneous flash of a painting, to "paint to the imagination," as Coleridge says (*BL* 2: 102), the poet must use the fewest possible verbal strokes.

Coleridge of course exaggerates, perhaps unwittingly, the instantaneousness of Milton's verbal picture. Though a pillared shade with loopholes cut in it may suggest a *camera obscura* with a pinhole through which the sun projects an image of itself, Milton's picture is not quite "flash'd . . . upon the eye."[66] It is rather made to grow before us as we discover in Milton's pillared shade not the projection of the sun—the reflected image of the outer world—but an inner world that gradually invites our introspective gaze even as the herdsman gazes out. Further, Coleridge himself notes that with "echoing walks" Milton invokes sound as well as sight to stimulate the eye of the mind (*BL* 2: 103). His verbal picture is therefore not the literal but the imaginative counterpart of a graphic one. In its exploitation of sound to excite vision as well as in its growing revelation of a shadowy enclosure that we are finally made to see as a whole, this is "poetic painting."

One other statement by Coleridge serves to show just how much he and Wordsworth too could appreciate the interpenetration of poetry and pictures. In the *Biographia Literaria*, Coleridge tells us that the *Lyrical Ballads* originated in conversations that

turned frequently on the two cardinal points of poetry, the power of exciting the sympathy of the reader by a faithful adherence to the truth of nature, and the power giving the interest of novelty by the modifying colours of imagination. The sudden charm which accidents of light and shade, which moonlight or sunset diffused over a known and familiar landscape, appeared to represent the practicability of combining both. (*BL* 2: 5)

The language Coleridge uses to describe the conception of poetry which engendered the *Lyrical Ballads* is unmistakably pictorial. He refers to the "modifying colours" of the imagination, and he compares its effect on the "truth of nature" to the distinctly pictorial effect of light and shade upon a "landscape"—which here of course means land beheld as if it were a picture. Significantly, however, the pictorial imagery does not simply set before us a static and opaque picture; it represents a process

65. For Lessing's discussion of this point, see Lessing 61–64.
66. On the history of the *camera obscura*, see Joel Snyder, "Picturing Vision" in Mitchell, *Language* 232–34.

of visible transformation that in turn symbolizes a process of imaginative transformation—the re-creation of nature in poetry. Like Wordsworth in "Tintern Abbey," Coleridge uses a verbally pictured landscape to give us the picture of a poet's mind.

Essentially, then, romantic poets responded to the sisterhood of the arts not by rejecting pictorialism but by fully assimilating it, reconceiving it in uncompromisingly "poetic" terms. But if poets could set the conditions under which painting entered the world of poetry, painters could not so easily do the reverse. They were caught in an almost irresolvable conflict between the pressure to be "poetic" and the special demands of their own medium.

In the eighteenth century, this conflict was generally suppressed by the belief that poetry could be translated into painting, and that even its techniques could be transferred from one medium to the other.[67] At the end of the century, in fact, when Turner and Constable were coming of age, Boydell and Macklin commissioned paintings that illustrated the works of Shakespeare and other English poets, built galleries to exhibit the paintings, and issued engravings of them. Yet these well-known galleries of "poetic" paintings—galleries, that Turner and Constable almost certainly visited—could hardly eliminate the fundamental problems inherent in any attempt to make pictures out of poetry.

A candid analysis of these problems can be found in the writings of Turner. Though Turner explicitly connected many of his own pictures with poems, and though he once stated flatly that "Poesy & Painting, being sisters agree intirely" (TMS BB, 22ᵛ), the very act of juxtaposing the sisters in his own work seems to have made him recognize the profound gap between them. About 1809, after ten years of quoting poetry under the titles of his exhibited pictures, he began to set down in words the difficulty of translating poems into paintings. If, he wrote, the painter departs from the poet to express his own vision, he is considered unfaithful to his original; if he follows the poet, "he is considered only secondarily as endeavouring to give to the most vulgar eye what has been admitted to be beautiful in the Poet, *by very different means.*" This difference of means decisively separates the poet from the painter, who "should omit, what is [in] many instances . . . from sentiment, the beauty of the poet, which in his language of Painting is inconsistent and Paradoxical" (TSB CVIII, 52ᵃ–51ᵃ). Citing Thomson's "Summer," lines

67. See Mitchell, *Blake's Composite Art* 17–18.

81–90, Turner insists that a painter cannot depict the "quality of motion" that Thomson gets into his sunrise: a time "beyond delin[e]ation, yet most truly drawn" (TSB CVIII, quoted in Ziff, "J. M. W. Turner" 198).

These thoughtful notes became the basis of a much more extended commentary on poetry and painting in Turner's fourth Academy lecture, first written 1810–12. In this lecture, Turner develops his analysis of Thomson's sunrise, and he also comments on another passage from "Summer," on one from Milton's "L'Allegro," and one from *Paradise Lost*. The purpose of these analyses is to show that no matter how pictorially descriptive poetry becomes, it will always frustrate the painter's attempts to put it on canvas. In "Summer," for instance, Thomson gives several "pictures" of the Nile at various stages: its "playful Youth, amid the fragrant Isles," its stately movement through splendid kingdoms, and its wild wandering "o'er solitary tracts" (lines 804–21). Citing this description, Turner notes that its individual scenes are all beautiful and "Poetic." But "to produce a whole" for the painter, he says, they "are almost all as to combination [an] impossibility"; and if you separate them, he asks, "where lies the majestic continuity of the Nile [?]" In Turner's eyes, Thomson's description of the Nile—along with his sunrise—paradoxically shows that "poetic description most full, most incidental, and display[ing] the greatest richness of verse is often the least pictorial" (TMS N, f. 8ᵛ). On the other hand, says Turner, "the opposite extreme of truth and pure simplicity" in poetry may be equally untranslatable to canvas. He quotes as follows Milton's description of twilight in *Paradise Lost*:

> Now came still Evening on and Twilight gray
> Had in his silvery livery all things clad.

Turner actually misquotes. In the original (4.598–99), the phrase is "sober Livery." But Turner was probably quoting from memory, and if the color denoted by "gray" and the sound of "livery" together prompted him to imagine a "silvery" light, his misquotation amounts to a painter's gloss upon the lines. For him at least, they suggest a light both somber and glowing, a light that cannot be realized on canvas. "Where," he asks, "can graphic art find incidents or aid, foil'd by a word of her own, gray? How define dignify'd purity without producing monotony of color?"[68] The

68. TMS N, f. 11. Contrast Diderot on Joseph Vernet's *Moonlight* in the Salon of 1763: "Il a rendu en couleur les tenebres visibles et palpables de Milton" (quoted in Wilton, *TS* 39).

answer to this rhetorical question is plainly implied, and Turner himself had already formulated it in the notes made about 1809. Recognizing that it was almost impossible for the painter to reproduce the "sentiments of the poet," he added: "Sentiments are his own and . . . he must embody them by known effects of nature, he should be allowed or consider'd equal [to the poet] in sentiments and having conquered his difficulties of mechanical [?] contradiction should be considered to have produced what is exclusively *his own*" (TSB CVIII, 51ᵃ–50ᵃ).

Turner's statement should be carefully weighed by anyone embarking on a study of Turner's relation to romantic poetry. In light of the fact that his interest in poetry continued unabated for the rest of his life, it could of course be read ironically. When Turner exhibits a painting entitled *Childe Harold's Pilgrimage*, as he did in 1832, is he presenting something "exclusively his own"? Strictly speaking, he is not. But the reference to Byron, like the reference to Thomson in the caption to *Buttermere*, chiefly serves to make us see the difference between the poet and the painter. We could say of Turner what W. J. T. Mitchell has said of Blake: that his refusal to provide visual translations of texts—whether his own or others—is "a basic principle in his theory of illustration" (*Blake's Composite Art* 19). It is also worth noting that most of the paintings Turner exhibited from 1812 to the end of his life were captioned with lines of a poem that was in fact his own, *The Fallacies of Hope*. If the romantic poets were determined to control the conditions under which painting could enter the world of their poems, Turner was equally bent on controlling the conditions under which poetry could enter the world of his paintings.

Yet precisely because of the acuteness with which he could define the limits of his art and the intensity with which he could defend its special powers, Turner dared to be "poetic" in a sense that Reynolds had forbidden. Reynolds had demanded in painting an absolute clarity and explicitness of presentation. For all his desire to promote painting by attaching it to the prestige of poetry, he could not approve in painting anything like the "poetic" practice of using "general indistinct expressions" which must be filled out and clarified by the imagination of the reader. Though he admits that "undetermined" sketches or drawings can make a poetic appeal to the imagination, he insists that everything in a finished picture be "carefully and distinctly expressed, as if the painter knew, with correctness and precision, the exact form and character of whatever is introduced into the picture."[69]

To this doctrine of explicitness—which Reynolds calls "a very fixed and indispensable rule in our art" (*D* 164)—Turner's theory and practice were decisively opposed. Though he brought to his work a profound and precise knowledge of forms, he ultimately aimed, as Hazlitt said, to represent not so much the objects of nature as "the medium through which they were seen" (4: 76n). And it is in Turner's representations of the interplay between atmosphere and form that we must seek the "poetry" of his painting.

If the *Discourses* of Joshua Reynolds can be read as a sustained attempt to gain for painting the intellectual prestige so long enjoyed by poetry, Turner's career can be seen as a lifelong struggle to gain for painting a virtually poetic kind of freedom: freedom to represent the infinite number of ways in which atmosphere transforms the natural world, and hence to explore and exploit the transforming power of painting. Turner's distinctive habit of captioning his pictures with poetry springs from the same impulse that caused him to ask in his will that two of his landscapes be hung beside landscapes of Claude in the National Gallery (Butlin and Joll 85). Just as he felt that his own work could withstand comparison with Claude's, so he believed that painting could withstand comparison with poetry, and could thereby reveal its own particular power.

But an equally important reason for the juxtaposition of landscape painting and poetry emerges from Constable's comments on the relation between the two. Though Constable did not regularly use poetic captions for his exhibited pictures, as Turner did, he quoted from *The Seasons* for the exhibition of *The Cornfield* in 1828 and of *Hadleigh Castle* in 1829 (Taylor 206; Leslie 176–77). He quoted Virgil, Thomson, Milton, Wordsworth, and several other poets in the letterpress for *English Landscape*, the set of twenty-two mezzotint engravings made from his pictures by David Lucas and published by Constable himself in 1833.[70] And as we

69. *D* 164. Reynolds says elsewhere, however, that the painter need not represent "minute particularities" or finish every hair.

70. Constable, *JCD* 8–27. On the title page printed for this set of engravings in 1833, the title given is *Various Subjects of Landscape, Characteristic of English Scenery* (*JCD* 7). Elsewhere, however, Constable speaks of the work as *English Landscape* (*JCD* 8, 11, 82), and I follow Beckett's lead in doing likewise.

have seen, his very last lecture on landscape—given at Hampstead in 1836—includes a lengthy quotation from *Paradise Lost*.

Here and elsewhere Constable uses poetry not so much for personal inspiration as for public demonstration that landscape had achieved in poetry the status it deserved to have in painting. As he says in one version of the prospectus to *English Landscape*,

It would be most gratifying to [the Artist] if . . . his humble efforts in Art, should in any degree tend to place English Scenery on the same footing in respect to Landscape [Painting] as that on which it has long stood with regard to Poetry. He is however convinced that it will eventually be acknowledged to be as capable of affording every material requisite for filling the canvas of the 'Landscape Painter' as it has been proved to be of supplying the finest imagery to our best descriptive Poets. (*JCD* 83)

Yet until the day that landscape painting stood with landscape poetry, Constable knew only too well that it could not speak for itself. It needed spokesmen like himself and Turner, and it likewise needed the supporting voices of the poets. What Turner and Constable both perceived about their art, in fact, clearly undermined the oft-repeated maxim that painting was universally and immediately intelligible, that in Dryden's words, painting spoke "the tongue of ev'ry land." [71] As applied to landscape painting, this was a polite fiction. It disguised the fact that in England at least, words spoke the only language understood and respected by all. Constable summed up the irony in a letter of 1833. Explaining why he had written commentaries for some of the pictures in *English Landscape*, he said tersely: "Many can read print & cannot read mezzotint" (*JCC* 3: 108).

The problem of reading mezzotint—or of interpreting any of the visual arts—remains as difficult and delicate for us as it was for Constable's contemporaries. The frequency with which Turner and Constable cite poetry and the compulsiveness with which Turner wrote it invite us to look for a visual poetry in their pictures, just as we may look for verbal pictures in the poetry of Wordsworth and Coleridge. But the distinctively poetic painting that Coleridge defines has its counterpart in the distinctively pictorial poetry produced by Constable and Turner. "Painting

71. "To Sir *Godfrey Kneller* (lines 124–27). The point was repeated in the eighteenth century by Samuel Johnson (2: 106), and in the romantic period by—among others—Coleridge (*BL* 2: 221) and Haydon (*LPD* 1: 221, 310).

is a science," said Constable, "and should be pursued as an inquiry into the laws of nature" (*JCD* 69). To compare the *Dedham Vale* that Constable painted in 1802 with the one he painted in 1828 is to see not so much the influence of the poetry he read in those years—including Wordsworth's—as the effect of his sustained inquiry into the laws of nature and of his own art: his relentless effort to find a pictorial language with which he could simultaneously express the complexity of natural forms, the shape of their movement, the life of the atmosphere, and—above all— the intensely concentrated power of his own feelings. What Constable said about the relation between painting and nature also reveals something about his conception of the relation between painting and poetry. "It is the business of a painter," he wrote, "not to contend with nature & put this scene (a valley filled with imagery 50 miles long) on a canvas of a few inches, but to make something out of nothing, in attempting which he must almost of necessity become poetical" (*JCC* 6: 172). The poetry of Constable's pictures lies not in their illustration of particular poems but in the power with which they make something out of nothing—that is, create something visually arresting from the intense observation of ordinary sights.

Sharing common aims, seeking to express at once the life of landscape and the life of the imagination, romantic poets and painters insisted on their separateness even as they continued to acknowledge not their parallelism but their triangular convergence, their inclination toward a "poetic painting" that unites representation with transformation, visual impact with imaginative import. But the task of defining this convergence is complicated by the fact that no significant influence flowed either way between the two major poets and painters of this study, or even between Turner and Constable. In spite of incidental evidence that has led some scholars to argue otherwise, I believe that Wordsworth and Coleridge were the only two of the four who formatively affected each other.[72] Consequently, any argument about what the poets and painters had in common must be based on a comparison of what they did in their respective arts and what they said about those arts in their essays, lectures, letters, notebooks, sketchbooks, and recorded conversations. Separated by all

72. Wordsworth's relations with Coleridge have been extensively studied. For a fine recent analysis of their complicated friendship, see McFarland 56–103. My reasons for believing that no significant influence flowed either way between the two major poets and painters of the present study are set forth in the Appendix.

the peculiarities of temperament which impede appreciation and under-standing, and divided too by all the differences between their arts, the poets and painters of this study were nonetheless bound by their common ambition to re-create the effect of landscape on their imaginations, to express their own perception of the outer world in such a way as to sig-nify the inner one. What Wordsworth said of poetry could be said of En-glish romantic landscape painting as well: that its business and duty "is to treat of things not as they *are*, but as they *appear*; not as they exist in themselves, but as they *seem* to exist to the *senses*, and to the passions" (*PrW* 3: 63).

Paradoxically, the correspondence I mean to explore grows out of an opposition to the traditional sisterhood of the arts. Inheriting landscape as a cultural phenomenon jointly created by painting, poetry, and land-scape gardening, the poets and painters of the romantic period had to reckon with the arts of landscape as well as with nature itself. But since the arts of landscape formed a crucial part of what they had to imitate, they redefined the relation between the arts in the very act of re-creating nature. With a "poetic painting" that transcends mere picture-making, Wordsworth and Coleridge reassert the metavisual powers of poetry. Likewise, with pictures that "make something out of nothing," that rep-resent the atmospheric transformation of the natural world, or that dras-tically revise the texts to which they are nominally attached, Turner and Constable reassert the independently "poetic" power of painting. The po-etry and painting of these four figures may therefore be seen not as paral-lel arts but as the lines of a triangle converging toward a common end from distinctively separate points.

To speak of the end as "common" is of course to risk the very reduc-tionism that the distinctive characteristics of painting and poetry will forever stubbornly resist. Yet we may reasonably begin to explore the correspondence between these two arts in the romantic period by consid-ering how Wordsworth, Constable, and Turner all displaced history: how Wordsworth overturned the traditional association of poetry with public history (the stuff of epic), how Constable made public history give way to the "natural history" of landscape as well as to the private history of his own relation to it, and how Turner made great historical moments con-tend with the power of the elements. To see what these three men did with the traditional authority of public history in painting and poetry alike is to understand one of the most important ways in which they re-created the arts of landscape.

CHAPTER 2

THE DISPLACEMENT
OF HISTORY

 THE MAJOR SHIFT in eighteenth-century art," says Ronald Paulson, "was from history painting to landscape as the norm of artistic expression" (*Literary Landscape* 16). This shift can certainly be documented, as Paulson himself has shown, yet no amount of documentation can explain why history should have continued to cast its shadow over landscape long after the end of the eighteenth century. Why did Constable's deliberate avoidance of historical subjects in favor of landscape cause him to be denied full membership in the Royal Academy until 1829? Why did Turner feel compelled—or impelled—to paint at least nominally historical canvases until 1850, the very last year he exhibited his work at the Academy? And correspondingly, in the first book of a poem that he began some seventy years after the appearance of Thomson's *The Seasons* and that was not even published until 1850, why did Wordsworth feel obliged to canvass traditionally historical subjects before settling down to write the history of his own relation to landscape?

These questions about romanticism and history arise with special force when we realize that much of romantic literature and art embodies the radically revolutionary desire to annihilate the past. "Drive your cart and your plow over the bones of the dead," says Blake in *The Marriage of Heaven and Hell* (*PPB* 35); essentially, this poem celebrates the overthrow of the ancien régime and the birth of the French republic, an event significantly marked in France itself by the origination of a new calendar wherein the year 1792 is suddenly displaced by the year 1, a radically new beginning. Hand in hand with this repudiation of the past goes the rediscovery of landscape as a prehistoric paradise unscarred by battle and unmarked by monument, a pristine spectacle never even represented before in any of the arts. Wordsworth strives to look at nature as if he were her first-born birth; Constable strives to forget the entire history of art when he makes a sketch from nature (Leslie 279). Even the history-obsessed hero of Byron's *Childe Harold's Pilgrimage* is periodically tempted to forget the past—his own and Europe's—when he gazes on the Edenic beauty of the Rhine, and in the resounding stanzas with which the poem concludes, he apostrophizes an ocean eternally unmarked by history: "Time writes no wrinkle on thine azure brow / Such as creation's dawn beheld, thou rollest now" (4: 1636–37).

To paraphrase Joyce, then, romanticism could be defined as the moment at which man awakens from the nightmare of history, or—in the words of Blake's *The French Revolution*—"from slumbers of five thousand years" (*PPB* 283). Yet as it awakened, the romantic imagination was like that of Milton's Eve when she wakes up after first being tempted by Satan in a dream (*Paradise Lost* 5: 28–93). Delighted to see Adam again, she is still profoundly troubled by what lingers in her memory, which now contains in embryonic form the whole history of Satan's rebellion against God: a history that she and Adam must be told and that they cannot afford to forget. The romantic poets and painters were likewise bound to confront history. Their recurrent longing to forget the past merely reveals the extent to which they were haunted by a consciousness of it.

Byron, for one, can never relinquish the past. Even as he idealizes an ocean on which time has written nothing, Byron himself is writing something, inscribing himself and his story—his history—in the history of texts. His own text—*Childe Harold's Pilgrimage*—is the record of a characteristically romantic alternation between the urge to forget and the compulsion to remember and record. Near the end of canto 3, after travelling through Switzerland and meditating on the literary remains of Rousseau, Gibbon, and Voltaire, he seems to turn from man to nature, from all texts—his own included—to the unmarked face of landscape:

> But let me quit Man's works, again to read
> His Maker's, spread around me, and suspend
> This page, which from my reveries I feed
> Until it seems prolonging without end.
>
> (3: 1013–16)

But the page is neither suspended nor forgotten; Byron continues to write and to remember, projecting his imagination through the clouds above him to the Alps, which lead him to anticipate Italy on the other side and hence inevitably to remember the first great crossing of the Alps by Hannibal:

> Italia, too! Italia! looking on thee,
> Full flashes on the soul of the light of ages,
> Since the fierce Carthaginian almost won thee,
> To the last halo of the chiefs and sages
> Who glorify thy consecrated pages.
>
> (3: 1022–26)

Just one stanza after proposing to quit man's works and suspend even the writing of his own page, Byron is back in the pages of history, caught up in a past which he is powerless to forget, enmeshed in a history to which he is even now adding his own.

The complexity of Byron's response to the past is at the very least matched by the complexity with which Wordsworth, Constable, and Turner defined their own response to it. Essentially, however, what their responses embody is a strategy of displacement.[1] Feeling inextricably bound to a past from which they sought to be free, they could neither forget nor obliterate history. What they could and did do, I shall argue, is to displace the kind of history they inherited: to make it give way to private history, natural history, or—most importantly—the history of man's relation to the natural world.

WORDSWORTH AND HISTORY

In the poetry of Wordsworth, the paradigmatic example of displacement is the poem customarily known as "Tintern Abbey." I say *customarily* because its full title is "Lines Composed a Few Miles Above Tintern Abbey, On Revisiting the Banks of the Wye During a Tour. July 13, 1798." It is a curiosity of literary history that the only part of this title we commonly use is the part referring to something nowhere mentioned in the poem itself and seldom mentioned even in critical commentaries on it. Yet unmistakably, the full title of "Tintern Abbey" invites us to see that the poem that Wordsworth might have written on the political and ecclesiastical history of a magnificent Cistercian ruin has been daringly displaced by a poem on the history of his own relation to the river Wye.[2]

---

1. Freud used *displacement* to mean the process by which, in dreams, material that seems unimportant takes the place and hence the value of psychically significant detail (215). I use *displacement* chiefly to mean the process by which natural phenomena, personal history, or rural episodes are made to assume the value and importance traditionally associated with scriptural episodes or sociopolitical history.

2. "A Wordsworthian landscape," says Karl Kroeber, "is inseparable from the history of the poet's mind" (*RLV* 103).

I speak of the displacement as daring because of the strength with which Wordsworth resists in this poem the almost irresistible appeal of his titular subject. Tintern Abbey—the monument, that is—is first of all a tangible thing, the only solid object which the lengthy title of the poem gives us. That is probably why we cling to this object when we refer to the poem, even as Wordsworth in his childhood grasped at a wall or tree to keep himself from falling into trances of idealism. Furthermore, the abbey in Wordsworth's time was—as it is now—a major tourist attraction. I have already noted that Gilpin called it a "splendid ruin" and that Turner exhibited a watercolor of it in 1794.[3] Doubly remarkable, it combined the visual appeal of Gothic tracery wreathed in foliage with the intellectual appeal of a history dating from the thirteenth century, from the age of monasticism to the age of the Reformation, when of course the monasteries were broken up. Visually rich and historically evocative, seated on a river and encircled by wooded hills, Tintern Abbey has been recently called "the most romantic Cistercian ruin in the country" (Rossiter 356). Yet Tintern Abbey is precisely what "Tintern Abbey" sets aside. In *The Prelude*, Wordsworth shows his admiration for the all-too-vulnerable delicacy of monastic shrines by the fervor with which he describes the Convent of the Chartreuse and the invasion of its solitude by French soldiers (6: 418–78). In "Tintern Abbey" he resists everything connected with the abbey itself—even the drama and pathos of its ruination. Given all the appeal of the abbey, Wordsworth's placing of himself a few miles above it is a daring act of self-assertion—an act whose significance deserves to be carefully weighed.

By this self-assertive act of displacement, Wordsworth is first of all doing what he much more elaborately does in book 1 of *The Prelude*, where the epic poem that he might have written on any one of the many historical themes he cites gives way to an autobiographical epic, the history of himself. Placing himself above Tintern Abbey, he presents himself as a figure not merely equal to it in historic importance but superior or, more precisely, anterior to it, above it in time as well as in space. The quest of *The Prelude* is a quest for unrecorded origins, for that ultimately unknown and unknowable source of what Wordsworth repeatedly calls the river of his mind.[4] Correspondingly, the opening lines of "Tintern

3. See above, p. 22. By 1818, if not sooner, Tintern Abbey had come to be regarded as a "hackneyed subject"—at least for painting. See the comments on the Royal Academy exhibition of 1818 in *Annals* 3: 293.

4. See for instance *Prelude* 2. 209; 9. 1–8; and 14. 193–202.

Abbey" speak of waters rolling from above the abbey, the waters of the Wye "rolling from their mountain-springs / With a soft inland murmur."

Yet the abbey is not simply set aside by the title and forgotten for the rest of the poem. The landscape of the opening passage is prehistoric rather than unhistoric, prefiguring the abbey that is not so much absent entirely as not yet there, waiting downriver in the flow of time. Consider the

> steep and lofty cliffs
> That on a wild secluded scene impress
> Thoughts of more deep seclusion; and connect
> The landscape with the quiet of the sky.
>
> (Lines 5–8)

The cliffs cannot be found above Tintern Abbey; Wordsworth moved them there from below the abbey to suggest, I think, the soaring walls of a natural cathedral.[5] The cliffs connect the landscape not only with the quiet of the sky but also with the quiet of the roofless ruin miles below them; they surround this wild secluded scene and thus convert it into a place of contemplation, an external sign of the depth, seclusion, and vastness of the human mind. The sense of monastic contemplation subtly conveyed here is reinforced a few lines later by the image of the hermit, the natural or prehistoric monk whose presence is merely suggested by the wreaths of smoke sent up in silence from among the trees

> With some uncertain notice, as might seem
> Of vagrant dwellers in the houseless woods,
> Or of some Hermit's cave, where by his fire
> The Hermit sits alone.
>
> (19–22)

The contrasting images of vastness and enclosure—the cathedral-like magnitude of the steep and lofty cliffs and the contracted space of the cave—together create a sense of prehistorically monastic seclusion. In

---

5. In *Cumberland and Westmoreland*, Gilpin reports that a towering rock over the entrance to a cave in Castleton is known as "the cathedral" (2: 215). In "Yew Trees," composed in 1803 (?), Wordsworth himself speaks of the trees forming a "natural temple" (line 29). See also Dorothy Wordsworth's Journal for 20 January 1798—just a few months before the composition of "Tintern Abbey": "Upon the highest ridge of that round hill covered with planted oaks, the shafts of the trees show in the light like the columns of a ruin" (1).

The Prelude, in fact, Wordsworth explicitly connects the figure of a hermit "Deep in the bosom of the wilderness" with the figure of a

> Votary (in vast cathedral, where no foot
> Is treading, where no other face is seen)
> Kneeling at prayers.
>
> (4: 362–64)

In this passage, the hermit and the votary are both presented as images of solitude. Together they make explicit what is implicit in the opening lines of "Tintern Abbey," where Wordsworth displaces the abbey itself by a natural monastery of solitude and contemplation.

Throughout the poem, the history of the displaced abbey subtly permeates Wordsworth's contemplation of his own history. It is in fact through its subtle connection with the abbey that the landscape of the Wye becomes enchambered, so to speak, so that it may symbolize the paradoxically enclosed vastness of the mind's own space as it emerges from the lonely rooms of urban confinement to the expansiveness of a setting in which all the mighty world of eye and ear can be encompassed and somehow contained—as Wordsworth will finally say to his sister Dorothy—in the dwelling place of memory, "the mansion for all lovely forms" (line 140).[6] Indeed, it is precisely by spatializing the mind that Wordsworth strives to make it permanent, to situate it above the flow of time. The survival of the abbey gives him reason to hope that he may do so. Situated on the banks of a river, it paradoxically embodies in its history both dissolution and permanence, violence and tranquillity, ruin and beauty; its *stand* against the destructiveness of time is precisely the stand that Wordsworth takes as he contemplates his own past, present, and future.

To withstand the destructiveness of time, the mind must gradually

---

6. In *The Art of Memory* (Chicago, 1966), Frances Yates shows that poets and orators traditionally used spatial forms to help them memorize their texts. Albert Wlecke notes that Wordsworth "consistently tends to speak of his mind in metaphors implying spatial extent," and he quotes Gaston Bachelard to confirm his interpretation of the hermit in the cave as a secret power lurking within the mind. The hermit's hut, says Bachelard (who is commenting on a legendary icon rather than on Wordsworth's poem), signifies "centralized solitude. . . . The hermit is *alone* before God. His hut, therefore, is just the opposite of the monastery" (32). I agree that the hut signifies centralized solitude, but rightly or wrongly, Wordsworth would not regard such solitude as antithetical to monastic life. In *The Prelude*, he treats the Convent of the Chartreuse as the embodiment of "*solitude*," a word he uses and italicizes twice in three lines (6. 419–21).

turn from a river into a kind of abbey, a place on the river, a place from which the flow of time can be serenely and imperturbably witnessed. This is the place or station that Wordsworth strives to assume in the poem. What he wants Dorothy to remember is the fact that they "stood together" (151) on the banks of the Wye, and that he stands guard over her maturation even as he contemplates his own. Yet critics have long recognized the irony in Wordsworth's claim that the mature pleasures of contemplation bring him "abundant recompense" (88) for the loss of his youthful vitality. When Wordsworth says that he neither mourns nor murmurs for this loss (86), the very intensity of the denial invites us to suspect the opposite, and when he dismissively describes his youth as "thoughtless" (90), he is willfully misremembering a period of his life when he was quite capable of thought.[7] Wordsworth fictionalizes his own history. As Paul Sheats has finely observed, he "constructs a past that he can relinquish without protest" (238). This "thoughtless" past of aching joys and dizzy raptures can be balanced, even overbalanced, by a double-meaning *present* of "other gifts" (86)—the gifts of contemplation, introspection, and recollection. Yet in this putative progression from the passionate instability of youth to the thoughtful stability of age, Wordsworth cannot fully relinquish his nostalgic yearning for wildness, disturbance, even instability. While describing the serenity of his present state, he speaks of a presence that "disturbs me with the joy / Of elevated thoughts" (94–95). While assuring Dorothy that her "wild ecstasies shall be matured / Into a sober pleasure" (138–39), he speaks repeatedly—almost obsessively—of her wild eyes (119, 148), and he uneasily anticipates a time when he can no more catch from those wild eyes "these gleams of past existence" (148–49). Wordsworth longs to recapture the very wildness that he claims to have relinquished and transcended. At the same time, in his putatively fixed stand upon the river, he must contemplate the inexorability of time even as he yearns to stand above it. Below him on the Wye is a violated monument to contemplation. Displaced as it is

---

7. In the opening section of *An Evening Walk*, first published 1793 but composed several years earlier, Wordsworth contrasts the melancholy mood of his present state with the happy wildness of his childhood and youth (lines 17–26). More pertinently, Mary Moorman suggests that when he describes himself in "Tintern Abbey" as having been a kind of fugitive in 1793—"more like a man / Flying from something that he dreads than one / Who sought the thing he loved" (lines 70–72)—he is recalling his attempt to flee "the torment of his own thoughts and memories" at a time when England had just declared war on a revolutionary France that he still fervently admired (Moorman 220–33). On the significance of denial in "Tintern Abbey," see Onorato 37–42, 67.

by his personal history, the history of that violated monument is subtly and ironically recalled when he assures his sister that nature can turn the mind into a place of inviolable serenity:

> for she can so inform
> The mind that is within us, so impress
> With quietness and beauty, and so feed
> With lofty thoughts, that neither evil tongues,
> Rash judgements, nor the sneers of selfish men,
> Nor greetings where no kindness is, nor all
> The dreary intercourse of daily life,
> Shall e'er prevail against us, or *disturb*
> *Our cheerful faith*, that all which we behold
> Is full of blessings.
>
> (125–34; italics added)

Standing above the ruined monument of a faith profoundly disturbed by the Reformation, Wordsworth assures Dorothy that their faith will be undisturbed. The act of displacement that he performs at the beginning of the poem now becomes an act of faith: faith in the benevolence of nature, faith in his own and his sister's capacity to withstand the ruinating ravages of time. In the concluding lines of the poem, where he speaks of himself as a worshipper of nature, he becomes a votary within the prehistoric cathedral that he has made of the landscape, a landscape that has now become a vertical structure as well as a spreading prospect in the mind. Profoundly internalized, the structure has been externalized for us in the fragmented architecture of the poem itself, with its soaring arches of transcendental vision and its broken buttresses—the gaps between past and present, the caesuras and half-lines that again and again in the poem suggest rupture, fracture, discontinuity, and disturbance. Yet just as the medieval abbey has survived the very disruption to which its ruined grandeur bears enduring witness, Wordsworth can imagine that his own faith will survive in the very words of the poem. In the end, he displaces the abbey and its history with a verbal monument to his own enduring struggle with time.

To read "Tintern Abbey" in these terms is to see its deep connections with a poem that Wordsworth wrote two years later and that in many ways seems quite different from it—namely, "Michael." While "Tintern Abbey" tells the intensely personal story of Wordsworth himself, "Michael" tells the story of an old shepherd and his family, so that the two poems seem to epitomize the two poles between which Wordsworth vibrated in this period: the pole of autobiographical self-expression on the one hand, and on the other, the pole of low mimetic narrative, the imitation of humble and rustic life—what Coleridge rather disdainfully called "ventriloquism" (*BL* 2: 209). Yet for all its differences from "Tintern Abbey," "Michael" shows us once again the displacement of history.

The opening lines of this poem invite us to turn from the public way and struggle up the tumultuous brook of Greenhead Ghyll. But the reward for this arduous climb is not the historically significant ruin that we might expect. It is rather an object of no apparent history or significance at all: a straggling heap of unhewn stones. In this poem of what is clearly "humble and rustic life," Wordsworth is again displacing the history of great public events and monuments with private history, the history of an old shepherd's pathetically frustrated struggle to monumentalize his relation to his land on the one hand and his son on the other. What is striking about the straggling heap of unhewn stones is that it is not only not a ruin of conventionally historic significance; it is not a ruin at all. It is not the relic of that which was but the unfulfilled promise of that which was to be. Here Wordsworth once again reverses historical perspective. Just as in "Tintern Abbey" he contemplates the prehistoric cathedral of the cliffs, here he contemplates at once the history and the prehistory of a sheepfold. The unhewn stones have barely begun to emerge from their unformed natural state into a structure of significant form, and they are doomed to remain forever in that state of incipient emergence. Nevertheless, the project of the poem is to make a history emerge from them, or— as Wordsworth goes on to suggest—to convert the oral, pretextual story of Michael into written history "for the sake / Of youthful Poets, who among these hills / Will be my second self when I am gone."[8] On a deliberately modest scale, Wordsworth is thus reenacting the genesis of the epic tradition, in which oral stories or oral histories of the Trojan War become Homeric texts. The great heroic history traditionally recorded in epic has been displaced by what Wordsworth calls at first a "story" and then "a history / Homely and rude" (lines 19, 34–35).

The significant shift from "story" to "history" in the opening lines of the poem shows us that Wordsworth is seeking to write a new kind of history. If history is the stuff from which literature—like painting—is

8. Lines 38–39. On the theme of literary legacy in "Michael," see Lea 55–68.

traditionally made, Wordsworth is determined to remake our concept of
history even as he remakes poetry. Before Wordsworth, the word "history" had been sometimes used to mean the record of a life which conventional history would not bother to record; the full title of Fielding's
Tom Jones (1749) is *The History of Tom Jones, a Foundling*. But Fielding's work is a comic epic explicitly linked to the tradition of serious
epic, conventionally historic in scope and social richness if not in the
status and stature of its central figure. No such kind of history can be
found in Wordsworth's story of an isolated shepherd. Furthermore, Wordsworth uses the word "history" not only for his own narrative but also—in
the plural—for the stories that Michael tells Luke on the eve of Luke's
fateful departure to London. Ironically seeking to bind Luke to him even
as he sends him away, Michael says, "I will relate to thee some little
part / Of our two histories" (336–37).

The word "histories" reminds us that the histories or history of their
relation has already been told once. Within the poem it is a twice-told
tale, and the second version of it—Michael's version—differs notably
from the first. In the first version, the poet-narrator tells us of the joy and
love that Michael felt for the young Luke, but also of the sternness with
which the old man tried to train him in the work of shepherding, reprov-
ing him

> if he disturbed the sheep
> By catching at their legs, or with his shouts
> Scared them, while they lay beneath the shears.
>
> (174–76)

The boy was

> Something between a hindrance and a help;
> And for this cause not always, I believe,
> Receiving from his Father hire of praise;
> Though nought was left undone which staff, or voice,
> Or looks, or threatening gestures, could perform.
>
> (189–93)

From the narrator, then, the picture we get is clearly that of a taskmaster
regularly chastising a wayward apprentice. Yet when Michael recalls this
period of Luke's life with him, the presumably factual history of their
relationship gives way to a fictive history, a history not derived from rec-

ollection but rather created by desire. Forgetting or repressing the memory of his efforts to train and discipline the boy in the work of shepherding, Michael says:

> we were playmates, Luke; among these hills,
> As well thou knowest, in us the old and young
> Have played together, nor with me didst thou
> Lack any pleasure which a boy can know.
>
> (353–56)

Michael is radically reconstructing the past even as he tries to determine the future, to perpetuate in the stone of the sheepfold both his love for Luke and his equally powerful love of the land. In the conflict between the two histories of Luke's childhood—between the story of play and pleasure and the story of a strained apprenticeship—lies also the irresolvable conflict between Michael's desire to possess Luke and his desire to possess the land for Luke. As he sends Luke away, Michael himself seems to realize painfully that he is not saving the land for Luke but rather sacrificing Luke for the land, and that in doing so he is doomed to lose both:

> I knew that thou couldst never have a wish
> To leave me, Luke: thou hast been bound to me
> Only by links of love: when thou art gone,
> What will be left to us?
>
> (399–402)

What is left is only the straggling heap of unhewn stones, a profoundly enigmatic monument to frustrated hope. Architecturally unformed and therefore meaningless to the conventional historian, the stones can be interpreted only by an historian of the heart, who gives them a permanent place in the architecture of his poem, who makes of them a lastingly rich and complex symbol of union and dissolution, permanence and change, possession and loss.

To move from "Michael" to *The Prelude* is to consider the displacement of history on a much larger scale. As I have already noted, Wordsworth reveals in book 1 of the poem that he began to write his autobiographical epic only after considering and rejecting a succession of the historical or quasi-historical themes that constituted the subject matter of traditional epic. Wordsworth regarded *The Prelude* as a fundamentally original work. On 1 May 1805, shortly before he finished the first version, he wrote with a mixture of sheepishness and pride about what he called its "alarming length! and a thing unprecedented in Literary history that a man should talk so much about himself" (*LW* 1: 586). In saying this, Wordsworth of course forgets or represses the double precedent of Augustine's *Confessions* and the *Confessions* of Rousseau, who himself forgets Augustine when he begins by declaring: "I have resolved on an enterprise which has no precedent."[9] Yet in certain fundamental ways, Wordsworth's *Prelude* is unprecedented, and not least in the daring with which the poet makes his own history take precedence over that of public figures and great events. We can see this clearly when we look at Wordsworth's account of his journey through the Simplon Pass in the light provided by Rousseau's account of *his* Alpine crossing made some sixty-two years before Wordsworth's. Having left his native Geneva at the age of sixteen to seek his fortune elsewhere, and having decided to seek it first in Turin, Rousseau crossed the Alps in a spirit of high adventure, acting out a metaphor for his own ambition, feeling that the height of the Alps would symbolize the height by which he would ultimately surpass his former comrades: "My heart," he says,

was full of young desires, alluring hopes, and brilliant prospects. Every object I saw seemed a guarantee of my future happiness. I saw in my imagination a country feast in every house and wild game in every meadow, bathing in every river and fishing from every bank; delicious fruit on every tree and voluptuous assignations in the shade; bowls of milk and cream on the mountain-sides, everywhere the delights of idleness, and peace and simplicity, and the joy of going one knew not where. (63–64)

This heaven of the hedonist is made still more glorious by the recollection of a great historic event, the same event that came to Byron's mind when he contemplated the crossing of the Alps in *Childe Harold's Pilgrimage*. For Rousseau adds: "To be travelling to Italy so young, to have seen so many countries already, to be following in Hannibal's footsteps across the mountains, seemed to me a glory beyond my years" (64).

9. Rousseau 17. Lindenberger (163) notes that Wordsworth owned an early French edition of the *Confessions* bound with *Reveries of a Solitary Walker*, but Wordsworth himself nowhere definitely refers to the *Confessions*. In his *Letter to the Bishop of Llandaff*, probably written in February or March 1793, he quotes from Rousseau's *Contract Social* (*PrW* 1: 36) and at several other points seems to echo its arguments (see *PrW* 2: 57, 59). He also cites Rousseau in his preface to *The Borderers* (written 1796–97), making what is apparently a reference to *Emile* (*PrW* 1: 76–77, 82), and in conversation he reportedly made a disparaging allusion to the "paradoxical reveries of Rousseau" (Peacock 335).

To read Rousseau's account—or Byron's, for that matter—is to realize how readily the recollection of Hannibal could spring to the mind of any literate traveller bent on crossing the Alps and filled with excitement at the prospect of doing so. Wordsworth himself refers to Hannibal in the "Essay, Supplementary to the Preface of 1815," when he says that a genuinely original author will have much in common with his predecessors, "but, for what is peculiarly his own, he will be called upon to clear and often to shape his own road:—he will be in the condition of Hannibal among the Alps" (*PrW* 3:80).

This is precisely the condition of Wordsworth as he describes his own crossing of the Alps in book 6 of *The Prelude*. But Hannibal's name is conspicuously absent from Wordsworth's truly unprecedented account of a crossing he made unconsciously when the way up over the Alps turned out to be—to his bewilderment and dismay—a way simply downwards. Wordsworth and his friend Robert Jones were following a band of travellers across the Alps to Italy. When the travellers got ahead of them, they had to find their own way, and they assumed that the right way was a steady climb upward, a mountingly glorious ascent. So when the road they took broke off at a stream, they assumed that the only thing to do was follow a track that led upwards on the other side. But this track did not lead them to the band of travellers who had gone ahead of them. On the contrary, they learned from a peasant that they would have to return to the stream they had crossed and follow the road that ran beside it—a road that ran steadily

> downwards, with the current of that stream.
> Loth to believe what we so grieved to hear,
> For still we had hopes that pointed to the clouds,
> We questioned him again, and yet again;
> But every word that from the peasant's lips
> Came in reply, translated by our feelings,
> Ended in this,—*that we had crossed the Alps*.
>
> (6: 585–91)

What Wordsworth discovered at this moment is that he had been literally translated, carried across the Alps without realizing it. Experience denied him the consciousness of crossing, the supreme moment of heroic daring and—insofar as he was walking in the footsteps of Hannibal—historic daring as well. To write about this Alpine crossing, he had to reckon with a frustrating absence at the very moment when he would have most wished for the memory of presence, had to acknowledge the painful fact that a would-be moment of supreme consciousness in his own history had been displaced by a moment of unconsciousness, so that there was no moment of crossing to remember.

As a traveller, then, Wordsworth lost his way. Yet as a poet, he finds it. Making his way through a verbal passage far more difficult and daunting than the Simplon Pass itself, Wordsworth is no longer following in the footsteps of Hannibal, as Rousseau did; the glory of Hannibal's crossing is utterly displaced by the glory of Wordsworth's realization that in striving to reenact a moment of physical crossing which he never consciously experienced and which he therefore cannot remember, he psychically crosses from recollection to revelation, from the measurable height of an Alpine pass to the immeasurable height of his own aspirations:

> Imagination!—here the Power so called
> Through sad incompetence of human speech,
> That awful Power rose from the mind's abyss
> Like an unfathered vapour that enwraps,
> At once, some lonely traveller. I was lost;
> Halted without an effort to break through;
> But to my conscious soul I now can say—
> 'I recognize thy glory.'
>
> (6: 592–99)

The glory of a great moment in ancient history is thus displaced by the glory of a great moment in the history of Wordsworth's imagination. Yet it is not only the memory of Hannibal's heroism that gives way here; it is the structure of memory itself, which gives way before the power of a revelation that Wordsworth experiences *as he writes*.[10] In this moment he is not recording the past, either Hannibal's or his own; soaring above the footsteps of memory, he is rather celebrating the power of imagination in time present.

Yet it is indeed the history of Wordsworth's imagination that finally displaces all others in *The Prelude*—even those that are explicitly acknowledged. Wordsworth plainly tells us that when he went to London, he felt the burden of its history. "A sense," he says,

10. Hartman rightly observes that Wordsworth in this moment is led "beyond nature" (*Wordsworth's Poetry* 46), but we must also recognize that he is led beyond history and memory as well.

> Of what in the Great city had been done
> And suffered, and was doing, suffering, still
> Weighed with me, could support the test of thought.
>   (8: 625–28)

He felt the weight of history signified by all the monumental sights that
he had come to see: St. Paul's Cathedral, the tombs of Westminster Abbey, the Giants of Guildhall, the carved maniacs of Bedlam, the gilded
equestrian statues in vast squares, "and that Chamber of the Tower /
Where England's sovereigns sit in long array / Their steeds bestriding"
(7.129–38). Yet all these sights and all of the history they signify were
in one blindingly revelatory moment obliterated for Wordsworth as he
made his way through the crowded streets of the city one day in a state of
dreamlike detachment:

> And once, far-travelled in such mood, beyond
> The reach of common indications, lost
> Amid the moving pageant, 'twas my chance
> Abruptly to be smitten with the view
> Of a blind beggar, who, with upright face,
> Stood propp'd against a Wall, upon his Chest
> Wearing a written paper, to explain
> The story of the Man and who he was.
> My mind did at this spectacle turn round
> As with the might of waters, and it seem'd
> To me that in this Label was a type,
> Or emblem, of the utmost that we know,
> Both of ourselves and of the universe.
>   (A 7: 607–19)

In this moment of revelation, the whole history of London gives way to
the story of a single human life written on a piece of paper: a story that of
course prefigures the story Wordsworth is even now writing about himself
on a piece of paper. In the revised version of this passage, the link between the beggar's paper and Wordsworth's whole poem becomes even
more explicit. The beggar wears the paper, we are told,

> to explain
> His story, whence he came, and who he was.
>   (7: 641–42)

Wordsworth's ultimate aim in the *Prelude* is precisely this: to explain not history but his story, whence he came and who he was. Recalling earlier in the poem a moment from his childhood, he asks, "How shall I trace the history, where seek / The origin of what I then have felt?" (A 2.365–66). In the latter part of *The Prelude*, this question is paradoxically answered by a structure that at first makes the history of a person give way to a personal history of the French revolution. In books 9 through 11, the story of Wordsworth's affair with Annette Vallon—a story that Rousseau would never have dreamed of suppressing—is displaced by political history, or more precisely by the story of Wordsworth's ecstatic affair with revolutionary idealism.[11] Yet in the end, the history of the French Revolution is itself displaced by the story of how Wordsworth recovered his imaginative strength after the collapse of revolutionary idealism left him in a state of despair. In the concluding lines of *The Prelude*, the revolution is literally reduced to a parenthesis in Wordsworth's statement of what he and Coleridge will reveal in their poetry about the human mind:

> what we have loved,
> Others will love, and we will teach them how;
> Instruct them how the mind of man becomes
> A thousand times more beautiful than the earth
> On which he dwells, above this frame of things
> (Which, 'mid all revolutions in the hopes
> And fears of men, doth still remain unchanged)
> In beauty exalted, as it is itself
> Of quality and of fabric more divine.
>
> (14.446–54)

CONSTABLE AND HISTORY

Nothing that precisely corresponds to Wordsworth's displacement of history in *The Prelude* can be found in the work of Constable and Turner, for a painting can hardly duplicate the structure of an autobiographical epic. Nevertheless, Turner and Constable had to contend with something

11. "Bliss was it in that dawn to be alive, / But to be young was very Heaven!" (11. 108–9). A disguised story of Wordsworth's affair with Vallon is told at some length in the early version of *The Prelude* (A 9. 555–934), then cut to a passing reference in the final version (9. 553–59). In 1820 Wordsworth published a version of the disguised story under the title "Vaudracour and Julia."

very similar to what Wordsworth faces in book 1 of *The Prelude*. As Wordsworth had to reckon with the long-standing assumption that epic poetry could be made only from the history of great events, Turner and Constable had to reckon with the well-established view that painting of the highest kind had to be "historic" in a broad sense, had to take its subject matter from what was commonly known as history, or from Scripture, mythology, or epic poetry. Throughout the eighteenth century and into the nineteenth, history painting in this broad sense ranked far above the painting of landscape, which was persistently regarded as a "low subject."[12]

Its status was not substantially changed even by the considerable achievements of Wilson and Gainsborough. The delicate, Italianate, and often subtly classicized landscapes of Wilson won him acclaim in Italy and some transitory fame in London, but the final price that he paid for his lifelong devotion to landscape was a final decade of poverty and neglect leading up to his death in 1782.[13] Gainsborough was far more successful, but his reputation and wealth came far less from his landscapes—on which I shall say more in the next chapter—than from his portraits.[14] In addition, though he produced only one major historical landscape himself and though he thought that history should in general be kept out of landscape, his "fancy pictures" of idealized rustics in the 1780s are directly traceable to the influence of biblical pictures by

12. Landscape painting was thus designated in 1725 by Jonathan Richardson, who also said that the "great business of painting . . . is to relate a history or fable, as the best historians have done" (iii–iv). In the *Analysis of Beauty* (1753), Hogarth puts landscape painting well below history painting, saying that it required only "mean abilities" (214–15). Joshua Reynolds speaks more respectfully of landscape painting in his *Discourses*, but he makes no effort to elevate its rank; on the contrary, he places even the landscapes of Claude among those works that deserve only limited praise because their subjects are "low and confined" (51–52).

13. In 1811 Turner castigated one of Wilson's rivals for having "defrauded the immortal Wilson of his right and snatched the laurel from his aged brow. . . . In acute anguish he retired, and as he lived he died neglected" (Ziff, "Backgrounds" 146–47). Leslie Parris notes that opinions changed about twenty years after Wilson's death, and "by 1814, when 88 pictures by (or attributed to) him were exhibited at the British Institution, Wilson was fully instated, with artists at least, as the founder of the British school of landscape and its first martyr" (29). For a full-scale study of Wilson, see W. G. Constable.

14. Prince Hoare wrote that Gainsborough "was so disgusted at the blind preference paid to his powers of portraiture, that, for many years of his residence at Bath, he regularly shut up all his landscapes in the back apartments of his house, to which no common visitors were admitted" (*Epochs of the Arts* [1813], quoted in Parris 41).

Murillo. *The Woodman*, for instance, which he painted in 1787—the year before his death—and which he regarded as his masterpiece, was apparently inspired by Murillo's *St. John in the Wilderness*.[15]

While landscape painting thus lay in the shadow of history, history painting itself was undergoing notable changes. Benjamin West's exhibition of *The Death of General Wolfe* in 1771 moved Joshua Reynolds to predict that it would prompt "a revolution in art" (quoted in Kroeber, "Experience" 325n). Instead of the toga and sandals traditionally used for costuming in historical pictures, West clothed his figures in modern military uniforms.[16] Furthermore, as Karl Kroeber has argued, the neoclassic "circle of repose" formed by Wolfe's attending officers was somewhat disturbed by the alien figure of the near-naked Indian who sits in the foreground gazing inscrutably at the general's sagging body.[17] Nevertheless, West's picture did not change the essential traditions of history painting, which required—among other things—that the principal figure be strongly and decisively emphasized. Nor did it materially alter the relation between history and landscape in painting. West's picture is dominated by the figure of the dying Wolfe, who draws all gazes to him; the mass of clouds at left, the tree at right, and the bits of field in the distance make up simply the background to an historical event.

Whether or not West's picture gave "a new impetus" to history painting, as Rothenstein suggests (72), this kind of painting unquestionably enjoyed more prestige than any other in the early decades of the nineteenth century. In the introduction to his *Biographical and Critical Dictionary of Painters and Engravers* (1813–16), Michael Bryan roundly declares that history painting "deservedly occupies the most exalted rank in the various departments of the art" (quoted in *Annals* 2: 527). It was admittedly not the most profitable kind of painting, and Royal Academicians were accused of neglecting it for the sake of portrait commissions (*Annals* 3: iv–vii). But West, president of the Academy from 1806 to 1820, was himself a history painter, and few Academicians in this period

15. See Hayes 1: 48, 51, 63. Gainsborough's historical landscape was the unfinished *Diana and Actaeon* of about 1784–85. *The Woodman* was destroyed by fire in 1810, though it had been engraved by P. Simon in 1791 (Waterhouse 104).

16. On "the goal of historical veracity" which emerges in French as well as English painting of this period, see Rosenblum 34ff. But James Barry was so outraged by West's flouting of classical conventions that he painted his own *Death of Wolfe* with the figures nude (Rothenstein 74).

17. Kroeber, "Experience" 328. The phrase "circle of repose" is Ronald Paulson's.

would have questioned the point made by the editor of the *Annals of the Fine Arts* in 1819: that "the encouragement of historical painting, ought to be the first object in any great nation that wishes to encourage art."[18]

It was precisely the prestige of historical painting that kept Constable out of the Royal Academy for much of his career. He was kept waiting, as he knew only too well, by "'highminded' members who stickle for the 'elevated noble' walks of art—i.e. preferring the *shaggy posteriors of a Satyr* to the *moral feeling of landscape*" (Constable, *JCC* 3: 18–19). Even when he finally became a full Academician in 1829 at age fifty-two, he was made to feel that a special favor had been done him. It was five years after *The Hay Wain* and two of his other paintings had made him a celebrity at the Paris Salon and won him a gold medal awarded by Charles X; but when he went to call on the Academy president, Thomas Lawrence (a portraitist), he was informed that he was "peculiarly fortunate in being chosen an Academician at a time when there were historical painters of great merit on the list of candidates" (Leslie 173).

To this tenacious prejudice in favor of history painting Constable and Turner responded in two different ways. Constable spurned history almost entirely in favor of landscape, which he defiantly regarded as "the most lovely department of painting as of poetry" (*JCC* 6: 182). Turner painted history throughout his career, but as we shall see, he made it strive for mastery with the powers of nature and with the force of his profoundly personal vision. In different ways, therefore, each of these two artists was challenging the dominance of history, exposing it to the pressure of something else.

Constable challenged the dominance of history painting by seeking to show that landscape painting had a history of its own. In his lectures he aimed "to separate [landscape] from the mass of historical art in which it originated, and with which it was long connected" (*JCD* 40). He therefore traced the history of landscape from its appearance in the background of scriptural works—where the sky is darkened for the crucifixion, for instance, or where rocks and trees surround the sepulchre—to its emergence as "a distinct branch of art" (*JCD* 41). Paulson argues that this amounts to a theory of subtraction: landscape painting is history painting with the history removed, but with the landscape arranged, ac-

18. *Annals* 3: iii. Perhaps in response to this exhortation, the Royal Academy offered in 1819 a gold medal for the best historical painting in oil and designated as the subject

tivated, and atmospherically charged "*as if* there were heroic figures contending within it, violently and passionately" (*Literary Landscape* 134). Paulson thus implies that the power of Constable's own landscapes depends, at least in part, on their capacity to stir historical associations, to make natural elements of landscape symbolically reenact historical moments. But the question which this penetrating suggestion raises is why Constable should have wished to provoke historical associations in an art that sought to declare its independence of history. The answer, I believe, is that Constable aimed to demonstrate the power of landscape painting as "a distinct branch of art" precisely by reminding us of what this art was contending against. If landscape was—in Constable's words—"first used as an assistant in conveying sentiment" (*JCD* 41), then elements such as light and darkness had prehistoric powers of their own, something they brought *to* history paintings. It is this that Constable seeks to revive—especially in works where "natural history," as he called it, worked to reinforce the impact of personal history.

Both are evident in the six-foot canvases that he began to exhibit in 1819: canvases whose very size and bravura, as Paulson notes, implicitly demand the respect normally reserved for history paintings alone (*Literary Landscape* 109). Constable's greatest works are studies in personal history. They recreate the intensity with which he saw and experienced his native ground—the valley of the Stour—during his childhood. To Fisher he wrote: "I should paint my own places best— Painting is but another word for feeling. I associate my 'careless boyhood' to all that lies on the banks of the *Stour*. They made me a painter" (*JCC* 6: 78).

In 1821, the very year he made this statement, Constable exhibited at the Royal Academy what is probably the best known of all the paintings based on his experience of the Stour: *The Hay Wain* (plate 6). As the title suggests, this picture seems to be organized around the hay wain itself. Caught in a pool of brightly reflected light and driving diagonally through the center of the picture, the horse-drawn cart and the figures in it command our attention, especially since one of the figures is pointing the way across the river and thus reinforcing the diagonal line in which the cart is moving. But the figures are small and nameless. Though the crossing of a river—like the crossing of a mountain range—can be

the Cave of Despair from Spenser's *Faerie Queene* (1: 9). The medal was won by Joseph Severn, now chiefly remembered as the faithful friend of Keats (*Annals* 4: 620).

charged with historic reverberations, the figures in this picture have neither heroic dimension nor historic significance.[19] The would-be moment
of political or military history here is displaced by a moment of what
Constable called "natural history": a moment in the ever-changing life of
the natural world.[20] The original title of this picture was not *The Hay
Wain* but rather *Landscape: Noon* (Taylor 200). The contracted shadows
of the trees, the cottage, the cart, and especially of the dog in the foreground tell us that the sun is directly overhead. The day is arrested, permanently caught in an eternal now, a moment of radiant calm; and in
spite of the diagonal movement of the cart and the energetic rondure of
the trees and clouds, the composition is dominated by the level of the
horizon, which cuts through the center of the picture and which is hardly
disturbed by the pointing arm of the figure in the cart.

I stress the pointing arm, however, because something like it occurs in
a painting that does give us a conventionally historic crossing: Jacques
Louis David's *Napoleon Crossing the Alps* (plate 8), painted in 1800 and
exhibited in London in 1815, when Constable may have seen it.[21] I do
not know whether Constable actually saw this picture, and I would not
want to claim that he was thinking of it when he painted *The Hay Wain*. I
juxtapose the two pictures merely to suggest the drastically different
ways in which two painters of the same period respond to the demand for
history in painting. With a pointing arm that barely gestures to the possibility of historic significance, Constable records the unhistoric crossing
of a river, an unimportant moment in the history of a rural day; by contrast, with an arm that points decisively skyward, a horse that leaps dramatically upward, and a figure that boldly occupies the center of the pic-

19. They may be contrasted with the figures in Thomas Sully's *Washington Crossing
the Delaware* (Boston Museum of Fine Arts), first exhibited in America in 1819—two
years before the *Hay Wain* made its first appearance in London. In Sully's picture, Washington points commandingly across the river.

20. Constable refers to the "natural history" of skies in the letterpress for *English
Landscape* (*JCD* 14). He may have borrowed the phrase from Gilbert White's *Natural
History and Antiquities of Selbourne* (first published 1789), which he acquired in 1821
after Fisher recommended it to him (Constable, *JCC* 6: 64, 66). His books include an
1833 edition of White's work (Constable *JC: FDC* 52), and his papers include a quotation
from it (Leslie 273).

21. For the London exhibition of David's picture, see Gage, *CT* 245 n. 114. Constable was in London during part of 1815, and whether or not he saw the picture then, he
definitely saw it in June 1835, when he scathingly attacked a group of three pictures that
included it (*JCC* 3: 126). Constable's assessment of David's other pictures and of his
work as a whole was consistently negative; see *JCC* 3: 126, and Leslie 313.

ture, David records a crossing of great historic impact: a crossing that openly recalls and reenacts the heroic feat of the ancient Carthaginian whose name is conveniently carved in stone just under Bonaparte's in the lower left corner of the picture. But David's picture has none of the subtlety and detail with which Constable catches a recognizable moment in the atmospheric history of a day. To turn from David's *Napoleon* to Constable's *Hay Wain* is to see how completely one kind of history has been displaced by another.

The displacement is even more striking in a picture that Constable painted some four years after *The Hay Wain—The Leaping Horse*. Constable did various versions of this picture; I refer to the full-size oil study done about 1825 and now at the Victoria and Albert Museum (plate 7). As compared with *The Hay Wain* and many of Constable's other pictures of the Stour, this one distinguishes itself by its emphatic elevation of the horse and rider. As Kenneth Clark observes, Constable puts them on a high stage, so that they achieve the dignity of monumental sculpture— or, Clark might have added, the grandeur of David's majestically mounted Napoleon.[22] Yet even as he suggests the dignity of monumental sculpture and the grandeur of a historic crossing, Constable displaces history with rural incident. The Pegasean steed in David's picture seems ready to leap the Alps in a single bound; in Constable's picture, a horse that significantly faces the other way is merely leaping over a stile, and the rider is anonymous. Nevertheless, Constable's horse decisively breaks the line between the earth and the sky, and even as it does so, it also cuts across the diagonals formed by the leaning buttress at lower right and the willow stump just above it. Given the muscular vitality of the trees at left, the surging of the clouds at right, and the churning of the water just below the bridge, the leaping horse seems to epitomize the very life of the landscape which surrounds it.

At the same time, the picture as a whole epitomizes Constable's determination to represent nature in a human context. In turning away from history to landscape, he did not simply spurn man for nature. On the contrary, he would have agreed with Blake that "Where man is not nature is barren" (*PPB* 37). His biographer Leslie writes that "the solitude of mountains oppressed his spirits. His nature was peculiarly social and

22. Clark 275. Clark likewise notes that in *Boat Building near Flatford Mill* (exhibited 1815) "the majestic architecture of the barge, set in an idyllic landscape, is the equivalent of a Greek temple in a Poussin" (270).

could not feel satisfied with scenery, however grand in itself, that did not abound in human associations. He required villages, churches, farmhouses, and cottages" (Leslie 18). The things of man can be seen in the very titles of Constable's pictures: *Flatford Mill*, *The Hay Wain*, *The Lock*, *The Valley Farm*, the seemingly endless versions of *Salisbury Cathedral*. What we do not see in Constable's pictures are great historic monuments dominatingly displayed. Even in the pictures of Salisbury Cathedral, which for him signified not so much history as his friendship with John Fisher, archdeacon of Salisbury, the cathedral is placed in the background of a world where man and nature vitally interact.

We can see this clearly in the greatest of his Salisbury pictures, *Salisbury Cathedral from the Meadows* (plate 9), exhibited in 1831. Here the foreground bristles with natural, unhistoric life of all kinds—human, animal, and vegetative. A good-sized wagon drawn by a team of one white and two brown horses makes its way conspicuously across a river curving around in front of us while a dog looks on from the near bank, a man on the far bank draws his boat into the weeds, birds hover low over the glittering water, a rough wooden footbridge crosses the river at lower right, and at left, a group of trees slants majestically upward. The austerely Gothic cathedral stands in the background with a somber majesty of its own, but the mottled tints of blue and green that permeate its gray stone seem to come from the clouds banked up behind it. Together with the framing effect of the rainbow curving down beside it, the rich chiaroscuro created by the breaking up of these clouds is largely responsible for the impact made by the cathedral itself. Within this powerfully charged landscape of so much natural vitality, the cathedral becomes a kind of prehistoric genus loci.[23]

In this respect *Salisbury Cathedral from the Meadows* recalls the quite different picture of *Old Sarum* (plate 10), where Constable represents the ruins of a fortress and cathedral just a mile and a half distant from Salisbury but hundreds of years older. This picture evokes history only to the extent that Wordsworth does in "Tintern Abbey," where the barely sug-

23. On the romantic response to the tradition of the genius loci, see Hartman, *Beyond Formalism* 311–36. Paul Schweizer has recently argued that because of the position of the sun in this picture, the rainbow is "meteorologically impossible" and is placed here as a biblical sign of peace and blessing to shelter the cathedral from the symbolic chaos of the clouds (426). But like the rainbow in Turner's *Buttermere*, Constable's rainbow hovers somewhere between a natural phenomenon and a biblical emblem; it stands on the margin of history.

gested presence of the hermit evokes the prehistoric condition of monastic solitude. In his letterpress to the mezzotint of *Old Sarum*, Constable writes at length of its history, of the "proud and 'towered' city" that once stood on this desolate site (*JCD* 24). But he does not try to depict this city in the pregnant moment of its ascendancy, as Turner does with Carthage in a picture I shall consider shortly. Instead, he shows us a mound of rock scarcely distinguishable from a natural formation, and the metaphorical "gloom, which clouds the dark history of the Middle Ages" in Constable's verbal commentary (*JCD* 25) appears in the painting itself as the literal or more precisely pictorial gloom of clouds swirling over the mound and symbolically levelling its proud towers. No great historic figures here enact an epitomizing moment in Sarum's past; Wordsworth's invisible hermit has his counterpart in the nameless shepherd who unobtrusively occupies the left foreground of Constable's picture and who thus seems to suggest that Sarum now antedates the history it has survived. But Constable does not simply give us a prehistoric pastoralism. The bloody conflicts that led to the destruction of Sarum and that might have been directly represented in a conventional history painting are here at once signified and displaced by the dramatic interplay of light and shadow in the oil picture and—in the mezzotint—by the still greater intensity of darkness virtually overpowering light.

Considerably more conspicuous than the levelled stones of *Old Sarum* is the strikingly vertical ruin in the left foreground of *Landscape Sketch: Hadleigh Castle* (plate 11), painted about 1828. Indeed, Paulson sees the ruin as one more example of the blocking agents that so often occupy the foregrounds of Constable's pictures and obstruct the viewer's way to open space beyond—whether sunlit meadow or open sea (*Literary Landscape* 126–33). Here, says Paulson, the picturesque elements that fill up the foregrounds of pictures like *The Leaping Horse*—with its muddy riverbank and mossy posts—give way to "a sublime power symbol, the ruined tower," which blocks the way "to a beautiful spot of rest in the far distance" (133). Yet two things sharply qualify the historical impact which this imposing monument seems to exert on the picture as a whole. One is that the ruin expresses not so much public history as the artist's own private feeling: the sense of loss and psychic ruin that he suffered when his wife Maria died in 1828, shortly before the work was painted.[24] Just as

24. Writing to Lucas not long afterwards, Constable said that he had added a ruin to the print of *The Glebe Farm* so as "to have a symbol in the book [*English Landscape*] of

important as the autobiographical significance of the ruin, however, is the competition established between its "sublime power" and the equally sublime energy of the oceanically turbulent clouds churning over the distant sea. What is opposed here, I think, is not the dark sublimity of the rugged ruin and the sunlit beauty of the tranquil sea, as Paulson suggests, but rather two kinds of sublimity: the one dark and brooding, the other bright and exultant. The historic authority of the dark ruin, which is charged with all the anguish of Constable's recent personal history, is ultimately overpowered by the sublime magnificence of the sunlit sky, which here becomes a symbol of renewal just as exhilarating as the sunrise that Wordsworth once beheld on his return from an all-night party (*Prelude* A 4.330–45). Where *Old Sarum* shows darkness virtually consuming light, *Hadleigh Castle* renders light rising triumphantly over darkness.

One other picture completed in Constable's last years shows just how determined he was to make historic monuments give way to the power of landscape. Ironically enough, the ostensible subject of this picture is the monument erected at Coleorton—George Beaumont's estate—to honor Joshua Reynolds, the indefatigable advocate of history painting. In the first version of *The Cenotaph at Coleorton* (plate 12), a pencil and wash drawing done in 1823, the monument occupies the center of the foreground, and a grove of rough-sketched trees provides an unobtrusive background. In the oil version, which he exhibited in 1836 (plate 13), Constable thrusts the monument back into the trees at right and left and adds busts of Michelangelo and Raphael—presumably his own invention. From one point of view, the result is that a simple clearing in Beaumont's wooded park has become an emblematically readable garden in the tradition of Kent. Situated between those he regarded as masters, respectively, of sublime energy on the one hand and pure beauty on the other (*D* 83–84), Reynolds is ostensibly presented as the heir to both. Yet there is a double irony here. Though he venerated Michelangelo and Raphael for their history painting, Reynolds himself was a portraitist, and though his monument is flanked by busts—sculptured portraits— which Constable presumably invented, there is no bust of Reynolds in this picture, even though Constable found one at Coleorton (*JCC* 6: 145).

---

myself" (*JCC* 4: 382), and to Leslie he wrote that "every gleam of sunshine is blighted to me in the art at least. Can it therefore be wondered at that I paint continual storms?" (*JCC* 3: 122). Likewise, Byron represents himself in Rome as a "ruin amidst ruins" (*Childe Harold's Pilgrimage* 4. 219).

Constable has therefore suppressed the bust of Reynolds, who is represented in the picture by his name alone, the only thing readable in the Wordsworthian verses inscribed to him on the cenotaph. The second irony is that the busts of the two great history painters have become unobtrusive adjuncts to a landscape painting, not central figures for which the landscape itself serves as an "assistant." The bust of Raphael is almost lost among the low trees on the extreme right, and the bust of Michelangelo is overshadowed by the towering tree in the foreground at left. Most strikingly, all three monuments to the history of art—and implicitly to history painting—must compete for our attention with the stag poised just to the left of center.

What is this stag doing here? Paulson argues that it represents Constable himself at bay, pursued and persecuted by those who disdained landscape painting (*Literary Landscape* 136–38). This seems to me improbable. Though Constable was doubtless familiar (as Paulson suggests) with literary and graphic portrayals of the persecuted stag, and though in *English Landscape* he himself illustrated the scene of Jacques and the wounded stag from *As You Like It* (2. 1), the vigorous and boldly upright beast in the *Cenotaph* bears no resemblance to the pathetically downed and stricken figure in the Shakespearean mezzotint. If the stag of the *Cenotaph* represents Constable, it expresses not a plaintive appeal to a hostile public but the confidence of one who had long since—in his own words—"found an original style" (*JCC* 6: 191). By the time he exhibited *The Cenotaph* in 1836, he no longer had reason to feel persecuted or neglected. He had been a full member of the Academy for seven years; he had been lecturing on landscape painting with considerable success for three years; and in 1836 itself he was a visitor to the Royal Academy life class (Leslie 261). The stag of *The Cenotaph*, therefore, is less likely a surrogate version of the persecuted artist than the concentrated symbol of the life embodied in the landscape as a whole, especially since the curving branches of the stag's uplifted horns strikingly repeat the sinuously animated lines of the tree limbs thrusting their way up through the top of the picture at left. In effect, the picture calls Michelangelo, Raphael, and Reynolds—two great practitioners of history painting and its one greatest exponent—to witness the fact that Constable has decisively cleared a space for his own kind of landscape painting in the history of art.

Constable thus displaces history by subordinating historic monuments to natural elements, or by giving to unhistoric incidents the stature and importance that painters like David reserve for great events. But since

Constable does not actually refer to historic events in his work, his challenge to the dominance of history is largely implicit. To see an explicit challenge to its dominance, we must consider the work of Turner, who was obsessed with history and yet determined to show that landscape could rival and even surpass it.

TURNER AND HISTORY

Turner aimed throughout his career to contend with the great tradition of history painting. The long succession of works that he based on biblical, classical, and strictly historical subjects begins with *The Fifth Plague of Egypt*, exhibited 1800, and continues to 1850, the very last year he exhibited his work, when he showed *Mercury Sent to Admonish Aeneas* and three other paintings based on Virgil's account of Aeneas's sojourn in Carthage.[25] But Turner could never accept the doctrine that landscape ranked inherently below history as a subject for painting. In his Royal Academy lectures he argued that landscape should be more than a background for historical subjects, that it deserved to be a subject in its own right. "To select, combine and concentrate what is beautiful in nature and admirable in art," he said, "is as much the business of the Landscape painter in his Line as in the other departments of art."[26]

25. The spirit in which Turner confronted the tradition of history painting may be gauged from a letter of 28 June 1822 which he wrote to J. C. Robinson, a publisher of prints. Proposing to have four of his historical works engraved and printed for Robinson to distribute, he refers to William Woollett's highly successful engravings of Richard Wilson's historical works, beginning with *Niobe* in 1761. Turner writes: "Whether we can in the present day contend with such powerful antagonists as Wilson and Woollett would be at least tried by size, security against risk, and some remuneration for the time of painting. The pictures of ultimate sale I shall be content with; to succeed would perhaps form another epoch in the English school; and if we fall, we fall *by contending with giant strength*" (*CCT* 86–87; italics added).

26. TMS I, f. 1ᵛ. Turner's defense of landscape painting may have been prompted in part by what he took to be attacks upon it by Henry Fuseli (1741–1825), the Swiss-born painter of Gothic fantasies and Shakespearean scenes who had become a professor of painting at the Royal Academy in 1799. Believing that Fuseli considered landscape painters "the map-makers, the topographers of art," Turner took "the part of elevated landscape against the aspersions of Map-making criticism" (quoted in Lindsay 184). But "mapwork" is a term Fuseli applied only to "that kind of landscape which is entirely occupied with the tame delineation of a given spot." He distinguished this "tame delineation" from the work of painters such as Titian, Rembrandt, Claude, and Wilson, who represented nature "in the varied light of rising, meridian, setting suns; in twilight, night, and dawn" (part 2, 185).

What Turner praised in this lecture were not landscape paintings per se, but paintings in which the power of landscape challenged the supremacy of history. Focusing on masters who combined "what was to them remarkable in nature . . . with the highest qualities of the Historic school," he cited Titian's *The Martyrdom of St. Peter* (plate 24) as a prime example.[27] In 1802, when he first saw this picture at the Louvre, he had suggestively noted that its "landscape tho natural is heroic" (TSB LXXII, 28ᵛ). In his lecture he called it a "triumph" of landscape. "Even over history," said Turner, Titian "felt not those puerile thoughts of making it subservient" (TMS I, f. 4ᵛ). Turner was clearly struck by the "eruptive expanding" of the trees in this picture, by the energy with which they rise up over Peter's prostrate form and connect him with the angels overhead, who shed the mellow gold of their beatitude "through the dark embrowned foliage to the dying martyr."[28] In Turner's eyes, Titian here demonstrated that landscape itself could be "heroic."

Turner's response to Titian's picture provides the key to what he does with history in his own historical paintings. I shall consider four done at various points in his long career: *The Fifth Plague of Egypt, Snow Storm: Hannibal and His Army Crossing the Alps, Dido Building Carthage,* and *Ulysses Deriding Polyphemus.* In different ways, these four pictures of biblical, classical, and strictly historical subjects show how Turner made the elemental powers of landscape triumph over the traditional authority of historic figures.

Significantly, what Turner depicts in *The Fifth Plague of Egypt* (plate 14), his very first history painting, is a manifestation of natural forces— albeit forces activated by supernatural intervention. Actually a painting of the seventh plague, it is meant to illustrate Exodus 9:23, which Turner quoted in the exhibition catalogue: "And Moses stretched forth his hands toward heaven, and the Lord sent thunder and hail, and the fire ran along the ground." To compare this text with the picture, however, is to see what Turner typically does with historic figures. Miniaturized and barely detectable among the shadows at lower right, the figure of Moses is all but overpowered by the triangle of carnage spreading out from the base of the picture, by the lurid glow of the burning city in the middle distance, and by the titanic swirling of fire-reddened thunderclouds over-

27. Painted in Venice between 1526 and 1530, the picture was destroyed by fire in 1867.

28. Lindsay 163, and Turner, TMS G, f. 27.

head. Turner thus rejects what even West's "revolutionary" *Death of General Wolfe* had preserved: the tradition of highlighting the central figure in an historical work.

Turner also departs from the kind of composition exemplified by Poussin, who used architectural form to furnish a background of imperturbable stability for the historic or mythological events he portrayed. In *Landscape with Pyramus and Thisbe*, for instance, which Turner greatly admired (Wilton, *TS* 72), the jagged streak of lightning at upper left points diagonally and appropriately to the leaning figure of Thisbe at lower right, but neither these diagonals nor the dark mass of clouds at upper right disturb the fundamentally horizontal stress of the picture, in which the line of buildings and low hills in the background is reinforced by a series of parallels running right up to the prostrate figure of Pyramus in the foreground. In *The Fifth Plague*, the decisively triangular white facade of the pyramid placed in the very center provides the compositional keynote, but triangular form in this picture is paradoxically made to signify disruption rather than stability. Surrounding the sharp, straight, upright triangle of the pyramid is a curved, inverted triangle of light opening out to the swirling clouds above: to the first hint of the elemental vortex which will come to epitomize in Turner's work the dominating power of natural forces.

This power is dramatically displayed in Turner's painting of what Byron could not help but remember, what Rousseau felt he was reenacting, what Wordsworth declined to recall in his journey through the Simplon Pass, and what David explicitly recalls in his picture of Napoleon: namely, Hannibal crossing the Alps. To compare Turner's *Snow Storm: Hannibal and His Army Crossing the Alps* (plate 15) with David's picture of Napoleon's crossing (plate 8) is to see how unheroic the painting of history can be. David's picture, which Turner saw at David's studio in 1802 (Gage, *CT* 100), presupposes a simple and fundamentally positive interpretation of Hannibal's act. In its straightforward evocation of paradigmatically heroic daring, *Napoleon Crossing the Alps* aptly illustrates what Karl Kroeber has said of neoclassic history in general: that its key unit "is the epitomizing occurrence, the episode revealing with rationalized clarity the pattern in which historical meaning resides" ("Experience" 330). This kind of history Turner rejects. Returning to the moment which David finds unequivocally exemplary, Turner exposes its sordidness and futility. What he sought to do in the picture is suggested by verses for the exhibition catalogue which he cited for the first time as coming from his

manuscript poem, "Fallacies of Hope." The verses speak of "craft, treach-
ery and fraud" inflicted on the rear of Hannibal's army, of soldiers and
their captives alike victimized by mountaineers, of Hannibal advancing
with a self-deluding hope through passes blanched with snowstorms and
bloodied with corpses, and finally of what lies ahead: the enervating lux-
uries of Capua (Butlin and Joll 79).

The daring and originality of the conception embodied in this picture
emerge still more clearly when we compare it with earlier pictures of
Hannibal and with Turner's own preliminary sketches. Before the appearance of *Snow Storm* in 1812, four other artists had exhibited pictures
based on Hannibal's life. Two of them enshrined what is unquestionably
an "epitomizing occurrence": the moment at which Hannibal takes an
oath against Rome at the behest of his father.[29] The other two pictures—
both now lost—showed Hannibal in the act of crossing the Alps, and
both seem to have given him considerable prominence. John Robert
Cozens's *A Landscape with Hannibal in His March Over the Alps, Showing to His Army the Fertile Plains of Italy*, exhibited sometime before
1797, was described in 1916 as consisting of "mountains, and soldiers
and elephants, one of which was falling down a ravine, and Hannibal in
purpel on horseback" (quoted in Matteson 387). It is probably fair to
assume that Hannibal was equally conspicuous in the other lost picture
of this subject—Richard Courbould's *Hannibal on His Passage Over the
Alps Pointing Out to His Troops the Fertile Plains of Italy* (exhibited 1808).

Turner could have known all of these pictures, and he certainly knew
the one by Cozens, which is said to have made a profound impression on
him (Matteson 386–87). In addition, recent research has shown that a
sketch he made about 1800 was probably based either on this lost oil or
on Cozens's monochrome drawing of the same subject, *Hannibal Showing to His Army the Fertile Plains of Italy* (ca. 1776).[30] The sketch shows
Hannibal poised on a ridge and pointing grandly ahead, with a ragged

29. Cited by Matteson 387, the pictures were Benjamin West's *Hannibal Taking the
Oath* (exhibited 1771) and Thomas Burges's *Hannibal . . . Swearing Eternal Enmity to
the Romans* (exhibited 1778). As further references will show, my analysis of Turner's
Snowstorm is considerably indebted to Matteson's admirable research. On the subject of
oath-taking in neoclassical art, see Rosenblum 68–80.

30. See Matteson 388–89. The drawing survives in a private collection in the United
States. Matteson takes the sketch as a "free variation" of the drawing, which Turner
could certainly have seen in the 1790s; but given the striking differences between the
drawing and the sketch, which Matteson notes (387), it seems to me just as likely that the
sketch was based on the oil.

column of soldiers struggling up the winding path behind him. We cannot know whether Turner was imitating the vertical and dynamic thrust that he may have seen in the lost oil (with its falling elephant) or was deliberately departing from the static and horizontal emphasis of the drawing, which shows Hannibal and his soldiers lined up on a level path like figures in a frieze. What we can see, however, is that Turner begins in the sketch to divert attention from Hannibal himself, to focus on the army struggling behind him.

From studies of climbing soldiers that Turner made about the same time as the sketch, we can infer that he may have originally intended to salute the heroism of Hannibal and the courageous determination he inspired in his men.[31] But by 1805, Turner had made a chalk study of Hannibal's crossing in which the figure of the proudly pointing general is entirely displaced by a mass of tumbling, writhing figures who are evidently meant to signify Hannibal's army under ambush from a stepped cliff rising on the left (Matteson 390). This change in Turner's approach to the subject of Hannibal could have been prompted in part by any one of several sources—most likely by Thomas Gray's description of an imaginary painting that might have been executed by Salvator Rosa: "Hannibal passing the Alps; the mountaineers rolling rocks upon his army; elephants tumbling down the precipices."[32] But what Turner did

31. The studies are TSB XL, 6a–7, and 13. Kroeber notes that Hannibal's courage is emphasized in Goldsmith's *History of Rome*, but it is not clear to me that this was Turner's literary source, as Kroeber says ("Experience" 329 n. 11).

32. *Poems of Mr. Gray*, ed. W. Mason (1775), quoted in Matteson 391. Gray's own source is Livy, whom he cites in one of the letters describing his own journey through the Alps (quoted in Wilton, *TS* 26–27). As an alternative source, Butlin and Joll suggest Ann Radcliffe's *The Mysteries of Udolpho* (1794), which also refers to the mountaineers' attack on the Carthaginian army, but the evidence for Turner's knowledge of Gray's description is considerably more persuasive (Butlin and Joll 79; Matteson 390–92). Matteson also notes (389–90) the similarity between Turner's lines on Hannibal's crossing and a passage in Thomas Gisborne's poem *Walks in a Forest* (first published 1794), which Turner quite possibly knew. But Gisborne's lines make no reference to attacking mountaineers or to the darker premonitions that shadow Hannibal's "hope" in Turner's lines.

The one other source commonly cited for *Snowstorm* is a thunderstorm that Turner reportedly saw and painted in 1810 while staying at Farnley Hall in Yorkshire. He is said to have predicted at the time that the drawing would in two years become "Hannibal Crossing the Alps" (W. Thornbury, *The Life and Correspondence of J. M. W. Turner* [1877], quoted in Matteson 386). But Gerald Wilkinson notes that the painting Turner supposedly made "doesn't seem to be in the Turner Bequest" (*TS 1802–20* 18), and while the story of the Yorkshire thunderstorm is attributed to the presumably reliable F. H. Fawkes, son of Turner's friend and patron, it comes to us in what Jack Lindsay

not get from any of his sources—either literary or pictorial—was the decision to suppress Hannibal altogether, and to subordinate even the attack on his army to the power of the elements.

Significantly, Hannibal cannot be found at all in the finished picture. While Moses is merely miniaturized in *The Fifth Plague*, Hannibal is banished utterly from the picture of an event in which he is supposedly the leading figure, and even in the title his name follows that of the dominant force: *Snow Storm*. In the center of the picture, where we might expect to see his monumental figure gloriously astride a horse or an elephant, we see the angular vortex of a predominantly black snowstorm consuming the sun even as it opens to view at left a beckoning ellipse of light. In the foreground is the sordid spectacle described in Turner's verses: soldiers being robbed and female captives being raped and killed by mountaineers. The figures are nameless, inglorious, and insignificant; they are Lilliputians caught in the great Brobdingnagian sickle of the storm, and the elephant profiled in the far distance, trunk upthrust, is a microscopic toy. The central figure in a great historic event is thus displaced by the elemental power of nature. While David's Napoleon is the modern-day heir to Hannibal's heroism, Turner's Hannibal anticipates the Napoleon who was victimized by the winter on his retreat from Moscow in 1812—the very year in which Turner exhibited this picture.[33] Commentators have interpreted the Turnerian vortex as a symbol of Turner's belief in the cyclic nature of history, or of its indeterminacy as a complex of movements without beginning or end.[34] But the snowy vortex in this picture ultimately signifies Turner's conviction that natural forces alone survive historic change. In Turner's eyes, the only thing permanently memorable and meaningful in Hannibal's crossing, which led ultimately to his defeat, was the menacing shape of the prehistoric energy unleashed by a storm.

---

has called "the most confused, haphazard, and slovenly work of biography in our language" (9).

Yet another possible—albeit improbable—source for the first appearance of the vortex in Turner's work is Cozens's monochrome drawing of Hannibal, which is placid and horizontal in itself, as I have already noted, but is done in the round.

33. On the possible connection of Turner's picture with Napoleon, see Kroeber, "Experience" 329, and Matteson 393–96.

34. See Clark 236–37. Comparing Turner's vision of history to Tolstoy's in *War and Peace*, Kroeber says that painter and novelist both represent the historic "hero" as a figure caught up in the interplay of confused, indeterminate, uncontrollable forces ("Experience" 329; Kroeber and Walling 161–64).

The power represented in *Dido Building Carthage* (plate 16), which Turner exhibited three years after *Snow Storm*, is of an altogether different kind. Here the sun shines from a misted but relatively cloudless sky upon a waterway flanked with the columned porticos and sculpted facades of nearly completed buildings, and the figures ranged about them seem busily engaged in productive work. The picture clearly recalls the delicate light and stately grandeur of Claude's *Seaport: Embarcation of the Queen of Sheba* (1648), beside which Turner asked that it be hung after his death (Butlin and Joll 85). Here, it would seem, nature smiles benignly on a scene of high commitment, on precisely the kind of significant, epitomizing moment that history painting traditionally enshrined. "Optimistic effort characterizes the scene," says Max Schultz. "No display of opulence as yet disfigures the city; rather industry and energetic resolution mark its every precinct" (411).

Careful inspection of the picture, however, shows that Turner is not so much enshrining as undermining the glory of an historic moment. There is little sign of industry or energetic resolution in the group of boys sailing a toy boat in the left foreground or in the woman gazing on them from behind; yet these are the most conspicuous figures in the picture. While Claude furnishes his seaport with several noteworthy ships, Turner's little boats trivialize the nautical ambitions of Carthage, which are otherwise just barely suggested by the two naked masts rising unobtrusively in the middle distance at left. Furthermore, Turner typically declines to emphasize the titular subject of his picture: Dido herself. In Claude's picture, the embarking queen descends the stairs at right with virtually all eyes upon her. In *Dido Building Carthage*, the difficulty of identifying Dido herself is revealed by the fact that two distinguished commentators have disagreed about whether she is the woman gazing on the boys or the barely detectable woman further back—the woman in white who seems to be consulting with a group of architects.[35]

The foregrounding of mock navigation and the deliberate diminution of the titular figure lead us to wonder just how much faith in historic significance this picture expresses. Kroeber notes the irony inherent in its inaugural grandeur; exhibited with the reference "—1st book of Virgil's Aeneid," it reenacts the creation of Carthage in terms of a literary work written long after the city was destroyed and in celebration of an

35. Kroeber thinks Dido is the woman gazing on the boys; Paulson thinks she is the woman in white further back (Kroeber and Walling 155, 168). I agree with Paulson.

Imperial Rome which was itself destroyed long before Turner painted his picture ("Experience" 325). The unfinished buildings here—especially the building at left with the fragments of stone around its base—already begin to resemble the ruins they will become, and thus to negate the high constructive purpose they are supposed to signify.

To compare this picture and its companion—*The Decline of the Carthaginian Empire* (exhibited 1817)—with the *Course of Empire* series that Thomas Cole painted in America some twenty years later is to see how ambiguous the representation of an historical moment can be. Each of Cole's five pictures unambiguously illustrates the condition designated by its subtitle: *Savage State, Pastoral State, Consummation, Destruction,* and *Desolation.* But even as *Dido Building* subtly prefigures the ruination of the city, *Decline* reveals the decadence latent in something remarkably similar to what Cole will later call *Consummation*: a spectacle of handsomely finished buildings, opulent statuary, gaily ornamented ships, and lavishly dressed crowds. In Turner's picture, all of these things are touched with the amber glow of a sun inexorably setting on Carthaginian glory. The sun is what finally triumphs in both pictures. In *Decline*, its burning yellow light brings out the tints of red and orange in the clothing of the figures massed on either side and thus portends a conflagration.[36] In *Dido Building*, it beams uninterruptedly down to the base of the picture. While Claude's *Seaport* shows a bank running straight across the foreground to enclose the harbor, Turner makes his sunlit waves run right up to the spectator, whose eye is thereby drawn from history to seascape. Indeed, as we look for significant action among the figures massed at left, we are led back down to the water by the gaze of the woman on shore, whose glance aligns her with the kneeling boys, the little toy boat, and the diagonal ripples of tide that stretch across the sunbeam just in front of us. Once again, therefore, the spectacle of a decisive and historic moment centrally portrayed is displaced by a natural phenomenon: this time by the shimmering of light upon water.

From one point of view, *Ulysses Deriding Polyphemus* (plate 17), exhibited in 1829, spectacularly contradicts what I have been arguing thus far. Here the impact of a poetically "historic" confrontation seems not so much displaced by natural forces as intensified by their interplay with

36. The verses Turner wrote for the exhibition catalogue describe the sun as "ensanguin'd" and "portentous" (Butlin and Joll 89). Earlier, above the setting sun in a sketch of about 1807, Turner wrote "Fire and Blood" (TSB CI, f. 9).

human and supernatural figures. Ulysses' ship clearly dominates the foreground, and the baroque flourish with which his crewmen unfurl its sails and flags grandly reinforces the gesture that Ulysses makes from the bridge, where he stands with arms defiantly upraised before the dusky monster looming up over him while the flag fluttering from the top of the mainmast—at the height of Polyphemus's head—visually proclaims what Ulysses is shouting at this moment: his own name. Furthermore, Ulysses' stance incorporates him within a triangle of mythological figures. Following the slant of the mast just beside him, his left arm points upward to the head of Polyphemus while the parallel lines of the mast and Ulysses' whole body also point downward to the star-crowned Nereids who play about the bow of his ship. From these the eye is drawn to the third point of the triangle at lower right, where the faintly outlined horses of Apollo—rearing upward and outward as they do on the east pediment of the Parthenon (Gage, *CT* 131)—exultantly erupt from the rising sun. Ultimately, the Parthenonian Apollo signifies the power of Athena, to whom the Parthenon was dedicated and by whom Ulysses will be guided successfully home. Thus the Apollonian sunrise promises a triumphant renewal of Ulysses' voyage even as Polyphemus threatens to end it in disaster, and the ghostly Nereids—not mentioned by Homer but signifying, as Gerard Lairesse had written, "the different qualities and various effects of water" (quoted in Gage, *CT* 129)—ambiguously offer to guide the mariners homeward or into the perilous waters that Ulysses alone will survive. For all his exultation, then, Ulysses seems caught in the grip of the mythological figures who will inexorably determine the destinies of himself and his crew. By his cunning triangulation of these figures, Turner implies what Homer's narration explicitly reveals: that in the very act of derisively disclosing his identity to the monster he has blinded and tricked, Ulysses gives him the means to wreak revenge by an appeal to his father Poseidon, whose power now lies hidden beneath the treacherously placid surface of the sea.

This reading of the picture, however, overlooks the extent to which its mythological figures have been incorporated into—or reclaimed by—the natural forces from which, as Blake puts it in plate 11 of *The Marriage of Heaven and Hell*, they were once imaginatively elicited by the ancient poets. Gage observes that the head of Polyphemus is represented as the peak of a smoking volcano which is possibly fed by the burning cavern at left, and he also notes that the starry Nereids embody the natural luminosity of putrescent matter in the sea—something Priestley had described in a work Turner knew (Gage, *CT* 129–30). Just as importantly, the rising sun all but dissolves or displaces the horses of Apollo, which are reduced to mere outlines, ghosts of antiquity, pentimenti vanishing in the primordial whiteness of the dawn. The rays of light fanning upward from the sun, in fact, not only overpower the Apollonian steeds; they also repeat and extend the fan-like spreading of the ship's three masts, which in turn repeat and extend the position of Ulysses' upraised arms. But of course the prime mover in this sequence of repetition is not Ulysses' arms. It is Turner's god, the sun. Ulysses' gesture simply imitates the spectacular radiance of the dawn, and by comparison with that, his upraised arms—and his whole figure—are Lilliputian. Miniaturized to the point of inconsequence, like Moses and Dido, he and his fictively "historic" moment are subsumed by a confrontation between darkness and light, sublimity and beauty, the destructive force of the volcanic fire burning in the cave at lower left and the regenerative power of the sun rising at lower right. Reflecting at once the darkness and the light of these two contending forces, the very surface of the sea is profoundly ambiguous, turning even the whiteness of the dawn into a liquid fire that reaches across the bottom of the picture toward the cavernous base of the volcano. Poseidon's vengeful rage is thus displaced by the indeterminacy of the sea itself, and in the picture as a whole, the personalities of the supernatural figures who shape the destiny of Homer's hero give way to the subtle and yet richly powerful conflict of natural forces.

LINEAR TIME AND TEMPORALIZED SPACE

The displacement of history that we have seen in both the landscape painting and the landscape poetry of the romantic period inevitably affected the long-standing assumption that literature and the visual arts are categorically divided by the difference between space and time. First systematically developed—though not in fact first enunciated—in Lessing's *Laocoön* (1766), this assumption is still very much alive. In *The Romantic Rebellion* (1973), Kenneth Clark says flatly: "Painting deals with stasis, with place, not with time" (220). In *The Language of Images* (1980), W. J. T. Mitchell says that language and imagery are "generally regarded as fundamentally different" because—among other things— "language unfolds in temporal succession; images reside in a realm of timeless spatiality and simultaneity" (3).

Plausible as it sounds, this formulation is open to strong objections. It has been challenged not only by those who argue, as Mitchell has, that "spatial form is a crucial aspect of the experience and interpretation of literature in all ages and cultures" (*Language of Images* 273), but also by those who insist that painting—not to mention cinema—can represent time. The latter point was in fact acknowledged by Lessing himself. Axiomatically declaring that "the material limits of Art confine her imitative effort to one single moment" (14), he said that the painter "must therefore choose the most pregnant [moment], from which what precedes and what follows will be most easily apprehended" (55). Nevertheless, as Wendy Steiner has recently observed, "the so-called pregnant moment . . . is obviously associated with historical and iconographical art, since it usually cannot function with full effect unless we already know the story captured in the moment of the painting" (40).

History painting, then, depends for its full effect on the spectator's knowledge of the history to which the painting can only refer by selecting from its succession of events just one synecdochically representative or "pregnant" moment. Le Brun claimed that in *Fall of Manna in the Wilderness*, Poussin had actually depicted a succession of moments in the Israelites' reaction to the manna (Lee 62), and Louis Marin has recently cited Poussin's picture to illustrate his definition of the historical painting, which—he implies—can be made to speak for itself.[37] Yet no matter how adroit the artist, a history painting can be "read" only by a viewer who comes to it with a textually acquired knowledge of the story it represents. Whether or not Poussin has succeeded in representing successive moments on a single canvas, his painting presupposes a familiarity with the twentieth chapter of the Book of Exodus.

What happens when a painter cannot presuppose a knowledge of the relevant text? In the eighteenth and nineteenth centuries, painters seeking an ever-wider audience felt compelled to provide such knowledge— sometimes at extravagant length. Here, for instance, is the full title of a lost painting by Fuseli exhibited at the Royal Academy in 1818: *Dante, in his descent to hell, discovers amidst the flights of hapless lovers whirled about in a hurricane, the forms of Paolo and Francesca of Rimini; obtains Virgil's permission to address them, and being informed of the dreadful*

37. "The historical painting," writes Marin, "is a painting whose 'tense' is present, whose time is the present moment when it is seen, and the only possible way of making the story understood by the viewer, or 'read' by him, is to distribute, all around this central represented moment, various circumstances that are logically connected to it by implications or presupposition" (297–98).

*blow that sent them to that place of torment at once, overcome by pity
and terror, drops like a lifeless corpse upon the rocks* (quoted in *Annals*
3: 292).

The need to presuppose or thus awkwardly to provide such before and
after information may be one reason why Constable eschewed history
paintings, and why Turner so often subsumed the pregnant moment of a
historical sequence in an atmospheric snowstorm, a sunrise, or a fiery
sunset. To fully understand *Ulysses Deriding Polyphemus* (plate 17), we
need to know *The Odyssey*; to fully grasp *Snow Storm: Hannibal and His
Army Crossing the Alps* (plate 15), we need some knowledge of Livy. But
neither of these pictures requires a literary or historical context to the
degree that a picture such as Fuseli's does; neither requires the viewer to
imagine a series of moments leading up to and down from the moment
actually depicted. Turner found a way to represent time in space, to displace the linear time of conventional history painting with his own kind
of temporalized space. In *Snowstorm*, for instance, the black jaws of a
storm which at once enclose the sun and open to view the sunlit plains of
Italy prefigure ultimate disaster for Hannibal even as the distant sunlight
treacherously promises success. Such a picture invites us to consider the
various kinds of temporalized space that we find in romantic poetry and
painting alike—and to see how far they call into question Lessing's fundamental concepts of space and time in literature and the visual arts.

Lessing's statement of this theory is worth quoting in some detail. "If,"
he writes

it is true that painting employs in its imitations quite other means or signs than
poetry employs, the former—that is to say, figures and colours in space—but
the latter articulate sounds in time; as, unquestionably, the signs used must
have a definite relation to the thing signified, it follows that signs arranged together side by side can express only subjects which, or the various parts of
which, exist side by side, whilst signs which succeed each other can express
only subjects which, or the various parts of which, succeed each other.

Subjects which, or the various parts of which, exist side by side, may be
called *bodies*. Consequently, bodies with their visible properties form the proper
subjects of painting.

Subjects which or the various parts of which succeed each other may in general be called *actions*. Consequently, actions form the proper subjects of poetry. (55)

Wendy Steiner has justly observed that Lessing's categorization of the
verbal and visual arts here is founded on the assumption that both are

iconically mimetic (26, 200). Ironically enough, in the very act of attacking those who would confuse the arts, Lessing ignored one of the fundamental distinctions they themselves typically acknowledged: the well-established (if also highly problematic) distinction between the "natural" resemblance by which a picture represents an object and the arbitrary convention by which a word signifies a meaning.[38] Lessing believed that painting and poetry must each have a "definite relation"—more precisely a "suitable" or "convenient" relation (*bequemes Verhältnis*), and emphatically not an arbitrary one—to what they signify. Hence it was equally suitable that the "spatial" art of painting should represent bodies juxtaposed in space, while the "temporal" art of poetry—whose signs succeed each other—should represent actions, which also succeed each other.

The problem inherent in this attempt to define poetry as an art of temporally linear succession is that language has the power to reorder the chronological flow of events—not only in the avant-garde literature which for Joseph Frank epitomizes "spatial form," but even in ordinary sentences. In "Before we arrived, the party had ended," the syntactic sequence reverses the chronological one; in "As we arrived, the guests were leaving," the syntactic sequence represents not chronological sequence but simultaneity. The fact that such sentences reverse or arrest the chronological flow of events does not in itself make either one of them "spatial" in form. But they do allow us to see the severe limitations in Lessing's basically mimetic approach to the relation between language and time: limitations singularly ironic in view of his desire to liberate poetry from the "bounds of painting" into which, he charged, other critics sought to force it.[39] Certainly there is nothing in Lessing's theory to account for the temporalization of space that we find in *The Prelude*.

---

38. Samuel Johnson, for instance, wrote in 1758 that poetry and painting differed "only as the one represents things by marks permanent and natural, the other by signs accidental and arbitrary" (cited in Abrams, *Mirror* 33).

39. Lessing 4. A closely related problem arises from Lessing's assumption that the poet "takes up each of his actions, as he likes, from its very origin and conducts it through all possible modifications to its final close" (17). In fact, says Roman Ingarden, "time-filling events are never represented in *all their phases*, regardless of whether it is a single event, constituting a whole, or a plurality of successive events. . . . It is always— to echo Bergson—only *isolated* 'segments' of 'reality' that are represented, a reality which is being represented but which is never representable in its flowing continuity" (237). Represented time is therefore analogous to represented space, which can never be more than a segment—or set of segments—of real space. The gaps between the seg-

Consider, for instance, Wordsworth's description of the way a shepherd sometimes appeared to him when he was a boy:

> him have I descried in distant sky,
> A solitary object and sublime,
> Above all height! like an aerial Cross,
> As it is stationed on some spiry Rock
> Of the Chartreuse, for worship.
>
> (A 8. 406–10)

This passage is explicitly spatial and even pictorial. Wordsworth locates the shepherd on a distant height with his solitary form sharply etched against the sky: an icon not merely pictorial but religious, the sublime effigy of Christ crucified. Yet this is no "pregnant moment" in a line of historical events. The historically insignificant shepherd is not even named, and the passage represents not so much an action as a *stance* detached from any necessary connection with a before and after, a previous action and a following one. The spatially defined figure is temporalized not by an implied historical context but by reference to what has preceded this moment in *The Prelude* and yet actually followed it in the unfolding of Wordsworth's life: his experience of the Chartreuse. Though he is here describing what he saw as a schoolboy, he did not see the cross of the Chartreuse until he travelled across Europe for the first time at the age of twenty—an experience he records in book 6. But in the temporally regressive progression that characterizes *The Prelude* as a whole, he returns to his boyhood in book 8 and draws on the chronologically later experience for a simile to describe the earlier one. The result is temporalized space: a description that evokes the fixity of an icon even as it reveals the growth of the poet's mind, the superimposition of mature experience upon a childhood impression. The icon thus evoked is the antithesis of the Baconian idol created by those who would spatialize truth absolutely, by "ye," says Wordsworth,

> Whose truth is not a motion or a shape
> Instinct with vital functions, but a Block
> Or waxen image which yourselves have made,
> And ye adore.
>
> (A 8: 433–36)

---

ments correspond to portions of space or time that are merely "co-represented," furnished or "taken as existing" by the imagination of the reader (222–24, 236–38).

The pictorial counterpart of temporalized verbal space—of the verbal icon instinct with vitally temporal functions—is the kind of painting that represents what Lessing said painting should not: action at its most transitory. All phenomena, said Lessing, that "break out suddenly and as suddenly vanish, . . . do, by the permanence which Art bestows, put on an aspect so abhorrent to nature that at every repeated view of them the impression becomes weaker, until at last the whole thing inspires us with horror or loathing" (15). For Lessing, the pregnant moment of historical painting had to be one of atemporal repose, the moment conceptually isolatable and stationed between an equally isolatable before and after, respectively apprehensible by inference as cause and consequence of the moment depicted. Yet to study a picture such as Turner's *Rain, Steam, and Speed* (plate 18), exhibited 1844, is to see not one distinct link in a chain of causes and consequences but rather the very shape of movement itself: the movement of the train rushing toward us, with its black locomotive leaping out of the rain into sharp and sudden focus.

Constable likewise sought to capture the shape of objects in motion—what Coleridge called "the universal motion of things in Nature" (*NC* 1: 591). In the introduction to *English Landscape*, Constable clearly indicated that he had tried in his pictures to do the very thing Lessing had proscribed:

to arrest the more abrupt and transient appearances of the CHIAR'OSCURO IN NATURE: to shew its effect in the most striking manner, to give "to one brief moment caught from fleeting time" a lasting and sober existence, and to render permanent many of those splendid but evanescent Exhibitions, which are ever occurring in the changes of external Nature. (*JCD* 9–10)

In thus dedicating himself to the proposition Lessing explicitly opposed—to the idea that art could successfully perpetuate the "evanescent Exhibitions" of atmospheric change, Constable defined himself as a painter of time, or more precisely of temporalized space. Significantly, it was during his visit to the Lake District in the fall of 1806 that he began trying to capture specific moments of a day—as in the drawing inscribed *Borrowdale 4 Octr. 1806 Noon Clouds breaking away after Rain.* Constable's mature work plainly reveals his determination to express time, and it was chiefly to explain how he had done so that he wrote commentaries on seven of the mezzotints in *English Landscape*, which first appeared in 1833. He treated *Stoke by Neyland*, for instance, as a picture of noon: "that time of day being decidedly marked by the direction of the shadows and the sun shining full on the south side of the Church." By contrast, he said that *East Bergholt* was meant to catch "the broad still lights of a summer evening, with the solemn and far-extended shadows cast round by the intervening objects, small portions of them only and of the landscape gilded by the setting sun" (*JCD* 21, 42).

Constable's faith in his capacity to temporalize space may well have been reinforced by his reading of Wordsworth, for the quoted phrase about "fleeting time" that appears in the introduction to *English Land-scape* comes from a sonnet Wordsworth wrote in 1811 to salute a land-scape painting by George Beaumont: a painting that is said to give "to one brief moment caught from fleeting time / The appropriate calm of blest eternity" (*PW* 3: 6). Constable quotes aptly, for Wordsworth ob-viously shared his belief in the value of pictures that perpetuated par-ticular atmospheric moments; he told Hazlitt that he "would not give a rush for any landscape that did not express the time of day, the climate, the period of the world it was meant to illustrate" (Hazlitt 11: 93). The striking unanimity between Constable and Wordsworth on this point ob-viously prompts us to compare Constable's pictures of fleeting effects with the "spots of time" enshrined in Wordsworth's poetry.

To do so conscientiously, however, is to see differences that at first seem to validate rather than undermine Lessing's argument about the op-position between literature and the visual arts. Geoffrey Hartman has noted that Wordsworth's "spots of time" fuse not only time and space but also stasis and continuity (*Wordsworth's Poetry* 212). Though Constable's landscapes typically express a particular time of day, it is hard to see how they can do what Wordsworth does in his spots of time: express the interaction of two discrete moments, the superimposition of one experi-ence on another, the convergence of different times in a single place.

We have seen how the description of the shepherd draws at once on the experience of the boy and the experience of the man in order to show the continuity in the growth of the poet's mind. The only two spots of time explicitly labelled as such in *The Prelude* involve a comparable con-vergence of different times and even different places. In the first spot of time, which significantly encompasses two spots of place, the "ordinary sight" of a beacon, of a windblown woman, and of a low pool is charged with "visionary dreariness" because the little boy who sees them has lost his way and has just left the "spot" where a murderer had once been hanged (A 11. 279–316). In the second spot of time there is just one spot of place; but instead of being caught at a single atmospheric moment, as in a landscape painting, this spatial spot is made to participate in the chronologically extended growth of the poet's mind.

The second spot of time (A 11. 345–89) occurred when Wordsworth was attending school at Hawkshead, and when, just before the Christmas holidays began, he had mounted a crag to watch for the horses that were being sent to bring him and his brother home. What he experienced was not a moment but a day of waiting, and the complex of emotions later associated with the place at which he waited actually developed over an extended period, the weeks of "Christmastime." On the day he waited, he was filled with eagerness to get home for the holidays and with mounting resentment that he was being made to wait so long ("Feverish, and tired, and restless"); but when his father died less than ten days after he got home, he recalled his resentment with feelings of guilt, and it was the succession of these feelings during the whole of this "dreary time" that gave such unforgettable vividness to the furniture of his waiting place: the old stone wall, the single sheep, and the blasted hawthorn. He remembers them not only because they were his immediate surroundings on the day when he waited with intense "anxiety of hope," but also because the death of his father gave the whole scene a deeper meaning in retrospect. Just as his eagerness to get home for Christmas was at first frustrated by the long delay of the horses, so the pleasure of the whole Christmas season was dashed by the death in the family, and the holidays at home for which the schoolboy had so impatiently waited (like a horse himself, straining at the bit) became a "dreary time." Such words as *expectation, resentment,* and *guilt* cannot of course exhaust the significance of the place that Wordsworth remembers, which comes to symbolize at once the pain of losing paternal guidance and the necessity of being guided—in a sense *re-fathered*—by the intercourse of his own imagination with nature.[40] But in any case, it is clear at least that this particular "spot of time" was not something snatched *from* but rather begotten *by* the passage of time, that the waiting place had to await the death of Wordsworth's father before it could truly become a spot of time.

To see what Wordsworth does with time and space in his poetry is to wonder whether anything genuinely comparable can be done in the vi-

---

40. On this point see Onorato 253–54. Note that in book 6 of *The Prelude*, Wordsworth likens the imagination to an "unfathered vapour" rising from an abyss (6. 594). Given the gradual discovery that his own imagination is ultimately autonomous, as Hartman has emphasized, it is not surprising that he should feel creatively regenerated by the memory of a spot indelibly linked with his father's death.

sual arts. Can a painting show how the experience of one place can affect the appearance of another, or how the memory of a particular place at a particular time has been modified—perhaps intensified—by the effect of another memory? To ask these questions is to ask again whether painting can move beyond the limits to which Lessing said it was confined: the depiction of a "single moment . . . from one point of vision" (14).

The history of art suggests that painting not only can but has transcended those limits. On the ceiling of the Sistine Chapel Michelangelo represents in a series of pictures the spiritual history of mankind, and in one of those pictures, *The Expulsion of Adam and Eve from the Garden*, he shows not only the expulsion itself but what preceded it—the taking of the forbidden fruit. In the art of our own time, the diagonally ranged cluster of figures in Duchamp's *Nude Descending a Staircase* represents the downward movement of a single figure, and in Picasso's *Portrait of Maia*, a face with nose in profile and both eyes visible represents a child seen from two different—and hence temporally distinct—points of view. Nevertheless, the immediate question is whether anything like Wordsworth's spots of time can be found in the work of Constable: whether Constable's pictures offer us anything more—temporally speaking— than the representation of a single moment.

To this question my own answer is yes. Constable's most characteristic paintings reveal, first of all, the effects of time. Sometimes, as in *Hadleigh Castle* (plate 11), he reveals its impact on historic ruins; more often he shows what it does to the natural objects and rustic structures that displace historic ruins in his work: to the blasted tree in the left foreground of *The Cornfield* (plate 20), to the big, conspicuously vegetating dungheap of *The Stour Valley and Dedham Village* (1814), to the "old rotten Banks, slimy posts, & brickwork" of which he writes so affectionately to Fisher in 1821 (*JCC* 6: 77) and which figure so prominently in paintings such as *The Hay Wain*. Furthermore, Ronald Paulson has noted that in pictures such as *Stour Valley and Dedham Village*, the relation between the mound of dung in the left foreground and the handsomely cultivated fields in the distance is decidedly temporal. In a process reaching back through the eighteenth century to Virgil's fourth *Georgic*, the rotting manure will be used to fertilize the distant fields, and decay will thus lead—in time—to regeneration (*Literary Landscape* 130).

This way of representing seasonal or vegetative renewal could of course be regarded as simply a dehistoricized version of Lessing's "pregnant moment," and even more, Constable's pictures of transitional weather—

of clouds breaking up or gathering for a storm—are clearly meant to signify at once what is and what is to come.[41] But Constable could do more with time than show its effects on natural objects or register the imminence of meteorological change. In *The Cornfield*, he subtly infuses the space of the "present" with the consciousness of his own past, and thus makes of a landscape painting something very like a Wordsworthian spot of time. For this reason the picture is worth examining in some detail.

Comparison of the finished picture with the medium-sized study (ca. 1826?), shows that the finished version was deliberately composed or invented rather than based on observation. Constable did this version in his London studio, and whether or not the sketch was also made there (as is generally thought), the finished picture includes a number of elements absent from the sketch: the dead tree, the drinking boy, the animals, the plough, the farmer at the gate, the distant laborers, and the still more distant church tower—which is not actually visible from the point depicted. Constable apparently took some of these elements—such as the plough—from individual sketches that *were* based on his own observation (G. Reynolds, *CE* 74–76; Parris, Fleming-Williams, and Shields 145–46). But the picture as a whole raises with particular insistence the question of its meaning: Just what is this carefully assembled configuration of elements meant to signify?

One answer is that it recalls the allegorical landscapes of the Renaissance by representing the "Ages of Man": a diagonal line connects the boy drinking in the lower left with the farmer at the gate (here serving as a passageway to manhood) and then leads to the distant laborers and finally to the church, an emblem of salvation in the life beyond.[42] The problem with this reading of the picture's temporality, however, is that it

41. In one of his 1836 lectures Constable himself explained how a winter landscape by Ruysdael "told a story" of the weather, showing that the wind had changed and that this change would bring a thaw (*JCD* 64).

42. Kroeber, *RLV* 31; and Paulson, *Literary Landscape* 23, 109. Constable said that allegory was "outside the reach of art" because when we look at a picture such as Ruysdael's *Allegory of the Life of Man*, we have no way of discovering that the ruins signify old age, the stream signifies the course of life, and the rocks and precipices signify its dangers (*JCD* 64). Yet Constable also said that he put ruins and storms into his own pictures to represent his own melancholy (see above, note 24). Is there contradiction here, as Paulson suggests (*Literary Landscape* 111)? Perhaps. But I am inclined to think that Constable is rejecting the impersonalism of traditional allegory for the personalism of symbolic self-representation. In any case, his statement about allegory should make us wary of reading *The Cornfield* in traditionally allegorical terms.

overlooks the powerful opposition between progressive and regressive movement: between the straightforward line that would take the boy through the gateposts to a life of spiritually rewarding work, and the circle that surrounds him: the circle made by the wooden fences, the sheep, the banks at left and right, the curving lane, the significantly idle plough, the gate itself oddly askew, the donkey standing maternally by its foal, and the trees at left. This powerfully enclosing structure makes the drinking boy in the foreground at least as important as the distant church, which—unlike the tower of the Dedham church in the Willoughby version of *The Leaping Horse* (ca. 1825, reproduced in Leslie, plate 38)—does not even break the horizon. Furthermore, the lane that starts so conspicuously in the center foreground leads not to the gate but away from it, down the hill to the right. Unless we believe that the farmer at the gate is coming to fetch the boy or even scold him for his idleness (like Wordsworth's Michael reprimanding young Luke), we have no grounds for supposing that the picture represents a boy being summoned to begin the pilgrimage of life,or to renounce—with a respectable nod to Hogarth—Idleness for Industry. The farmer by the gatepost is himself at rest. Neither exemplifying industry nor signifying (by any gesture) admonition, he is—so far as we can tell—simply contemplating the drinking boy. And if the viewer's eye is led up through the gate to the church beyond, it too is just as powerfully drawn back to the figure of the boy, who draws to himself the dog's glance as well as the farmer's gaze.

"The Drinking Boy," in fact, is what Constable himself often called this picture, and the boy could well represent Constable's boyhood self. We know that the lane in the foreground is the one he regularly took to school, that about 1810 he had made an oil sketch of a boy lying down to drink from a stream (G. Reynolds, *CE* 76), and that a few years before painting *The Cornfield* he had written to Fisher what I have already quoted in part: "I should paint my own places best—Painting is but another word for feeling. I associate my 'careless boyhood' to all that lies on the banks of the *Stour*. They made me a painter (& I am gratefull) that is I had often thought of pictures of them before I had ever touched a pencil" (*JCC* 6: 78). If we can plausibly infer that Constable was thinking of himself when he painted *The Cornfield*, the picture of a drinking boy has distinctly Wordsworthian overtones. When Wordsworth recalls his own vivifying recourse to the memory of the spot where he had waited as a schoolboy, he tells us that all that he saw and heard at this spot were "spectacles and sounds to which / I often would repair and thence would drink / As at a fountain."[43]

Constable did not know *The Prelude*, so he could not have chosen deliberately to literalize Wordsworth's metaphor. What Constable knew intimately, however, and what he drastically revised in this picture is the structure of a painting on which—as we have seen already—he also drew for his two quite different versions of *Dedham Vale*. I refer to Claude's *Landscape: Hagar and the Angel* (plate 3), where the trees framing the vista of the slanting bridge make a mirror image of the trees framing the vista of Constable's slanting cornfield, and where the biblical figures occupy precisely the place in which Constable puts the drinking boy: the left foreground. Displacing biblical history with his own history, Constable represents the boy he once was: the boy who carelessly drinks from a wayside stream with one sock slipped halfway down his calf, the boy who could see the scenes around him reflected—as it were depicted—in the very stream from which he was drinking and who could thus think of pictures of these scenes before he ever touched a pencil (or a paintbrush). We can now see that the farmer looking back on this boy probably stands for the mature Constable contemplating his own past. Working in his London studio, he locates his surrogate present self in the world of man's order and cultivation, beside the straight posts of the gate and against the academically strict diagonal of the cornfield slanting down behind him. But this surrogate present self gazes back on the circle of a world in which a boy lies down to drink, donkeys nibble leaves, sheep saunter along, and the shepherd dog who is supposed to guide them momentarily forgets his duty. The picture is a spot of time in which the present is revitalized by the past, in which Constable represents himself in the very act of seeing again the boy he once was in one of the scenes that "made me a painter."

Of course it is possible to read this contemplation of the past quite unsympathetically. John Barrell has argued that Constable's landscapes reflect a subtly oppressive pictorial tradition which stresses the poetically pastoral beauty of the landscape while suppressing reference to the labor required to produce it (*Dark Side* 131–64). Since the only two fig-

43. A 11. 383–85. The drinking metaphor here takes its place with the pervasive references to water in Wordsworth's poem, beginning with his earliest recollections of the river Derwent, where as a five-year-old child he "Made one long bathing of a summer's day" (A 1. 295). I have already noted that he repeatedly speaks of his growing mind as a river.

ures actually laboring in *The Cornfield* are mere specks on the distant edge of the field, this picture seems to confirm Barrell's thesis. Constable himself said that it offered "more eye-salve" than he usually supplied (*JCC* 6: 217), and to an unsympathetic viewer, its foreground cluster of boy and animals could easily recall Gainsborough at his most sentimental. Yet sentimentality is precisely what Constable avoids by locating the farmer and the carefully cultivated field on the very edge of the boy's world—as a vantage point from which to view it. The plough by the gate—though momentarily idle—is meticulously depicted by an artist who reveals in his own work a profound respect for the work and the tools of others. Constable suppresses the laborers here no more than Wordsworth does when he recalls the dawn that he witnessed on his return from an all-night party: the dawn in whose magnificent light he felt himself at once summoned to and liberated for the work of poetry at the very moment when "Labourous [were] going forth into the fields" (*Prelude* 5. 349). At such moments, as Jeffrey Baker has shown, Wordsworth's imagination moves triumphantly beyond the temporal imperatives of the conventional working day to the "deliberate holiday" of a vocation at once self-exploratory and self-liberating (Baker 153–54). Constable's mature surrogate in *The Cornfield* symbolically aspires to the same end. He is a liminal figure standing at the gateway to the world of man's work and yet stirred—in an enduring moment of idleness—to the work of remembering, perceiving, imagining, and finally re-creating the life of the boy. In this spot of time that draws the present back through the gateway to the past, the conventions of labor and the conventions of history are alike displaced by a painter determined to re-create his own history.

Karl Kroeber has written that "romantic historical vision is founded upon the impossibility of any definitive, that is, rationally unchanging, representation of historical phenomena" (Kroeber and Walling 161). One way of summarizing the displacement of history which I have examined in this chapter is to say that English romantic poetry and painting displaces one kind of history with another: moments of clear and enduring significance dominated by one or two major figures give way to moments of indeterminate significance dominated by no one in particular. But this is only a partial explanation of what happened to history in the romantic period. Besides losing its stability as a source of exempla virtutis, a tradition that grew moribund in England even as it was revived in France, the history of great public events ceased to maintain its supremacy over

CHAPTER 3

THE INTERNALIZATION
OF PROSPECT

IN LOOKING AT OBJECTS of Nature while I am thinking, as at yonder moon dim-glimmering thro' the dewy window-pane, I seem rather to be seeking, as it were *asking*, a symbolical language for something within me that already and forever exists, than observing anything new.

— COLERIDGE (*NC* 2: 2546)

> before the vernal thrush
> Was audible, among the hills I sate
> Alone, upon some jutting eminence
> At the first hour of morning, when the Vale
> Lay quiet in an utter solitude.
> . . . .
> Oft in those moments such a holy calm
> Did overspread my soul, that I forgot
> That I had bodily eyes, and what I saw
> Appear'd like something in myself, a dream,
> A prospect in my mind.

— WORDSWORTH (*Prelude* A 2. 360–71)

 TO CONSIDER the displacement of history in English romantic poetry and painting is to discover one of the most important points of correspondence between the two arts: their preoccupation with private history, and in particular the history of an individual's relation to landscape. This line of investigation leads to the very center of romanticism: to autobiography, to the self-consciousness that is inevitably bound up with romantic nature-consciousness, to the art of representing landscape as if it were a prospect in the mind, or an emblem of the mind in the very act of creation, which is what landscape becomes in the concluding book of *The Prelude*.

Recent criticism has approached this center of romanticism in various ways. M. H. Abrams argues that romanticism makes man assume the role once played by God, reading nature as a reflection of his own inherent powers and yet (unlike God) using it to guide his development and elicit his self-knowledge.[1] Northrop Frye interprets romanticism as a "recovery of projection" in which the imagination reclaims as its own creations God, heaven, hell, and nature—everything it has traditionally projected onto a world external to man (3–49). Harold Bloom treats romanticism as "the internalization of quest romance" the transformation of an external journey into an interior quest for the self and its origins ("Internalization" 3–24). And Thomas Weiskel has shown that romanticism profoundly internalizes the sublimity that eighteenth-century aestheticians chiefly imputed to external spectacles.

The question I wish to raise now is to what extent this process of internalization so variously manifested in romantic poetry can be found in romantic landscape painting. Part of the answer is readily available. If we define internalization as autobiography, we can certainly find it in a picture such as Turner's *Snow Storm—Steam-boat off a Harbour's Mouth* (plate 37), exhibited 1842, for the full title of this picture actually includes an autobiographical statement: *The author was in this storm on the night the Ariel left Harwich.* Ruskin tells us that Turner had himself lashed to the mast so that he might observe the storm, and that he was there for four hours. "I did not expect to escape," he reportedly said, "but I felt bound to record it if I did" (quoted in Butlin and Joll 224). Turner's comment is at once objective and subjective. Though Ruskin was struck by his use of the word *record*, which suggests a detached, impersonal representation of a snowstorm at sea, the word *author* in the very title of the picture is equally telling. Turner's painting is a work not of self-effacement but of survival and triumphant self-assertion. Looking at the picture itself, with its dramatically pitched-up horizon and its swirling vortex, we cannot doubt that this is the "record" of a profoundly personal experience.

Romantic landscape paintings furnish no simple equivalents for the self-revelation we so often find in romantic poetry.[2] Yet for this very rea-

---

1. Abrams, *Natural Supernaturalism* 88–117. Geoffrey Hartman likewise notes that Wordsworth's poetry—which paradigmatically illustrates Abrams's definition of romanticism—springs from the union of nature consciousness with "an answering self-consciousness" (Abrams, *English Romantic Poets* 123).

2. It is startling to realize that the two most important painters in what we have come to regard as an age of supreme self-consciousness produced only three known self-portraits between them—far fewer than we have from Rembrandt, whom they both

son, they prompt us to reexamine the assumption that poetry is an art of the inner world and painting an art of the outer one, that poetry—as Burke said—displays "the effect of things on the mind" while painting presents "a clear idea of the things themselves" (172). It is not only that pictures such as *Snowstorm* and *The Cornfield* can be autobiographically interpreted, or even that a substantial portion of Constable's work can be read as the expression of his successively frustrated, gratified, and finally shattered love for Maria Bicknell.[3] In romantic painting as well as in romantic poetry, the internalization of prospect goes well beyond autobiography, beyond the record or history of an individual life. Essentially, it is the process by which landscape is re-created to represent the mind, or more precisely the mind's interaction with nature. In this chapter, therefore, I will examine two contrasting ways in which romantic poets and painters make the outer world express the inner world. One is by representing scenes of enclosure or "refuge" from the world at large. The other is by eliminating stable or elevated viewpoints: an elimination that leads to the absorption of self in prospect, the merging of nature-consciousness and self-consciousness, the experience of a sublimity at once external and profoundly internalized.

THE REFUGE OF SELF

We may approach the study of refuge in English romantic poetry and painting by first considering the contrast between refuge and prospect in eighteenth-century representations of landscape. As Jay Appleton defines these terms, the landscape of prospect affords the maximum opportunity to see and the landscape of refuge the maximum opportunity to hide. Psychologically, therefore, the most satisfying landscape is one that combines these two features by offering an unobstructed view from an enclosure: the maximum opportunity to see without being seen (74). A classic example of this combination is Claude's *Landscape: Hagar and the Angel* (plate 3), where groups of trees at left and right in the foreground provide a refuge from which we can see the bridge in the middle distance

---

greatly admired. Turner painted two, one about 1793 and the other about 1798; Constable did a pencil sketch of himself in 1806.

3. See Paulson, *Literary Landscape* 127–52. Karl Kroeber sees in *Hadleigh Castle* (painted the year after Maria Bicknell died) something like the "deep distress" with which Wordsworth commemorates the death of his brother John in "Elegiac Stanzas Suggested by a Picture of Peele Castle" (*RLV* 44).

(itself another refuge) and the mountains beyond it stretching to infinity. The practice of thus defining a view by means of wing-screens or coulisses became common in eighteenth-century English landscape painting. In Richard Wilson's *Holt Bridge on the River Dee* (ca. 1762), a pair of trees at left and a wooded cliff at right frame a vista of bridge and distant mountains. More dramatically, Joseph Wright's *A Cavern: Morning* (1774) puts the viewer within a cave whose shadowy mouth dramatically encloses the sunlit Gulf of Salerno.[4]

In poetry and landscape gardening as well as painting, however, most landscapes tend to be dominated by either prospect or refuge rather than poised between the two. In the development of English landscape gardening, for instance, the winding paths and grottoes designed by Kent provided a refuge from the prospect-dominated layout of French gardens; "Capability" Brown's creation of large open spaces was an attempt to revive the sense of prospect; and the reaction against Brown's "shaven" expanses in the name of "picturesque" intricacy and concealment was a renewed expression of the desire for refuge. In painting, pictures such as George Lambert's *Hilly Landscape with a Cornfield* (1733) provide broad, light, panormaic views, while Gainsborough's *The Market Cart* (1786–7) has large, dark, and almost cavernous trees surrounding the central figures. The corresponding contrast in eighteenth-century poetry can be seen in the movement from the sunlit expanses described in *The Seasons*, where—as Hunt suggests—Thomson tends to lose his identity in panoramic views, to the moments of sublime obscurity in poems such as Collins's *Odes* and Edward Young's *Night Thoughts*, where darkness provides a refuge and release for the self, and where verbal pictures of the outer world give way to verbal evocations of the inner one.[5]

Nevertheless, to link darkness with refuge, as Appleton does, is to ignore the more obvious and powerful link between darkness and danger:

4. In book 5 of *The Prelude*, Wordsworth describes himself as seated within a rocky cave looking out at the sea when he falls asleep and dreams of the Arab bearing the stone and the shell (5. 58–140). Hillis Miller takes this rocky cave as "an example of those many nooks or caves in Wordsworth's verse emblematic of subjectivity looking out on the world" (142).

5. See Hunt, *Figure* 124, 135–36, 173, 179–80; and Weiskel 110. I do not mean to imply that Thomson's poetry was uniformly impersonal; the opening lines of "Winter" seemed to Constable "a beautiful instance of the poet identifying his own feelings with external nature" (Leslie 328). But on the whole, Thomson's effort to join the inner and outer worlds was hampered, as Hunt says, "by either a mimetic instinct or a too generalized formulation of the subjective, perceiving mind" (*Figure* 124).

a link to which Burke significantly devotes two full sections of his *Philosophical Enquiry* (144–47). Likewise, to think of refuge as a place of safety for the self is to ignore the terrors that lurk within the self: the "fear and awe" that fall upon us, as Wordsworth says, "when we look / Into our minds" (*PW* 5: 4). What Appleton calls refuge symbolism may be a way to the self, but this is often perilous and uncertain, as the poetry of sensibility shows. Much of it vacillates between the evocative language of obscure introspection and the pictorial language of description, with allegory and personification struggling to mediate between the two. Thus in Collins's "Ode to Fear" (1747), a personified Danger

> stalks his Round, an hideous Form,
> Howling amidst the Midnight Storm,
> Or throws him on the ridgy Steep
> Of some loose hanging Rock to sleep.
> And with him thousand phantoms join'd
> Who prompt to Deeds accurs'd the Mind.
>
> (Crane 731)

With his lingering attachment to iconography, Collins gives us a figure at once vaguely visual ("an hideous Form" recalling Milton's "Death") and evocatively auditory ("Howling"). But the inner feelings suggested here are projected onto an outer world populated by phantoms. In a darkness that breeds not so much introspection as confusion, we have lost the clear picture of the outer world, but we have not yet found our way to the depths of the inner one.[6]

A more tangible alternative to the panorama of Thomson's *The Seasons* is provided by Cowper's *Task* (1785). In place of Thomson's expansiveness, Cowper offers a concentrated vision of local detail, minute particulars, and intimate scenes. Yet Cowper is a poet not so much of psychic as of habitational interiority. As a refuge from outer space, he characteristically seeks the inner space of a cottage, a hut, a weather house, or—in its most minimal form—the sofa that he "sings" at the beginning of *The Task*. The sofa itself aptly symbolizes Cowper's way of domesticating nature. Calling to mind the joint stool and even the "rugged rock" on

---

6. At the end of the poem, says Paul Sherwin, "we are left with a voice constraining a void, the urgency of the voice deriving from a blind effort to possess on the affective level what it already possesses" (77). Elsewhere Sherwin notes that Collins "cannot transcend his isolate ego" (61). But I must add that Sherwin's book is a fine and searching study of Collins's attempts to do so.

which the "hardy chief" of yore reposed his weary limbs (1. 12), the sofa mediates between indoors and outdoors, literally providing a humble seat from which one may contemplate nature—with a subtle pun, perhaps, on the much grander "seat" of the nobleman whose imposing estate keeps nature at bay. Cowper studies nature at close range, but he does so by converting it into habitable space. When he leaves the modern indoor sofa in order to ramble through the countryside, he inevitably finds his way to a "herdsman's solitary hut," to a weather house, or to what he calls a "*peasant's nest*" (1. 168, 211, 227).

William Free rightly observes that the difference between Thomson and Cowper is nowhere more evident than in their treatments of winter (Free 112–20). For Thomson, winter is a forbidding outdoor season of wind, mist, "Vapours, and clouds, and storms"—a magnificent specimen of the external sublime, complete with Alpine avalanches. For Cowper, winter is an indoor season, "king of intimate delights" (4. 139), an occasion for domestic intimacy, for hearthside gatherings in which a small, self-contained society basks in the warmth of fire and friendship, and the art of needlepoint creates a little garden that cannot fade (4. 150–57). To the extent that nature is present here, it has been imported into the cottage, which in this case is literally a refuge from the prospect of ice and cold. But it is not a vantage point from which to view external sublimity; it is not like the mountainside hut that looks out on "wilds and swelling floods" in Collins's "Ode to Evening" (Crane 738). Cowper notices raging frost and rough wind outside only as they "endear / The silence and the warmth enjoy'd within!" (4. 150–57).

Thus the interaction between mind and nature in Cowper's work occurs within a relatively narrow range. Outer space shrinks to a habitable enclosure—a room, a cottage, a sofa, a grove. But inner space expands to accommodate more than one person, so that while Cowper explores the literal inner space of a human dwelling, he does not cross the threshold into the individual consciousness. He keeps us in an outer room, where the movement toward introspection is checked by the firm if benevolent pressure of society.

Cowper is therefore a particularly good example of a tendency observable in much of the art as well as the poetry of the eighteenth century: the tendency to domesticate or appropriate outdoor space. In Gainsborough's *Mr. and Mrs. Andrews* (1748), the gracefully curved wrought-iron bench on which the figures sit domesticates the fields around them and subtly proclaims their ownership. In Joseph Wright's *Sir Brooke Boothby*

(1781) an elegantly dressed country gentleman turns the ground itself into a luxurious sofa by the way he lies upon it. In Francis Wheatley's *The Wilkinson Family* (ca. 1776–78), an outdoor portrait, the turf beneath the splendidly attired figures is virtually indistinguishable from a carpet. And even in Gainsborough's later portraits, where the settings become primitive, the primitivism is softened by an atmosphere of domesticity. The title figure in *Mrs. Sheridan* (1783) sits on a rock—like one of Cowper's hardy chiefs—with the wind ruffling her hair and her diaphanous dress. But it is not at all clear whether she becomes a part of nature, as Paulson suggests (*Emblem* 218), or nature becomes a part of her. Paradoxically, the bristling cornstalks in the proprietary landscape of *Mr. and Mrs. Andrews* are distinctly more realistic than the powder-puff leaves in the ostensibly open landscape here, where the shapes of the foliage repeat the oval of the lady's face and the ground beneath her feet repeats the filmy texture of her dress.

The case of Gainsborough is nonetheless a special one. If we are tempted to think of his work as in some sense artificial, Paulson reminds us that he sought in many ways to make it natural: to replace history, iconography, meaning, morality, and textuality in art with plainness and simplicity (*Emblem* 204; "Gainsborough's Landscape Drawings" 107). To some extent he even anticipates the "natural painture" of Constable, who praised not only the "fine sentiment" of Gainsborough's work but the "exquisite" treatment of natural forms and masses in his black-and-white chalk drawings—some of which were made directly from nature.[7] But Gainsborough did not regularly work from nature. He once declined a request for a painting of a specific scene because, he said, "with respect to real views from Nature" in England, he had "never seen any place that affords a subject equal to the poorest imitations of Gaspar or Claude," and he added that any landscapes he would paint "must be of his own brain" (Waterhouse 15). Gainsborough's brain was a storehouse of generalized forms, and most of his landscapes—especially the later ones—give us a generalized version of nature: a nature re-created indoors. Indeed, in light of the complex relation between refuge and prospect, indoors and outdoors, psychic inner space and natural outer space, it is striking to note that many of Gainsborough's drawings were based

7. Leslie 233–34, 270; Hayes 30. Though Constable told Farington in 1799 that he found Gainsborough's later work "so wide of nature," Hayes notes that a group of drawings in the Huntington Gallery provides "real evidence for Gainsborough's influence on the young Constable" (75).

on the literal importation of natural objects into his studio. "From the fields," Joshua Reynolds tells us, "he brought into his painting-room, stumps of trees, weeds, and animals of various kinds; and designed them, not from memory, but immediately from the objects" (*D* 250).

Gainsborough's landscape drawings, then, give us a nature that has been imported into his house and thereby transformed. It is not clear that the drawings emerge from a subconscious manipulation of "pure form," as Paulson suggests, or that Gainsborough's method is really akin to the technique popularized by Alexander Cozens, who recommended a meaningless shape or "blot" as the starting point for a landscape design (Paulson, "Gainsborough's Landscape Drawings" 108; Hayes 14; Wilton, *BW* 26–27). Most of the time, Gainsborough used natural objects rather than blots or purely mental forms. Nevertheless, we know that he worked from a domesticated version of nature, using lumps of coal as models for rocks, broccoli and herbs for woods, and bits of mirror for water (Hayes 33). Working at night by candlelight, Gainsborough turned these forms into deeply shadowed objects of landscape, in patterns that slant repeatedly or even obsessively downward. "The prototypical Gainsborough landscape," says Paulson, "shows banks and slopes converging to make a single path that drops into darkness" (*Emblem* 218–19).

The meaning of this pattern can only be guessed at. Unlike Hogarth and Reynolds, who give us explicitly readable structures often accompanied by actual texts, Gainsborough offers expressive structures without readable meaning.[8] What then can we make of his darkening and descending way? We have no way of knowing for certain, but it is at least clear that Gainsborough turns from prospect to refuge, from the sunlit, spreading vistas of Claudian outer space to what is at least potentially the mind's inner space. His drawings exploit and expose all the ambiguities of the refuge, which is at once protective and suffocating, a womb and a grave. A few of Gainsborough's landscapes look outward to a dis-

---

8. Paulson, *Emblem, passim*. The singularity of Gainsborough's style prompted Joshua Reynolds to say that he was like men speaking a language which they themselves—let alone their auditors—"can scarce be said to understand" (*D* 258). But Reynolds is talking here of Gainsborough's portraits, which on balance he commends; so far from criticizing them for their unintelligibility or for a uniqueness antithetical to the standards of a conforming group, as Eaves suggests (75), Reynolds praises them for the "general effect . . . [of] striking resemblance" which (he thought) their unfinished manner actually helped to create (*D* 259). Nevertheless, though Reynolds also commends Gainsborough for bringing natural objects into his studio and for working by candlelight (*D* 250–51), he has nothing to say about the landscapes produced by these methods.

tant horizon, but most look downward. Unlike Richard Wilson, who translated Claude into English terms but kept his prospective vision, Gainsborough is profoundly introspective.

He achieved this introspection, however, at the cost of external particularity. In his drawings of the early 1750s, when he often worked outside, Gainsborough carefully renders tree trunks, limbs, and even individual leaves. In the later drawings, which were done chiefly inside, limbs and branches tend to disappear; trees become scalloped puffs of foliage; and the bristly texture and angularity of the early work give way to smoothness and undulation (Hayes 32). The dangers of preoccupation with such a deeply internalized landscape are essentially those that Wordsworth experienced in his childhood, when he communed with everything he saw as if it were part of his own nature, and often "grasped at a wall or tree to recall myself from this abyss of idealism to the reality" (*PW* 4: 463). Gainsborough's later drawings do not represent the abyss of idealism, but it is noteworthy that the trees in these pictures seem hardly substantial enough to be grasped. They come not from continually renewed study of nature but rather—in Gainsborough's words—from "his own brain."

The conversation between mind and nature in Gainsborough's landscapes, then, finally becomes the mind's soliloquy. To the extent that Gainsborough's drawings pursue a darkening and descending way, his vision is the antithesis of that primordial vision granted to Milton's Adam from the highest hill in paradise, a hill "from whose top / The hemisphere of earth in clearest ken / Stretcht out to the amplest reach of prospect lay" (*Paradise Lost* 11. 378–80). Gainsborough abandons this outer vision for an inner one of darkened and darkening self-consciousness: a vision disarmingly reminiscent of the fallen Satan's in book 1 of *Paradise Lost*, where in a hell that significantly serves as both prison and refuge he sees "no light, but rather darkness visible" (line 63). If it is fanciful to associate Milton with a painter who claimed that he "scarcely ever read a book" (quoted in Waterhouse 16), there is nothing fanciful about the association of paradise and hell with prospect and refuge more generally. In the resoundingly Miltonic "Prospectus" to *The Recluse* (lines 3–6), Wordsworth sets himself a double goal: to fathom the mind of man, more fearful than "the darkest pit of lowest Erebus" (line 36), and to rediscover paradise in "this goodly universe" (line 53). In these terms, the romantic struggle to re-create landscape in painting and poetry can be seen as the struggle to balance prospect and refuge, to reconcile a heaven of sunlit prospect with a hell of darkened self-consciousness.

Of course the darkness of refuge cannot be simply equated with Milton's hell. In Coleridge's "Frost at Midnight," it is hard to see anything hellish or Satanic in the apparently benevolent mood with which the poet contemplates the fire and the frosted windows of his darkened cottage on a winter night. Coleridge's account of what his "idling Spirit" (line 20) finds in a fluttering flame actually seems to echo Cowper's description of himself before a fire on a winter night, contemplating a shadow "dancing uncouthly to the quivering flame," seeing houses, faces, and other shapes in the red cinders, superstitiously reading the films of flame upon the bars as portents of some stranger's approach, and on the whole regarding the fire "in indolent vacuity of thought" (*The Task* 4. 276–97). But Coleridge's mood is subtly different from Cowper's. While Cowper contentedly contrasts the "raging" frost and rough wind of the outdoors with "the silence and the warmth enjoy'd within" (4. 310), Coleridge anxiously contrasts the silence of the frost and of the windless night outside with the fluttering film within, "the sole unquiet thing" which mirrors and matches the stirrings of his own unquiet soul (16–23). There are Dantean if not Miltonic reverberations here; we are reminded of the flaming souls that shake when they speak in canto 26 of *The Inferno*. But in any case, the comforting habitational interiority of Cowper has given way to a psychic interiority, a sense of deep and vexing disturbance within the dark refuge of the self.

The counterpart of this introspective tendency in the poem is the prospect of a psychically liberating future for the baby who now sleeps in the protective refuge of his cradle but who will, Coleridge predicts,

> wander like a breeze
> By lakes and sandy shores, beneath the crags
> Of ancient mountain, and beneath the clouds,
> Which image in their bulk both lakes and shores
> And mountain crags.
>
> (54–58)

Though a place beneath crags and clouds suggests enclosure, the net effect of the passage is one of expansion and prospect—both psychic and visual. After retrospectively withdrawing into his own confined schooldays, "pent 'mid cloisters dim" at Christ's Hospital in London (52), Coleridge prospectively travels into open space, where Hartley, he says, will see and hear the shapes and sounds of God's eternal language. The movement from refuge to prospect is thus a movement from one self to another, and from *a* self to the landscape at large, which now becomes the earthly paradise, the mediator between God and man.

A still more striking example of the way Coleridge bridges the gap between the problematic refuge of self and the prospect of landscape is a poem written several months earlier than "Frost at Midnight"—"This Lime-Tree Bower My Prison." The structure of this poem recalls that of John Dyer's *Grongar Hill* (1726, Crane 655–58), the paradigmatic prospect poem of the eighteenth century. Dyer starts from "mossy cells" of "silent shade" (lines 15–17), winds his way to the "mountain's brow" from which a brilliantly cloudless landscape opens up to a panoramic view (41ff.), and then returns to the "humble shade" of groves (131–58). Coleridge likewise moves from the shaded recesses of bower and dell (1–19) to an open space "beneath the wide wide Heaven" (21), and then returns to the shadowy bower. But there the resemblance to Dyer's poem ends. While Dyer makes a topographical, largely impersonal survey of the ground beneath him, as Lambert does in *Hilly Landscape*, Coleridge merely imagines the prospect that his friends are actually seeing. Throughout the poem, he remains a prisoner of the bower, into which he must import the landscape seen by his friends:

> Well, they are gone, and here must I remain,
> This lime-tree bower my prison! I have lost
> Beauties and feelings, such as would have been
> Most sweet to my remembrance even when age
> Had dimm'd mine eyes to blindness.
>
> (1–5)

The casual tone of these opening lines masks their complexity. In a situation that disarmingly recalls that of Milton's Satan at the beginning of *Paradise Lost*, Coleridge is condemned to a dark prison where he contemplates lost beauties. But the beauties lost are at once prospective and retrospective, anticipated and proleptically regretted by a poet who foresees in the shadow of the bower a fate like Milton's: the deeper shadow of blindness in old age. In this deeply introspective mood, we are offered no prospect of landscape; the opening lines promise only a poem of dark, vague, possibly solipsistic self-exploration. Yet Coleridge no sooner regrets the "lost" beauties he will be unable to remember in a blind old age than he begins to find them in his memory now. By the inward eye of memory, the blindness which seems to engulf him in the bower turns into a vision of what his friends are even now seeing: friends whom he melodramatically thinks he "never more may meet again" (6) but whom in fact he accompanies in his imagination as they wander on springy heath, wind their way down to a dell, or "emerge / Beneath the wide wide heaven" (20–21). Within the dark bower and refuge of his own memory, Coleridge rediscovers the light of landscapes remembered with uncanny precision: the file of dripping weeds in the dell, the covertly oxymoronic *still trembling* of yellow leaves that "tremble still" (15), the purple shadow of the sea, the distant groves in the yellow light of the setting sun. These things are so much a part of him that we can scarcely say whether the poem is excursion or incursion, whether Coleridge goes out of the bower or landscape comes into it. Either way, however, he joins the inner world and the outer one, dark refuge and brilliant prospect, solitude and companionship, "blind" present and sighted past. The result is a fusion of matter and spirit:

> Ah! slowly sink
> Behind the western ridge, thou glorious Sun!
> Shine in the slant beams of the sinking orb,
> Ye purple heath-flowers! richlier burn, ye clouds!
> Live in the yellow light, ye distant groves!
> And kindle, thou blue Ocean! So my friend
> Struck with deep joy may stand, as I have stood,
> Silent with swimming sense; yea, gazing round
> On the wide landscape, gaze till all doth seem
> Less gross than bodily; and of such hues
> As veil the Almighty Spirit, when yet he makes
> Spirits perceive his presence.
>
> (32–43)

In the light of this landscape, which is both external and profoundly internalized, a prospect in the mind, Coleridge returns to contemplation of his shadowy refuge, which is now subtly re-created as a prospect:

> Pale beneath the blaze
> Hung the transparent foliage; and I watch'd
> Some broad and sunny leaf, and lov'd to see
> The shadow of the leaf and stem above;
> Dappling its sunshine!
>
> (47–51)

Like the burning clouds that he has just been contemplating with his
mind's eye, the foliage seen in time present now becomes a thing of ethereal radiance, and the elements of the scene assume the character of a
concentrated prospect, with one leaf shadowing another and dark ivy setting off the lighter elms. Even as the outer world penetrates the inner
one, light and shadow interpenetrate here. In the final passage, Coleridge's reflections on the solaces of confinement (56–67) recall Dyer's
self-chastening wish to be contented "with an humble shade" (131), and
the creeking of the rook "when all was still" in Coleridge's poem (73–74)
recalls the sound of the thrush "while all is still" in Dyer's (158). But
Coleridge's treatment of light and shadow is far more complex than Dyer's.
While Dyer simply contraposes the sunlit prospect with "humble shade,"
Coleridge fuses the two, and his final lines on the rook are a final demonstration of just how subtle this fusion can be:

> My gentle-hearted Charles! when the last rook
> Beat its straight path along the dusky air
> Homewards, I blest it! deeming its black wing
> (Now a dim speck, now vanishing in light)
> Had cross'd the mighty Orb's dilated glory,
> While thou stood'st gazing; or, when all was still,
> Flew creeking o'er thy head, and had a charm
> For thee, my gentle-hearted Charles, to whom
> No sound is dissonant which tells of Life.
>
> (68–76)

Like the black wing of the rook that vanishes into a dusky light rather
than into darkness, the line between light and darkness itself becomes
virtually invisible. Correspondingly, the gap between Coleridge and his
excursioning friend closes. Coleridge seems to see as well as hear the
homeward-bound rook, and thus to share as well as imagine Lamb's vision of it against the setting sun. Paradoxically, the mood of introspection
generated by the bower leads to a final act of imaginative excursion.

Since nothing short of a surrealist painting could superimpose an
imagined prospect on a bower represented as actually seen, the union of
refuge and prospect that Coleridge achieves in "This Lime-Tree Bower"
has no precise counterpart in the work of Turner and Constable. What
their paintings do show us, however, is a preoccupation with refuge—
with enclosed and often mysterious spaces. To study their work is to see

them each pursuing their own alternatives to the representation of mere prospects or "views."

Writing in 1824 of a spectacular view which he had just seen, Constable termed it "unfit" for depiction. "It is the business of a painter," he wrote, "not to contend with nature & put this scene (a valley filled with imagery 50 miles long) on a canvas of a few inches, but to make something out of nothing, in attempting which he must almost of necessity become poetical" (*JCC* 6: 172). By "nothing" Constable meant an object of no evident importance. "My limited and abstract art," he said elsewhere, "is to be found under every hedge, and in every lane, and therefore nobody thinks it worth picking up" (*JCC* 3: 59). Constable's art, then, stands at the opposite extreme from that of such nineteenth-century American landscapists as Henry Lewis, whose works include *Mammoth Panorama of the Mississippi River* (exhibited 1849), and Frederick Edwin Church, whose *Heart of the Andes* (1859) measured just over 66 by 119 feet (Novak 23, 26). Even Constable's large canvases, which were barely more than six-feet wide or tall at most, typically concentrate on distinctly "limited" scenes set within relatively dark enclosures. In *The Cornfield*, the panoramic view that Lambert offered in his *Hilly Landscape with a Cornfield* shrinks to a narrow vista of light. The two large groups of trees nearly touch in the center of the picture and cast most of the foreground in shadow. In the *Hay Wain*, the horses and cart move through a pool of light, but the river they cross flows from the powerful shadow under the bank at right to the equally powerful shadow under the looming trees at left, and it is into this shadow that the horses are headed and toward it that the man facing us points. The view across the river is confined to the right third of the picture, and even there it stops at the far side of the field, where a further row of trees and a sky full of clouds precludes anything like the sensation of infinite distance we so often get from the landscapes of Claude. Constable in fact used clouds as much as trees to enclose his pictures. In *Hadleigh Castle*, the view across the sea is blocked by a wall of them; in *Coast at Brighton, Stormy Day* (1828), the mass of heavy clouds appears as a low ceiling inexorably sinking to the sea.

What is the meaning of these enclosing forms? I have already noted that Paulson sees in Constable's pictures a structure of psychically significant blockage wherein a dunghill or sublime ruin in the foreground obstructs the view to the beautiful open meadow or sea in the distance, and thus symbolizes the frustration of Constable's love for Maria Bick-

nell. But this pattern of frustration blocking the prospect of ultimate happiness will only partly explain what Constable does with the traditional—
or more precisely Claudian—kind of blockage: wing-screens framing a
vista. The skies reaching up behind the blocking agents in Constable's
pictures do not lead to infinite serenity. The clouds with which he characteristically fills them either create a prospect of sublime and regenerative turbulence, as in *Hadleigh Castle*, or cast the viewer back into the
shadows from which the mind is only provisionally released. The *Hay
Wain*, for instance, subtly projects the structure of a bower. Though Constable deliberately widens the river to suggest the scale of a panoramic
view, the picture contains even as it expands. In the very center is exactly what Coleridge sees before him in "This Lime-Tree Bower": pale,
transparent foliage hanging beneath the blaze of an unseen sun. The fact
that Constable's trees loom almost as large and high as his clouds makes
these two elements partners in the creation of what is at once prospect
and refuge, a picture of exploded interiority. While Coleridge contrives
to rediscover the light of an oceanic prospect within the shadow of a
bower, Constable extends the structure of a bower into the space of a
prospect, making it symbolize the mind's capacity to contain the outer
world.

To move from the subtly internalized prospects of Constable to the
world of Turner is to enter a distinctly deeper realm of introspection.
Turner actually said in one of his lectures that painting ultimately derives not from rules or even from "Nature and her Effects" but from "the
imagination of the artist enthroned in his own recess, incomprehensible
as the cause [of] darkness" (TMS H, f. 41–42). His own imagination
characteristically projects itself as a glow of light, but as John Dixon
Hunt observes, we do well to recall what Burke said about extreme light:
it could resemble the sublimity of darkness in its capacity to obliterate
forms (Burke 80; Hunt, "Wondrous Deep" 140). Turner's work demonstrates this paradoxical resemblance. In *Trancept of Ewenny Priory*, an
early watercolor (1797), an arch of enveloping shadow stands beside an
arch of equally enveloping light. And Hunt notes that Turner frequently
created this effect with bridges, using them to frame mysterious sources
of light and compelling the spectator to "[fill] the void with his own definition" ("Wondrous Deep" 142).

Yet it is not so much in what lies behind as in what sometimes lies
beneath Turner's bridges that we discover something like a visual locus
of self-consciousness. In *The Devil's Bridge, Pass of St. Gothard*, a water-

color sketch done on the spot in 1802 (TSB LXXV, 34), the bridge is a delicate arc stretched over a dark, apparently bottomless gorge and flanked by steep cliffs rising through the top of the picture. Wilton notes that unlike William Pars, whose 1770 watercolor of the bridge has an "insistent horizontal stress" that helps provide a reassuring stability, Turner creates a mood of "dizzying instability" by fully exploiting the verticality of his subject (*TS* 116). He does so not only here but in an oil painting of ca. 1803 based on this sketch, in another on-the-spot sketch of the gorge as seen from the bridge (TSB LXXV, 33), and in two finished pictures based on this other sketch—one a watercolor of 1804 and the other an oil called *The Pass of St. Gothard* and painted ca. 1803–4 (plate 21). All of these pictures—especially those of the gorge as seen from the bridge—reveal Turner's fascination with the combination of seemingly infinite height and depth.

In romantic poetry, the combination of infinite height and depth typically helps to define moments of sublimity, which are experienced within the mind but may be articulated by reference to natural forms or spatial relations.[9] Kant defined the sublime as a consciousness of unattainability leading to transcendence; since the sublime cannot be grasped by the senses or represented in sensible form, the sublime is that, says Kant, "the mere capacity of thinking which evidences a faculty of mind transcending every standard of sense" (98, italics romanized; see also 119). This supersensible faculty of mind is Kant's "reason," but as Thomas Weiskel observes, the mind's discovery of its own supersensible powers can be and typically is expressed in terms of height or depth. "The sublime moment," says Weiskel, "establishes depth because the presentation of unattainability is phenomenologically a negation, a falling away from what might be seized, perceived, known. As an image, it is the abyss. When the intervention of the transcendent becomes specific, however, the image is converted into a symbol, and height takes over as the valorizing perspective" (24–25).

We can see this vertical movement most conspicuously at work in what might be called the poetry of altitude—a word significantly derived from the Latin *altitudo*, which means height *or* depth. In the poetry of altitude, descent signifies self-exploration and ascent signifies transcen-

9. On the internality of the sublime, see Kant 93: "For the beautiful in nature, we must seek a ground external to ourselves, but for the sublime one merely in ourselves and the attitude of mind that introduces sublimity into the representation of nature." See also 104.

dence. In Shelley's *Mont Blanc*, for instance, the poet describes himself as gazing down upon the dark, unfathomably deep Ravine of Arve before looking up at the white peak of the mountain "Far, far above, piercing the infinite sky" (line 60). In a sense, he prepares himself to look up by first looking down and "as in a trance sublime and strange" seeing his own mind imaged in the ravine, where the wandering wings of his thought alternatively float above its darkness and descend to the shadows passing by "In the still cave of the witch Poesy" (34–44). Similarly, in Wordsworth's description of what he saw from the summit of Snowdon, the sea of moonlit mist contains "a blue chasm; a fraction in the vapour, / A deep and gloomy breathing-place through which / Mounted the roar of waters."[10] The spectacle spread out before him is largely created by the light of the moon, which stands above him "at height / Immense" (*Prelude* A 13. 41–42), but it is in the gloomy chasm that Wordsworth first locates "the Soul, the Imagination of the whole" (65). Even in the final version of the passage, which drops this line, he interprets the entire spectacle as the emblem of a mind that "broods / Over the dark abyss, intent to hear / Its voices issuing forth to silent light" (14. 71–73). Like Shelley, Wordsworth echoes Milton's description of the creating God as a dove-like spirit "with mighty wings outspread" hovering over "the vast abyss" and making it pregnant (*Paradise Lost* 1. 17–22). But for Shelley and Wordsworth, the abyss now becomes the symbol of the creating self, the source of the voices which speak through poetry, or—in Shelley's Platonic image—of the shadows reflected in it.

What then of Turner's Alpine gorges? Can the simple representation of seemingly infinite height and depth signify a state of consciousness? Like the earlier question about Constable's enclosures, this one has no easy answer. Yet insofar as a painter can express a state of mind, can signify at once the profundity of the self and its aspirations to infinite height, Turner does so in the St. Gothard pictures—most especially in the pictures of the pass as seen from the bridge. What we find in these pictures is that the mountain track leading diagonally upwards from the lower left corner draws us not to the sight of a spreading prospect or infinite vista, as we might expect, but to a visual impasse: a cloud of mist backed by soaring mountains, with the merest glimpse of distant peaks

10. *Prelude* A 13. 56–58. Lindenberger notes that Wordsworth "was more centrally concerned with depths rather than heights, with the continually intensified inwardness suggested by the interaction of water, air, and rock in the deeper regions of the earth" (89). On this point see also Wlecke 25.

and sky at the top of the picture. Like Wordsworth in the Simplon Pass, the spectator becomes a halted traveller, balked in his forward progress through the picture, forced to look downwards and upwards rather than outwards and thus to confront the dimensions of his inward self. Turner's pictures of the St. Gothard Pass provide a visual counterpart to the language in which Wordsworth and Shelley define self-exploration. The oil version of ca. 1803–4 (plate 21) even seems to anticipate their allusions to *Paradise Lost*, a poem Turner greatly admired, since it depicts a group of birds hovering over the gorge with outstretched wings. But whether or not Turner was thinking of Milton here, he was clearly showing just how far a painter could represent in landscape the refuge of his own inner world. Implicitly at least, Turner follows the advice once offered by his German contemporary Caspar David Friedrich, who said that the artist "should not merely paint what he sees in front of him" but "what he sees within himself" (quoted in Eitner 55).

Friedrich's counsel could also be illustrated by his own *Wanderer uber dem Nebelmeer* (ca. 1818), in which a figure standing on a hump of rock and with his back to us gazes out on mountain peaks engulfed by a sea of mist. Here, as in Wordsworth's account of the misted hills he saw from the summit of Snowdon, we are invited to look not at the beholder but within him, to enter his consciousness, to see with his eye as he contemplates the kind of spectacle Wordsworth considered "the emblem of a mind / That feeds upon infinity" (*Prelude* 14. 70–71). As Michael Fried has noted in connection with Courbet, "the effect of the figure portrayed from the rear is . . . to remove all sense of confrontation between painting and beholder and thereby to facilitate the virtual merging of the latter into the former" (111). Yet this is only one of the strategies by which, says Fried, the painter could transform the conventional relation between painting and beholder—a relationship in which the painting is a kind of theatrical event performed *for* a spectator, designed precisely to be beheld. The other way of overcoming this "primordial convention," as Fried calls it, is "to reduce to an absolute minimum all sense of distance and indeed of separateness between representation and beholder, as a step toward absorbing the beholder into the painting in an almost corporeal way" (110–11). Fried uses the contrast between theatricality and absorption to explain how the essentially dramatic style of David and his followers was transformed by Courbet in mid-nineteenth-century France. But Fried's terms can also be used to explain how the English romantic poets and painters draw the beholder into their landscapes and thus seek to dissolve the opposition between the outer world and the inner one, between nature consciousness and self-consciousness, between the sublimity we sometimes impute to natural objects and the sublimity that Kant says is discoverable only in the mind.[11] It is this kind of internalization that I wish to explore now.

THEATRICALITY AND RECIPROCAL ABSORPTION

When we turn from history painting in France to landscape painting in England, the theatricality that Fried finds in the works of David and his followers has its counterpart in such pyrotechnically spectacular canvases as Joseph Wright's *View of Naples with Vesuvius Erupting*, one of several Vesuvian pictures that Wright did after his trip to Naples in 1774.[12] What is at once notable and typical about this kind of picture is that its theatrical effect is reinforced by the presence of spectators within the picture—in this case by a number of sailors and fishermen watching the distant smoke and flame from boats floating safely in the foregrounded bay. Sometimes the act of beholding or even of depicting could itself become the subject of a picture. In Richard Wilson's *View Near Tivoli* (1760s), a peasant in the left foreground points to a far-off plain while an artist in the middle distance paints the town on the hilltop at left. In Thomas Hearne's pen and wash drawing titled *Sir George Beaumont and Joseph Farington Painting a Waterfall* (1777–78?), the waterfall is hardly more important than the men depicting it, who are firmly established with their easels on a set of rocks in the left foreground, attended by a servant, and sheltered from the sun or the spray by no less than three parasols or umbrellas—it is not clear which. But perhaps the grandest treatment of spectatorship in the history of landscape painting is an American canvas done in the middle of the nineteenth century: Asher Durand's *Kindred Spirits* (1849), which shows Thomas Cole and William Cullen Bryant serenely contemplating a ravine in the Catskills from the safety of a high and solid ledge.

11. Kant 93. Fried uses "absorption" in two ways. On one hand it denotes the process by which the painter represents himself in the very act of painting, "reconstitute[s] pictorially his absorption in his live bodily being" (102). On the other hand it denotes the process by which the viewer is drawn into the picture. The second kind of absorption is what chiefly concerns me here, but to be drawn into a picture, I will argue, is also to be drawn into the state of mind that the picture represents.

12. Ross Watson 14–15. Turner did a watercolor of the same subject in 1817; see Wilton, *TAL* 137.

Not all of these works have the spectacular impact of Wright's volcano. But different as they are, they all share a mode of presentation that decisively separates and where necessary protects the viewer from what is viewed. Viewers placed within the picture look out on a scene that is presented as such to us, and they set us an example of how to look at it: with aesthetic detachment and secure self-possession. Where the scene is one of violence or upheaval, the need for protective separation is of course intensified, and the sense of theatrical display is correspondingly heightened. We can see this not only in Wright's picture but also in a better known work by Philip James de Loutherbourg: *An Avalanche in the Alps* (plate 22), exhibited 1803. De Loutherbourg's picture shows how readily an artist could theatricalize the sublime. Burke applies the term to whatever excites "delight" by appealing to our sense of self-preservation without actually threatening us: by giving us "an idea of pain and danger, without being actually in such circumstances." [13] Using "delight" to mean not "positive pleasure" but "the sensation which accompanies the removal of pain or danger" (36–37), Burke implicitly defines the experience of the sublime as a spectator sport, something violent or terrible to be enjoyably witnessed from a safe distance. This is exactly what de Loutherbourg's *Avalanche* offers us. As Hugh Honour notes, it was apparently designed to have the kind of effect that de Loutherbourg regularly created at his Eidophusikon, the miniature theater that he opened in 1781 for the purpose of showing spectacular painted scenes animated by colored lights (33–34).

What *Avalanche* represents is not a disaster but the transformation of a disaster into a theatrical event. At lower right, a small shelter is being shattered in the rush of snowy boulders, and one figure is being rather comically engulfed like Breughel's Icarus, while another scampers away, his mind presumably busy with thoughts of self-preservation. We can afford to be amused, however, because at lower left we have a safe and apparently solid ledge from which to witness this sensational spectacle. The ledge is part of a roughly diagonal fortress of rock which protects us from the churning avalanche, and on it are three figures: a man clasping his hands in supplication, a woman running away, and, furthest from

13. Burke 51. Burke's definition sounds most appropriate to the representation of terrifying spectacles in works of art, but it is broad enough to include also any real-life situation that makes us think of danger without actually threatening us. De Loutherbourg's *Avalanche* represents a traveller's response to precisely such a situation, which is real for him though merely depicted for us.

danger, another man stretching out his arms in astonishment, a traveller obviously thrilled by the show he has come to see. From the red blanket-roll on the back of this traveller to the rich puffs of pink in the clouds over the avalanche, the whole conception of the painting is essentially theatrical. There is pain and danger here, but it does not really threaten our spectator, who is at once entertained and glorified by what he sees. We are never more swollen with triumph, says Burke, "than when without danger we are conversant with terrible objects, the mind always claiming to itself some part of the dignity and importance of the things which it contemplates" (50–51). De Loutherbourg's spectator epitomizes this condition. Startled by a scene of cataclysmic devastation but essentially undisturbed by either sympathy for its victims or fear for himself, since he is out of danger, he stretches out his arms not in desperation but in triumph—as if the avalanche had become a symphony which he was suddenly, amazingly, and apotheistically appointed to conduct. If anything, the word *delight* understates the magnitude of his pleasure.

A fundamentally different picture of the same subject was painted by Turner, who knew de Loutherbourg's *Avalanche* but radically departs from its theatrical style in *The Fall of an Avalanche in the Grisons* (plate 23), exhibited 1810. Turner's picture precludes spectatorship by removing any vantage point from which the avalanche might be safely viewed.[14] While de Loutherbourg visually protects us with a diagonal of solid rock, Turner gives us a steep diagonal of falling ice; and while de Loutherbourg shows soft, blue-gray, rounded stones falling from clouds of pink into billows of cottony white, Turner shows jagged, angular chunks of harsh chalk white rushing down the middle of his picture. Gray-black streaks of wind and snow drive diagonally against them, and just below the center of the picture, the lines of force converge to make a wedge of churning devastation. There are no figures in this picture, nor any safe place on which they might stand. Where de Loutherbourg carefully separates solid rock from rushing boulders, Turner shows the rocky ground disintegrating at the base of his picture. What crushes the cottage is not falling ice or snow, but a massive thumb of rock and tree-sprouting earth

14. It thus differs not only from de Loutherbourg's *Avalanche* but also from Thomas Cole's *Snow Squall, Winter Landscape in the Catskills* (ca. 1825–26), of which Bryan Jay Wolf has written: "A foreground promontory or cliff thrusts itself forward at a diagonal to the picture plane. Its stark and dramatic placement, following the canons of the Burkean sublime, exposes the spectator to the terrors of the scene while protecting him in its dark and sheltered spots from the dangers he views" (184).

thrown up by the force of the avalanche. The only sign of a human presence here is the cottage itself, which is being devastated, and the only thing that softens the stark brutality of the scene is a touch of pink sky at upper left—an ironic allusion to the rosy theatricalism of de Loutherbourg. By thus attacking the whole conception of spectatorship and eliminating the distance that conventionally separates the viewer from the "sublime" spectacle, Turner makes us feel and experience the overwhelming destructiveness of what he represents.[15] He himself wrote for the exhibition catalogue lines that recall the description of a devastating avalanche in Thomson's "Winter" (lines 414–23):

> The downward sun a parting sadness gleams,
> Portentous lurid thro' the gathering storm;
> Thick drifting snow on snow,
> Till the vast weight bursts thro' the rocky barrier;
> Down at once, its pine clad forests,
> And towering glaciers fall, the work of ages
> Crashing through all! extinction follows,
> And the toil, the hope of man—o'erwhelms.
>
>   (Butlin and Joll 69)

But it overwhelms, of course, neither painter nor spectator. The paradox of a picture which perpetuates the very moment of overwhelming destruction is that it elicits the viewer's capacity to absorb and transcend that destruction, to possess it even as it threatens to possess him. Insofar as is possible in the pictorial representation of landscape, the elimination of a secure vantage point leads to a reciprocally absorptive merging of inner and outer worlds: a merging in which the viewer absorbs or internalizes the very spectacle that by its thrusting immediacy seems to absorb him. Turner thus invites us to connect if not identify *The Fall of*

15. Andrew Wilton finds this effect especially evident in Turner's seascapes, which become most absorptive, he says, around 1810—the year of *Avalanche*: "The progression from *Dutch Boats in a gale . . .* of 1801, to the *Shipwreck* of 1805, to the *Wreck of a Transport Ship* of about 1810 is one of gradually increasing involvement of the spectator in the scenes depicted. In the first a minor incident at sea is presented objectively as an external event; in the second a more serious incident is shown, the composition catching us up in a swirl of water and rocking vessels. The third is no longer an external event at all: the spectator is wholly absorbed into what is happening, actually in the water which reels and towers about him, a victim of the catastrophe that he witnesses" (*TS* 46). Wilton gets carried away here, for of course the spectator is not actually in the water. The relation between picture and viewer in a case like this is reciprocally absorptive.

an Avalanche with a kind of sublimity that is ultimately and essentially internalized.[16]

An apt example of this sublimity is Shelley's *Mont Blanc*, which describes the annihilative effect of an avalanche in words that strikingly recall Turner's picture:

> a flood of ruin
> Is there, that from the boundaries of the sky
> Rolls its perpetual stream; vast pines are strewing
> Its destined path, or in the mangled soil
> Branchless and shattered stand; the rocks, drawn down
> From yon remotest waste, have overthrown
> The limits of the dead and living world,
> Never to be reclaimed. The dwelling-place
> Of insects, beasts, and birds, becomes its spoil;
> Their food and their retreat for ever gone,
> So much of life and joy is lost. The race
> Of man, flies far in dread; his work and dwelling
> Vanish, like smoke before the tempest's stream,
> And their place is not known.
>
> (Lines 107–20)

Like Turner's picture, Shelley's poem conveys a vision of absolute annihilation. But this whole process of relentless destruction is, in the words of Shelley's opening lines, simply part of the "everlasting universe of things" that "flows through the mind," and the mind can encompass not only violent destruction but also the invisible "Power" that stands behind it.[17] Paradoxically, the peak that embodies this power is "still, snowy, and serene" (61). Violence flows from the stillness of an unmoved mover and ultimately returns to serenity as the "tempest's stream" undergoes a tranquillizing sea change: "Rolls its loud waters to the ocean-waves, / Breathes its swift vapours to the circling air" (125–26). At once

16. Martin Meisel sees Turner's apocalyptic works—including such pictures as *Fall of an Avalanche*—as unquestionable manifestations of the internal sublime. "In Turner of the apocalyptic imagination," he says, "one sees the fullest transformation in painting of the sublime into a subjective terrain, the sublime as the affective dissolution of material forms in light" ("The Material Sublime," in Kroeber and Walling 214). But this description applies less to a picture such as *Avalanche*—which has a kind of brutal materiality—than it does to the visionary canvases of Turner's last decade.

17. For a full discussion of this point, see Wasserman 222–38.

beautiful and terrifying, sublime beyond the categories of Burke, Mont Blanc here is profoundly internalized. While the mind through which the universe flows is universal and transcendent, this universal mind is represented by the very ravine in which—as I have already noted—Shelley sees his own mind.[18] Furthermore, the concluding lines of the poem implicitly affirm the dependence of all natural objects on the human imagination. "And what were thou," the poet asks the mountain,

> and earth, and stars, and sea,
> If to the human mind's imaginings
> Silence and solitude were vacancy?
> (142–44)

The human mind gives a meaning to silence and solitude, and thus demonstrates its capacity to understand the Power that governs the universe. In a sense, Shelley felt that he possessed Mont Blanc. Writing to Thomas Love Peacock about his first impressions of the mountain and the scenery around it, he said: "All was as much our own as if we had been the creators of such impressions in the minds of others, as now occupied our own" (*Letters* 1: 497).

One of the most searching analyses of the process by which the mind thus appropriates the external power of a sublime spectacle can be found in an uncompleted essay written by Wordsworth in 1811 or later.[19] This essay shows the probable influence of Burke and the possible influence of Kant. Besides following Burke in saying that we must be free of "personal fear" to experience the sublime, Wordsworth resembles Kant in his emphasis on the internality of the sublime as well as on the consciousness of unattainability which it entails.[20] But whether or not Wordsworth

18. Wasserman says that Shelley distinguishes between the individual mind and the "One Mind, which constitutes total Existence and of which each individual mind is a portion" (223). But the distinction is not rigorously maintained; it tends to blur as the outer and inner worlds merge.

19. It remained in manuscript until 1974, when it was published in *PrW* 2: 349–60, under the editor's title, "The Sublime and the Beautiful." The editors assign this fragmentary essay to the years 1811–12; in my review of their edition, I have offered reasons for assigning it to 1825 or later (Heffernan, Review 558–60).

20. Wordsworth, *PrW* 2: 354, 357, 456–67. A case for Wordsworth's dependence on Burke's *Enquiry*—which Wordsworth nowhere cites—has been made by W. J. B. Owen (67–68). Wordsworth is closest to Kant in saying that "Power awakens the sublime . . . when it rouses us to a sympathetic energy & calls upon the mind to grasp at something towards which it can make approaches but which it is incapable of attaining" (*PrW* 2: 354). Kant says that the sublime is "an object (of nature) the representation of which determines the mind to regard the unattainability of nature ('die Unerreichbarkeit der

knew Kant's theory of the sublime, of which he may have heard from Coleridge, he moves well beyond Burke in his analysis of the extraordinarily complex relation between internal and external power.

The concept of power is essential to Burke's definition of the sublime. "I know of nothing sublime," he wrote, "which is not some modification of power" (64). But Burke was far more concerned with the effect of power *on* the mind than with any corresponding power awakened *in* the mind. Wordsworth strives to encompass both. The sublime involves, he says,

impressions of power, to a sympathy with & a participation of which the mind must be elevated—or to a dread and awe of which, as existing out of itself, it must be subdued. (*PrW* 2: 351–52)

After thus implying that sublimity will be either elevating or humiliating, Wordsworth complicates his formula. "Power awakens the sublime," he says,

either when it rouses us to a sympathetic energy & calls upon the mind to grasp at something towards which it can make approaches but which it is incapable of attaining—yet so that it participates force which is acting upon it; or, 2dly, by producing a humiliation or prostration of the mind before some external agency which it presumes not to make an effort to participate, but is absorbed in the contemplation of the might in the external power, &, as far as it has any consciousness of itself, its grandeur subsists in the naked fact of being conscious of external Power at once awful & immeasurable. (*PrW* 2: 354)

The either/or formula now becomes alternate versions of a both/and. On the one hand, we experience the sublime when the power of a natural object moves the mind to approach what it cannot attain, to "participate" in a force that transcends it; on the other hand, we experience the sublime when the mind is humiliated by the consciousness of external power yet also filled with grandeur—"its grandeur"—as a result of that very consciousness. In either case, external power elicits internal power. The grandeur which the mind experiences in itself paradoxically derives from its consciousness of being acted on by a force outside itself—"external Power at once awful & immeasurable." Whether we rise toward the unattainable or sink before some external agency, "absorbed" in contemplation of its immeasurable might, we feel power within as well as without; the way up and the way down become one.

Nature') as a presentation of [reason's] ideas." (Here I quote the translation given by Weiskel [22] rather than by Meredith [Kant 119].)

Wordsworth's theory of the sublime thus implies a vertical structure—something he commonly uses, as we have already seen, to signify self-exploration. One of the most conspicuously sublime passages in *The Prelude* is in fact a study in the verticality of a landscape which at once absorbs the poet and elicits his power to absorb it. I refer to Wordsworth's description of what he saw and heard during the journey that he and his friend Robert Jones took through the narrow, gloomy Gondo Gorge just after they had unknowingly crossed the Alps:

> The immeasurable height
> Of woods decaying, never to be decay'd,
> The stationary blasts of water-falls,
> And every where along the hollow rent
> Winds thwarting winds, bewilder'd and forlorn,
> The torrents shooting from the clear blue sky,
> The rocks that mutter'd close upon our ears,
> Black drizzling crags that spake by the way-side
> As if a voice were in them, the sick sight
> And giddy prospect of the raving stream,
> The unfetter'd clouds, and region of the Heavens,
> Tumult and peace, the darkness and the light
> Were all like workings of one mind, the features
> Of the same face, blossoms upon one tree,
> Characters of the great Apocalypse,
> The types and symbols of Eternity,
> Of first and last, and midst, and without end.
>
> (*Prelude* A 6. 556–72)

Coming as it does immediately after the interruptive passage in which Wordsworth says that his imagination "rose from the mind's abyss / Like an unfathered vapour" and that the soul's innate beatitude is "like the flood of Nile / Poured from his fount of Abyssinian clouds" (lines 594–95, 614–15), this description of the gorge is clearly charged with psychically symbolic import. As Hartman suggests, Wordsworth here seems to actualize some of the images which he has just used figuratively to describe his own mind (*Wordsworth's Poetry* 45). These actualized images intensify the sense of verticality suggested by the earlier passage and thus exemplify the complex relation between inner and outer world that Wordsworth postulates in his theory of the sublime. The poet-traveller unquestionably confronts "external Power at once awful and immeasurable"—a power revealed in the "immeasurable height" and immeasurable durability of the woods ("never to be decayed"), in the paradoxical spectacle of "stationary blasts" and "torrents shooting from the clear blue sky," in the vertiginous prospect of the raving stream, and in the reversion to something like primordial chaos with "winds thwarting winds, bewilder'd and forlorn"[21] From immeasurably far above him to below him and even beside him at his ears, Wordsworth is enveloped by this landscape. But he is not overpowered by it. Besides projecting his own feelings and powers into its elements, which are called "bewildered," "giddy," and capable of something like speech, he also constructs from these warring and turbulent elements a single sentence with a decisively internalizing predicate: "were all like workings of one mind."

It is just here that the conflicting elements of the gorge may seem not so much internalized as overdetermined by what Weiskel calls an "excess of the signified" (26), a phrase he uses to distinguish between the positive and negative sublime. In the negative or Kantian sublime, says Weiskel, the mind is overwhelmed by "an excess on the plane of the signifier," by consciousness *that* a particular object means, yet defies the mind's ability to understand *what* it means; the mind's inability to grasp the object fully then becomes "a symbol of the mind's relation to a transcendent order" (23). In the positive sublime, the flow of time is apocalyptically abrogated, and "the word dissolves into the Word" (26–27). Weiskel believes that this is what happens in the passage just quoted, which explicitly designates the elements of the gorge as "types and symbols of Eternity" and which ends, as he notes, with an allusion to the morning hymn that Adam and Eve sing to God in *Paradise Lost*: "Him first, him last, him midst, and without end" (5. 165).

But Weiskel's account of the overdetermination in this passage is itself overdetermined. In Wordsworth's revision of Milton's hymn, the "Him" is significantly expunged, and Wordsworth's "embrace of traditional ontology," as Weiskel calls it (195), fails to include the Godhead on whom that ontology is based. Even the impersonal eternity signified by the gorge is a state perpetually verging on the very chaos to which the Miltonic eternity is so decidedly opposed. To say that the conflicting elements of the gorge were "all like workings of one mind" is not to impose

21. Compare Milton's description of the "furious winds" raging in the abyss before God begins to create the universe (*Paradise Lost* 7. 210–15).

an ultimately determinate signification on those elements, but rather to expose the indeterminacy of the "one mind" which they putatively signify. In effect, Wordsworth translates indeterminacy from the plane of the signifier to the plane of the signified. As his own essay on the sublime plainly implies, the price he must pay for what he calls "participation" in the power of landscape is the surrender of determinate categories. Only after his mind has given up its claims to intellectual sovereignty over nature can he lay claim to a transcendent sovereignty—by being

> first
> In capability of feeling what
> [Is] to be felt.
>   (*Prelude* A 8. 634–36)

It is nonetheless true, as Weiskel suggests, that Wordsworth detemporalizes experience in this passage and very nearly depersonalizes it as well, with but a single muted reference to himself in "our ears." Far more personal is the way he internalizes landscape in book 1 of *The Prelude*, where he tells us what he saw one evening while rowing a stolen boat across a lake. Indeed, if his lines on the Gondo Gorge seem impersonal and typologically overdetermined, his description of an apparently rising cliff is so charged with hints of personal fear that it precludes any suggestion of sublime "delight." [22] What makes the sublimity of this episode distinctively Wordsworthian is the extent to which the boy's own fear generates the power that seems to rise up over him. Facing sternwards in his boat and fixing his eyes on the summit of a ridge to guide him, he can at first see nothing but stars above the ridge. But as he steadily rows away from shore, he begins to see something else:

> from behind that craggy steep till then
> The horizon's bound, a huge peak, black and huge,
> As if with voluntary power instinct
> Uprear'd its head. I struck and struck again,
> And growing still in stature the grim shape
> Towered up between me and the stars, and still,

22. Weiskel reads this episode as an instance of the negative or Kantian sublime: the boy's perceptional imagination struggles to grasp something that it cannot comprehend, and its very failure to do so gives it "extension and . . . power," access to a supersensible realm of "unknown modes of being" (100–102). But Kant's formula does not adequately explain the relation between fear and power in this passage.

> For so it seemed, with purpose of its own
> And measured motion like a living thing,
> Strode after me.
>
> (1. 377–85)

Rowing steadily away from the cliff ("I struck and struck again"), the boy sees more and more of the peak behind it, rising with a "measured motion" that precisely follows the cadence of his rowing. Because his gradually increasing distance from shore lets him gradually see more of the peak, his attempt to escape it only makes it seem higher and higher. Thus fear elevates the peak as well as animating it. All unknown to the boy, the power that makes the peak seem to tower up over him comes from the boy himself, whose mind—in the words of Wordsworth's essay on the sublime—totally "participates [in the] force which is acting upon it."

Different as this passage is from the one on Wordsworth's journey through the Gondo Gorge, both of them share a perspective at once vertical and absorptive. Looking up to something like infinity—to the immeasurable height of woods or to the uncontrollably rising peak—the viewer is enveloped by what he sees, powerless to detach himself from it, and thus compelled somehow to internalize it. In the Gondo passage, Wordsworth says that the things he saw and heard "were all like workings of one mind"; in the stolen boat passage, he says that after the episode his "brain / Worked with a dim and undetermined sense / Of unknown modes of being" (1. 392–94). In both cases the perspective is such as to force the outer world down upon and, so to speak, into the viewer, who thus takes possession of the very thing that threatens to possess him.

Strikingly enough, this vertically enveloping perspective is precisely what we find in a picture greatly admired by both Turner and Constable: Titian's *The Martyrdom of St. Peter* (plate 24).[23] In this picture of a Dominican monk being attacked by an assassin while his companion flees in terror, a group of three trees rises majestically over the three figures and St. Peter himself lies under the tree in the center with his body facing us, his right elbow on the ground, his head looking up, and his raised left hand pointing up to the angelically winged *putti* directly above him. This

23. On the history of this picture and Turner's first-hand knowledge of it, see above, p. 81. Constable never saw the picture itself, but he owned an engraving of it as well as a copy presumably made by John Partridge, the portrait painter (*JC: FDC* 25, 218).

powerful stress on verticality fascinated Turner and Constable alike. In the coruscating light and "eruptive" composition of the picture Turner saw "a struggling in the ascent from Earth towards Heaven" (Lindsay 163). Constable noted that Titian achieved this ascensional effect only after making preliminary sketches with the head of St. Peter facing down or toward his assassin. "The composition," says Constable, "was then heightened, the vision of angels introduced, and the head of the saint again altered, so as to look up to the glory that now beamed down upon him" (Leslie 305). Everything in the picture works to reinforce and intensify the upward-looking aspirations of its central figure, who yearns for heaven even as he is driven to earth. "Amplitude, quantity and space," says Turner, "appear in this picture given by the means of Trees opposed to a blue sky and deep sunk horizon not more than one-sixth the height of the picture, across which rush the knotted stems of trees with dark brown and leafy foliage, stretching far their leafy honours" (Ziff, "Backgrounds" 135). The treetops actually reach beyond the top of the picture, so that their height seems as immeasurable as that of the Alpine woods described by Wordsworth. Furthermore, since the figures under the trees preempt the entire foreground, there is virtually no place on which a spectator could stand to look at the scene without looking up. On the contrary, Peter and the figure at left, who is also looking upward but angled forward in what Turner calls "unshackled obliquity," are both made to look as if thrusting their way out of the picture—"impelled forward," says Turner, upon the spectator (Lindsay 163; Ziff, "Backgrounds" 140). At the same time, because the picture offers no separate vantage point, the spectator is absorbed by the upward-looking figure of Peter and made to see the angels and the infinitely soaring treetops with his eyes. Titian thus draws us and the whole of his landscape into the mind of the martyr at the moment of his death.

I have dwelt at some length on this picture by Titian because the comments it provoked from both Turner and Constable may help us to understand just how far they themselves used the outer world to express the inner one, or more precisely how they used verticality and preempted foregrounds to absorb the spectator, to dissolve the opposition between the viewer and the viewed. Curiously enough, there is virtually no sign of these effects in the one painting by Turner which was demonstrably influenced by Titian's picture: *Venus and Adonis*, painted ca. 1803–5.[24]

24. Turner's *Holy Family* was originally based on the composition of Titian's picture (Butlin and Joll 32), but the present version is not. In *Venus and Adonis* Turner borrows

But we do find them in an extraordinary drawing made by Constable in 1820—*Fir Trees at Hampstead* (plate 25). Though nothing in this drawing readily recalls Titian's picture, though there are no angelic *putti* overhead and no figures of any kind on the ground, which is occupied entirely by trees, there is nonetheless a remarkable similarity between the shape of the tall tree rising through the center of Constable's picture and the central line of Titian's compositional structure.

First of all, the angle at which the straight base of Constable's tree slants to the right duplicates the angle of the straight line running from Peter's right elbow, which is on the ground, to his upraised left wrist. In effect, Peter's strictly aligned arms supplant the base of the tree which rises from directly behind them, and Constable preserves the line of Peter's arms in the base of his own tree while characteristically using the tree to displace the historical figure of Peter himself. Secondly, the undulating line of Constable's tree essentially repeats the contraposto structure that Titian builds into the middle of his picture. In Titian's picture, the tree that rises from behind the rightward-slanting line of Peter's arms leans to the left, in the direction of his pointing finger, and then divides into branches bending left and right, with the slant of the right branch reinforced by the rightward lean of the angels hovering just above it. Correspondingly, Constable's tree leans right, slants left at midpoint, then sends out branches to left and right, with the slant of the right branch reinforced by the rightward lean of the branch above it—the one that rises just through the top of the picture.

I cannot say for certain that Constable set out to re-create Titian's picture in naturalistic terms, to recall its central tree and the central line of its composition even as he utterly displaced its historical subject matter. But we can be virtually sure that by the time he drew *Fir Trees* he had acquired a profound admiration of *The Martyrdom of St. Peter*, which in his lectures of the 1830s he treated as a "central epoch" in the history of landscape painting, "the foundation of all the styles of landscape in

from Titian the trees rising up over the central figures and the *putti* hovering overhead, but the figures are definitely—almost theatrically—recessed from the foreground, and they are looking not upwards but at each other—in loving farewell. The thrust of the picture is lateral rather than vertical. The horizontal position of Venus on her couch is reinforced by the figure of the *putto* crawling on the ground just beneath her and by the nearly horizontal left forearm of the standing Adonis, which in turn leads the eye of the spectator leftward—to the dogs straining at their leashes for the hunt in which Adonis will meet his death. I do not know why Turner borrowed elements of a decisively vertical picture to represent a subject that in fact required this fundamentally lateral emphasis.

every school of Europe in the [seventeenth] century."[25] Given the similarities I have noted, it is at least possible that Titian's picture also
served as the foundation of Constable's.

Whether or not it did, Constable's picture perfectly illustrates the absorptive effect of a compositional structure that requires the viewer to
look sharply upward. With such a structure Constable abandons the relatively high viewpoint that eighteenth-century English landscape painting
had inherited from Claude.[26] Claude's trees sometimes reach to and even
beyond the tops of his pictures, but they always serve as side screens
framing a prospect that stretches out to infinity, and which is thus presented to the viewer as a distant scene. Constable's trees work altogether
differently. By rising from the very bottom of the picture, by preempting
its foreground, and by dominating its center, the tallest tree obstructs the
view into the group of trees behind it and compels us to look up.

The upward thrust of this tree is accentuated by the appearance of
resistance overcome. Surging up through the apex of a triangle suggested
by the two lower trees leaning into it from either side, rising from pyra-
midal strength below to a line of sinuous beauty above, the tall tree towers over us like the rising cliff that towered over Wordsworth in his stolen
boat. By forcing us to look up, it makes us reckon with ourselves as look-
ers as well as with what we are looking at. In this fusion of self and other,
of nature-consciousness and self-consciousness, Constable represents
far more than a natural object. *Fir Trees* was the drawing, I believe, that
excited the admiration of no less a figure than Blake, who thought natural objects per se inimical to the imagination but who, while looking
through one of Constable's sketchbooks, "said of a beautiful drawing of
an avenue of fir trees on Hampstead Heath, 'Why, this is not drawing,
but *inspiration*.'"[27]

25. Leslie 294. Though Constable seems to have made no recorded reference to *The
Martyrdom of St. Peter* before the 1830s, we can be reasonably sure that he learned of
this celebrated work during his Royal Academy student years, which began in 1799 or
1800 (see Leslie 8). In 1801 he would have heard Fuseli lecture on Titian's mastery of
landscape in terms that anticipate his own later tribute. "Landscape," said Fuseli,
"whether it be considered as the transcript of a spot, or the rich combination of congenial
objects, or as the scene of a phenomenon, dates its origin from [Titian]" (2: 64–65).
26. John Barrell notes that "a fairly high viewpoint" is one of several compositional
features in the landscapes of Claude, and Claude's arrangement, he says, became "a
standard one" in eighteenth-century landscape painting (*Idea of Landscape* 7–11). Barbara Novak says that an upward-looking point of view is rare in the painting of any period
(180).
27. The report comes from Leslie (280). Graham Reynolds says that *Fir Trees* is "pos-

What I have chiefly tried to explore in this chapter are the ways in which poets and painters alike used the outer world to represent the inner one. Though the landscapes of Turner and Constable furnish no simple equivalent for the self-revelation to be found in romantic poetry, we have seen in the shadowy enclosures of Constable as well as in the mysterious recesses and Alpine abysses of Turner the imagery of refuge: the imagery with which the romantic poets characteristically signify self-exploration. We have also seen in their work the internalizing effect of reciprocal absorption. By dissolving the barriers that conventionally separate the viewer from the viewed, by eliminating any stable vantage point from which a distant or theatricalized scene may be detachedly witnessed, a picture such as *Fall of an Avalanche* absorbs the viewer even as it provokes him to absorb and possess it, to become conscious of his own participation in the sublimity which he experiences. Likewise, by lowering the viewpoint from its conventionally elevated position and thus compelling the viewer to look up, a picture such as *Fir Trees* creates the kind of vertically enveloping effect that we find in Wordsworth's description of the Gondo Gorge and of the rising peak. The viewer is made to look simultaneously upward and inward, and the immeasurable height of the outer world thus becomes the immeasurable depth of his own all-absorptive self-consciousness.

To define romantic poetry and painting in these terms, however, is to exacerbate rather than resolve the problem of solipsism—the problem that first confronted Wordsworth in his childhood, when he was "often unable to think of external things as having external existence, and . . . communed with all that [he] saw as something not apart from, but inherent in, [his] own immaterial nature" (*PW* 4: 463). The poet or painter who perceives or represents the outer world as a projection of his own inner one inevitably risks plunging into the Wordsworthian "abyss of idealism" (*PW* 4: 463), and the risk must be honestly recognized. If solipsistic tendencies seem far from Constable, with his hard-won grasp of natural texture and atmospheric vitality, we can nonetheless see them in Wordsworth's moments of "holy calm," in Coleridge's moments of blissful reverie, and especially in the form-dissolving world of Turner, which— for all of Ruskin's insistence on Turner's dedication to the facts of na-

---

sibly" the drawing Blake spoke of (*CCC* 133), but I do not know what other drawing by Constable would fit Leslie's description. On Blake's attitude toward nature per se, see *PPB* 655: "Natural Objects always did & now do Weaken deaden & obliterate Imagination in Me."

CHAPTER 4

THE LANGUAGE OF
TRANSFORMATION

AMONG THE MANY seeming inconsistencies that permeate and complicate the preface to *Lyrical Ballads* is one involving a conspicuously pictorial metaphor for the process of imaginative transformation: "colouring." Wordsworth uses the word in the 1802 version of the preface, where he gives us a fuller statement of his poetic aims than he offers in the original version of 1800. In the 1800 version he says that his chief object was "to make the incidents of common life interesting by tracing in them . . . the primary laws of our nature: chiefly as far as regards the manner in which we associate ideas in a state of excitement" (*PrW* 1: 122, 124). In the 1802 preface, he says that he has aimed in his poems "to choose incidents and situations from common life, and to relate or describe them, throughout, as far as was possible in a selection of language really used by men, and, at the same time, to throw over them a certain colouring of imagination, whereby ordinary things should be presented to the mind in an unusual aspect" (*PrW* 1: 123). Two things about this revised formulation give pause. One is that some years after Wordsworth is supposed to have shaken off his allegiance to picturesque habits of observation and description, he is using the very word with which Gilpin defined "picturesque description" in a book Wordsworth himself owned (Heffernan, *WTP* 21–22). The other is that later on in the 1802 preface Wordsworth uses "coloured" in a distinctly pejorative sense. "The dramatic parts of [poetic] composition are defective," he says, "in proportion as they deviate from the real language of nature, and are coloured by a diction of the Poet's own, either peculiar to him as an individual Poet or belonging simply to Poets in general" (*PrW* 1: 142). Clearly the word "coloured" here means adulterated or falsified rather than heightened, intensified, or imaginatively transformed, which is presumably what happens to ordinary things when they are touched by "a certain colouring of imagination."

The two quite different senses in which Wordsworth uses "colouring" and "coloured" indicate that he felt a certain ambivalence not only toward pictorial metaphor but toward the whole process of creative transformation in poetry. And Wordsworth's ambivalence points in turn to a larger ambivalence, or at least a larger problem. As applied to poetry, "colouring" is a metaphor for a transformation that may falsify or enhance natural objects; in painting, color is part of what Augustan and romantic commentators alike called the "language" of art.[1] This language too could falsify or enhance. On the one hand, neoclassic theorists and their romantic descendants—of which Blake is the most conspicuous example—often treated color as ornamental, sensuous, and even treacherous, at best inferior to and at worst subversive of that intellectual order which could only be insured by a well-drawn line.[2] On the other hand, Turner and Constable both criticized the French for their preoccupation with line and their corresponding failure to recognize the value of shade and tone. About 1809, when he was preparing his Royal Academy lectures, Turner noted that the French look "with cool indifference at all the matchless power of Titian's glowing tones because precision of detail is their sole idol" (Ziff, "Backgrounds" 128), and at about the same time, he wrote even more caustically of

The French school, where drawing stands first, second, and third,
Without the aid of shade or tone
But indivisible alone
Seems every figure cut from stone.

(Turner, Sunset Ship 125)

1. Jonathan Richardson in 1725 compared finishing, color, and chiaroscuro in painting to "language, rhime, and numbers" in poetry (vii). In 1771 Joshua Reynolds observed: "The powers exerted in the mechanical part of the Art have been called *the language of Painters*" (*D* 64). Constable often referred to "the language of art"; see for instance *JCD* 46 and Leslie 97. In our own time, E. H. Gombrich has said "that the phrase 'the language of art' is more than a loose metaphor" (*AI* 87).

2. See Eaves 12–22. Eaves makes an important distinction between Blake's linearism and the linearism he inherited. For neoclassicists, says Eaves, "drawing is primary in art because it is best suited to the imitation of Lockean primary qualities in nature perceived by the impersonal human intellect. In Blake's view line is primary for a quite different reason: it is the direct expression of imagination" (175). For a sample of the neoclassical distrust of color, see Pope's *Essay on Criticism* (1711), where judgment and good sense threatened by false learning are like "*lines* . . . drawn right" but disgraced by "ill *Colouring*," and where the impermanence of language is compared to the fading of "*treach'rous Colours*" (1. 19–25, 484–93). It is nonetheless hazardous to claim that the Augustans were generally less sensitive to color than their romantic successors. While Fuseli in the early nineteenth century rails against the "debaucheries of colour" and de-

1. J.M.W. Turner,
Buttermere Lake
(1798).
Tate Gallery, London

2. William Kent–
N. Tardieu, *Spring*
(1730).
*By permission of the
Houghton Library,
Harvard University.*

3. Claude Lorrain,
*Landscape: Hagar and
the Angel* (1646).
National Gallery, London.
Reprinted by permission.

4. John Constable,
Dedham Vale (1802).
Victoria and Albert Museum, London.

5. John Constable, *Dedham Vale* (1828).

National Gallery of Scotland, Edinburgh.

6. John Constable, *The Hay Wain* (1821).
National Gallery, London. Reprinted by permission.

7. John Constable, *Full-scale Study for "The Leaping Horse"* (1824–25).
Victoria and Albert Museum, London.

8. Jacques-Louis David, *Napoleon Crossing the Alps* (1799).

Musée Nationale du Chateau de Malmaison.

9. John Constable, *Salisbury Cathedral from the Meadows* (1831).
By permission of Lord Ashton of Hyde.

10. David Lucas (after John Constable), *Old Sarum: First Plate, 1830*
(from *English Landscape Scenery*, London, 1830).
Yale Center for British Art, New Haven. Paul Mellon Collection.

11. John Constable, *Landscape Sketch: Hadleigh Castle* (?1828–29).

Tate Gallery, London. Reprinted by permission.

12. John Constable, *The Cenotaph
at Coleorton* (1823).
Victoria and Albert Museum, London.

13. John Constable, *The
Cenotaph at Coleorton*
(1836).
National Gallery, London.
Reprinted by permission.

14. J.M.W. Turner, *The Fifth Plague of Egypt* (1800).
Indianapolis Museum of Art, Gift in memory of Evan F. Lilly.

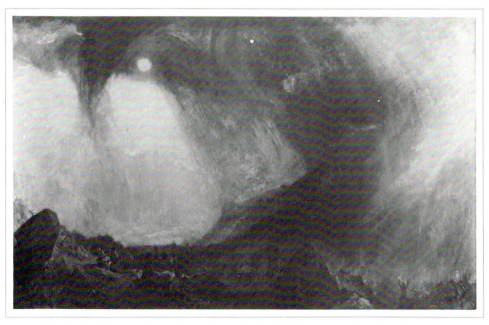

15. J.M.W. Turner, *Snow Storm: Hannibal and his Army Crossing the Alps* (1812).
Tate Gallery, London.

16. J.M.W. Turner, *Dido Building Carthage* (1815).
National Gallery, London. Reprinted by permission.

17. J.M.W. Turner, *Ulysses Deriding Polyphemus* (1829).
National Gallery, London. Reprinted by permission.

18. J.M.W. Turner, *Rain, Steam, and Speed—The Great Western Railway* (1844).
National Gallery, London. Reprinted by permission.

19. J.M.W. Turner, *Old London Bridge* (ca. 1796–97), TSB XXXIII-U.
British Museum, London. Reprinted by permission of the Trustees.

20. John Constable, *The Cornfield* (1826).

National Gallery, London. Reprinted by permission.

21. J.M.W. Turner, *The Pass of St. Gothard* (ca. 1803–4).
Reprinted by courtesy of Birmingham Museum and Art Gallery.

22. Philip de Loutherbourg, *An Avalanche in the Alps* (ex. 1804).
Tate Gallery, London.

23. J.M.W. Turner, *The Fall of an Avalanche in the Grisons* (1810).
Tate Gallery, London.

24. Martino Rota after Titian,
The Martyrdom of St. Peter
(1526–30).
*British Museum, London. Reprinted by
permission of the Trustees.*

25. John Constable, *Fir Trees
at Hampstead* (1820).
Victoria and Albert Museum, London.

26. Rembrandt, *The Mill* (1650).
National Gallery of Art, Washington. Widener Collection 1942.

27. J.M.W. Turner, *Norham Castle, Sunrise* (ca. 1835–40).
Tate Gallery, London.

28. J.M.W. Turner, *Mortlake Terrace: Early Summer Morning* (1826).
Copyright the Frick Collection, New York.

29. J.M.W. Turner, *Mortlake Terrace . . . Summer's Evening* (ex. 1827).
National Gallery of Art, Washington. Andrew W. Mellon Collection 1937.

30. John Constable, *A Cottage and Road at East Bergholt* (1817?).
Victoria and Albert Museum, London.

31. John Constable, *Study of Cirrus Clouds* (ca. 1822).
Victoria and Albert Museum, London.

32. J.M.W. Turner, *Sky Study* (1817). TSB CLVIII, f. 24.

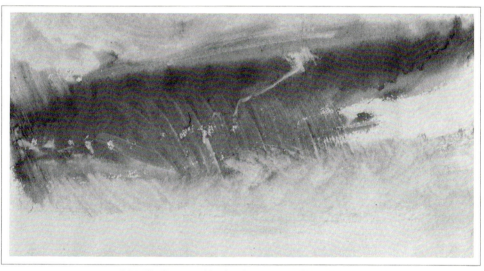

33. J.M.W. Turner, *Sky Study* (1817). TSB CLVIII, f. 32.

34. J.M.W. Turner, *Yacht Approaching the Coast* (ca. 1840–45).
Tate Gallery, London.

35. J.M.W. Turner, *Slavers Throwing Overboard the Dead and Dying—*
Typhoon Coming On (1840).
Courtesy, Museum of Fine Arts, Boston. Purchased, Henry Lillie Pierce Fund.

36. J.M.W. Turner, *Calais Pier* (1803).

National Gallery, London. Reprinted by permission.

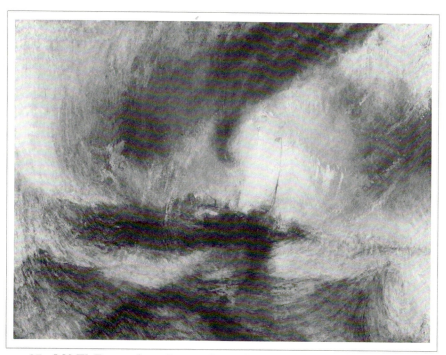

37. J.M.W. Turner, *Snow Storm—Steam-boat off a Harbour's Mouth* (1842).

Tate Gallery, London.

38. J.M.W. Turner, *Keelmen Heaving Coals by Moonlight* (ca. 1835).
National Gallery of Art, Washington. Widener Collection 1942.

39. J.M.W. Turner, *The Fighting 'Temeraire'* (1839).
National Gallery, London. Reprinted by permission.

40. J.M.W. Turner, *Willows beside a Stream* (ca. 1807).
Tate Gallery, London.

41. J.M.W. Turner, *The Dogana, San Giorgio, Citella,
from the Steps of the Europa* (1842).
Tate Gallery, London.

42. John Constable, *Water-meadows near Salisbury* (1829).
Victoria and Albert Museum, London.

43. J.M.W. Turner, *Burning of the Houses of Parliament* (1834).
Cleveland Museum of Art, Bequest of John L. Severance. Reprinted by permission.

Constable likewise found French painting petrified by linearity; in his own lectures he spoke of it as populated with "stern and heartless petrifactions of men and women—with trees, rocks, tables, and chairs, all equally bound to the ground by a relentless outline, and destitute of chiaroscuro, the soul and medium of art" (*JCD* 60).

Constable and Turner thus redefine the relation between line and tone. For neoclassical theorists, as Eaves says, line alone could represent the rational and scientific truth that lay beneath appearances (15). But Turner and Constable demanded a new respect for color and chiaroscuro precisely because they believed in the truth of appearances, in the value of representing things—as Wordsworth said—"not as they *are*, but as they *appear*" (*PrW* 3: 63). For the romantic poets and painters, color also symbolized the freedom of the creative process, the spontaneous life of an imagination liberated from the constraints of line and the analytical divisiveness that would separate light into seven distinct colors. *Buttermere* (plate 1) is Turner's tribute to the truth of appearance overlaying the rationally separable hues of the Newtonian spectrum, but it is also a declaration of imaginative independence, a demonstration of what Coleridge would say some twenty years after *Buttermere* was painted. Lines, says Coleridge (in his 1818 "Fragment of an Essay on Beauty"), belong "to the shapely (*forma, formalis, formosus*), and in this, to the law, and the reason; and [colours belong] to the lively, the free, the spontaneous, and the self-justifying" (*BL* 2: 251).

Can color symbolize creative freedom and yet also insure—or help to insure—that a work of art is made faithful to the truth of appearances? The fact that Wordsworth can use "colouring" to signify falsification as well as creative transformation clearly indicates that the relation between coloring and truth is highly problematic. And the problem persists when we turn from the metaphorical to the literal, or more precisely to the graphic. Wordsworth's objection to the falsifying colors of poetic diction has its counterpart in Turner's objection to "historical color," the brown or mellow golden tone that was often spread over landscape paintings in order to make them look like "historical" works of the old masters. In 1798, Turner told Farington that his own pictures had been criticized for tending too much "to the *brown*" and that to correct this habit

---

nigrates the ornamental sensuality of the Venetian school (cited in Eaves 12), Jonathan Richardson in his *Theory of Painting* (1725) treats color as a source of both pleasure and truth (cited in Eaves 16), and Joshua Reynolds in 1782 salutes "the beauty and brilliancy of the colouring" in the works of Titian, greatest of the Venetians (*D* 196).

he was "attending to nature" (Farington, FDT 5: 1333). Later, in public, he criticized historical color in the works of the old masters themselves, noting in his sixth Academy lecture that Poussin's "love for the antique" produces "a colour that often removes his works from truth" (Ziff, "Backgrounds" 143). Yet Turner does not rest with a simple disjunction between historical and "natural" color; he makes his own characteristically impassioned case for colors that may emanate from the painter's imagination. Commenting in his fifth lecture on the "lurid, watery, subjugated interval of light" in Poussin's *Deluge*, he says that it

sets aside all comparative theory, however obtained; tho drawn from nature and her effects, these are the materials and instruments of [our] representations and our perceptions. 'Tis here that aerial perspective has her limits; and if theory dared to stipulate for aerial hues, peculiar colors or tones of color, she would step to self-destruction. It is here the utmost range of art that should tell. [The] imagination of the artist dwells *enthroned* in his own recess [and] must be incomprehensible as from darkness. (Quoted in Gage, *CT* 208–9)

Even without this remarkable statement, no one who sees the dazzling glow of chrome yellow that radiates again and again from Turner's late work can doubt that Turner believed in his right to transform natural objects by the modifying colors of his own imagination. But how can we reconcile Turner's claims for the prerogatives of an enthroned imagination, as he calls it, with his defense of "truth" and "nature" against the encroachments of historical color? To answer this question adequately, to reckon fairly with all its implications, we much see how the language of transformation is spoken in both the poetry and painting of the romantic period.

TRANSFORMATION AND TRUTH

In a useful corrective to M. H. Abrams's observation that painting "almost disappears" as a model for poetry in the romantic period (*Mirror and Lamp* 50), Roy Park has argued that painting "taught a new generation of poets and critics to interpret all art as a revelation of reality" (*Hazlitt* 136). Park's claim is at once problematic and provocative. It is probably impossible to prove that painting had such an influence, which Park himself admits was the "least tangible" of its effects. But Park helps us to realize that at the very least, major romantic poets and painters shared a strong desire to reveal the essential, unadorned conditon of human nature and the natural world: to make their respective arts express what Heidegger calls the "unconcealedness of Being" (164).

Wordsworth articulated this desire in its most fundamental form. In the "Prospectus" to *The Recluse*, his great but uncompleted philosophic epic, he announced that he would awaken his readers from the sleep of death and sensuality "by words / Which speak of nothing more than what we are" (*PW* 5.5). Behind this elementary formulation stands the whole argument of the preface to *Lyrical Ballads*, where Wordsworth declares that poetry can be made with "the real language of men" and that it should be purged of "poetic diction"—an "absurd and extravagant" kind of phraseology that obliterates "the plain humanities of nature" (*PrW* 1: 161–62). Significantly, this is one point on which Wordsworth won the agreement of Coleridge. Though Coleridge seriously questioned Wordsworth's contention that poetry could and should be made with "the real language of men," he seconded Wordsworth's attack on the use of figurative language without natural passion to motivate it: on figures of speech "which, stript of their justifying reasons and converted into mere artifices of connection or ornament, constitute the characteristic falsity in the poetic style of the moderns" (*BL* 2: 28).

In like terms Constable criticized much of what he saw in painting. I have already noted that in 1802—the very year Wordsworth first published his "Appendix" on poetic diction—Constable wrote to John Dunthorne about the seductiveness of what he called "manner," which soon ensnared any painter who imitated the old masters or simply reproduced his own style instead of continually "referring to nature." [3] Given this attitude, it is not surprising to find that Constable shared Turner's aversion to the brown, autumnal tones of "historical color." He simply could not accept the reigning pictorial doctrine that "Nature must be stripped of her green livery, and dressed in the browns of the painters, or confined to her own autumnal tints in order to be transferred to canvas." [4] Constable thought just the reverse. To Leslie he wrote: "I never did admire Autumnal tints in nature—so little of a painter am I in the eye of commonplace connoisseurship—I love the exhilarating freshness of spring" (*JCC* 3: 103).

3. Constable, *JCC* 2: 32; see also Leslie 274–75, and J. Reynolds, *D* 225. Park notes that in his *Essay on the Nature, the End, and the Means of Imitation in the Fine Arts* (1837), Quatremere de Quincy "attributed the Romantic rejection of poetic diction to the influence of painting" (*Hazlitt* 137n). But this seems to me at best a remote possibility. The evidence indicates not so much a causal connection as a coincidence of attitudes.

4. Henry Matthews, *Diary of an Invalid* (1820), quoted in Constable, *JCC* 6: 64.

This is what we find in pictures such as *The Lock*, painted 1823–24 (Philadelphia Museum; reproduced in Taylor, plate 100). The dominant colors here are blue and green, which not only permeate the group of trees at right but also invade the white-gray clouds churning around them, so that the windblown boughs seem to be virtually exploding into the sky. There are touches of yellow-brown in both the foreground and distant meadow, and the waistcoat of the figure leaning in the center offers the spot of red that by this time had virtually become Constable's trademark. But for the most part, instead of warm browns and yellows, this picture gives us the almost icy shock of white, blue, green, and gray. In May 1824, when the picture was being exhibited, Constable wrote to Fisher that "its light cannot be put out, because it is the light of nature— the Mother of all that is valuable in poetry, painting or anything else" (*JCC* 6: 157). And in 1825, when the picture was back in his studio, he wrote again to Fisher: "It looks most beautifully silvery, windy & delicious—it is all health—& the absence of everything stagnant" (*JCC* 6: 200).

Constable struggled to preserve this freshness. He spurned Beaumont's suggestion that his pictures be colored like an old Cremona fiddle, and when a fellow academician ventured to glaze *Hadleigh Castle* just before it was exhibited in order to soften the apparent harshness of its lights, he said, "There goes all my dew," and carefully removed the glaze.[5] But Constable's method cannot simply be defined in terms of negation. The removal of the glaze exposed something *added* to the picture: white flecks of paint. If we ask what distinguishes these flecks from the glaze that he insisted on subtracting, we may be led to an answer by what Constable says in one of his lectures, where he compares the foregrounds of Reynolds's pictures to the minute depiction of foliage in the foreground of Titian's *The Martyrdom of St. Peter*. In Reynolds's foregrounds, says Constable, "we often find . . . rich masses of colour, of light and shade, which, when examined, mean nothing. In Titian there is equal breadth, equal subordination of the parts to the whole, but the spectator finds, on approaching the picture, that every touch is the representative of a reality" (*JCD* 48). The difference between the glaze and

5. Leslie 114, 177. As a result, his pictures were often considered "very unfinished." See Leslie 96, 207, 227; Constable, *JCC* 4: 38; and Crabb Robinson's reaction to what was probably *The Leaping Horse*, exhibited 1825: "Why does he spot and dot his canvas?" (*Diary* 2: 295).

the white flecks is like the difference between Reynolds's generalized masses and Titian's particularized texture. While a glaze signifies nothing but the artist's wish to make his picture look mellowed by time, the white flecks signify dew. The reality they represent is something added to actual landscapes by atmosphere, which transforms what it touches.

Constable's remark about his dew recalls what Coleridge said about his reaction to Wordsworth's *Guilt and Sorrow* when—shortly after the two men first met—he heard Wordsworth himself recite it. He was most of all struck, he says, by the poet's "original gift of spreading the tone, the *atmosphere*, and with it the depth and height of the ideal world around forms, incidents, and situations, of which, for the common view, custom had bedimmed all the lustre, had dried up the sparkle, and the dew drops" (*BL* 1: 59). This statement must of course be distinguished from Constable's remark. Constable's "dew" is visible; Coleridge's "dew" is a metaphor for the ideality with which Wordsworth heightens the impact of his forms, incidents, and situations. Yet if we are properly wary of blurring the differences between Constable's remark and Coleridge's critical formulation, we should be likewise wary of overstating the differences. Constable's "dew" is no more literal than Coleridge's. It refers not to natural moisture but to white flecks—to marks that may look like spots of whitewash, as Turner said (Constable, *JCC* 3: 21), but that nonetheless signify natural moisture in the language of Constable's art. In different ways, Coleridge and Constable are both describing what the language of their respective arts imposes on the forms and situations that it represents. Constable's white flecks transform his representation of the seacoast just as surely as the metaphorical "dew drops" of Wordsworth's ideality transform his narration of a murder and its aftermath in *Guilt and Sorrow*. Thus, even as Constable proclaims his determination to represent nature in all its pristine freshness, he gives us fresh cause to ponder the complex relation between transformation and truth.

As we ponder this relation, we may turn again to the statement in which Wordsworth says that he has sought to relate common incidents in real language and also "to throw over them a certain colouring of imagination, whereby ordinary things should be presented to the mind in an unusual aspect" (*PrW* 1: 123). This highly problematic sentence involves a series of shifts. It first of all shifts from saying to seeing, from the language of the tongue to the language of the eye. It is thus one of many reminders that Wordsworth's determination to make poetry speak the real language of men is bound up with his determination to "look steadily at [his] subject" (*PrW* 1: 132), to make his language correspond with what men really say and with what he really sees. But in this sentence, the characteristic shift from saying to seeing is complicated by a further shift: an implied turning from the naked actualities of sight and speech to the "shift" of the imagination, the garment of color that it throws over ordinary things. At once pictorial and sartorial, Wordsworth's metaphors clearly suggest that as a poet, he has added something to reality in the process of representing it.

What he has added could be called "atmosphere" in the purely metaphorical sense used by Coleridge. A good example from the *Lyrical Ballads* of 1800 is the distinctly unpictorial atmosphere which is made to surround the "straggling heap of unhewn stones" in "Michael." Though its roughness and variety could have made it visually arresting, Wordsworth introduces this object by deliberately dismissing its potentially picturesque appeal, speaking of it as something "which you might pass by, / Might see and notice not" (lines 15–16). The connoisseur of the picturesque, says Martin Price, "turns to the sketch, which precedes formal perfection, and the ruin, which succeeds it."[6] But for the eye, a straggling heap of unhewn stones is neither a sketch nor a ruin, neither form in the making nor form dissolving. We later learn that the stones have simply been gathered up and thrown together by Michael (326–28), and as such, they are nothing but raw material waiting to be cut and formed. Only by reading the story that "appertains" to the stones can we learn of the purpose that was to have formed them, and only then do we see that the absence of form in the stones is precisely designed to represent the frustration of that purpose. What "distinguishes these Poems from the popular Poetry of the day," said Wordsworth in the preface of 1800, is "that the feeling therein developed gives importance to the action and situation and not the action and situation to the feeling" (*PrW* 1: 128). In the end, it is the feeling of Michael that makes the stones important, that makes them express his profound and poignant incapacity to build the sheepfold:

> and 'tis believed by all
> That many and many a day he hither went,
> And never lifted up a single stone.
>
> (463–66)

---

6. "The Picturesque Moment" in Hilles and Bloom 277.

Wordsworth's language here has none of the intricate light and shadow demanded by the rules of picturesque description; the potentially picturesque accumulation of unhewn stones has now become a single stone, isolated and unadorned by so much as a single descriptive adjective. Yet for all its plainness, we are made to feel that the weight of this stone is both physically and psychically unbearable.

The atmosphere with which Wordsworth invests the stones in "Michael," then, is purely metaphorical. Yet if Wordsworth could demonstrate the transforming effect of emotional atmosphere, he was equally capable of revealing what actual atmosphere could do to the natural world. In fact, except where this actual atmosphere is entirely displaced by an emotional one, as with the heap of stones in "Michael," Wordsworth's determination to represent the real appearance of natural objects paradoxically but inevitably leads him to represent the lights, colors, and shadows in which they are naturally clothed. In the sonnet "Composed upon Westminster Bridge, September 3, 1802," the city of London is said to be "bare" and yet also impalpably dressed: "This City now doth, like a garment, wear / The beauty of the morning" (lines 4–5). Wordsworth's simile is the verbal counterpart of a visible paradox. The garment of beauty leaves the city bare, yet at the same time clothes it in a light that makes of it a landscape: "Open unto the fields, and to the sky; / All bright and glittering in the smokeless air." A transformation wrought by actual atmosphere is thus reenacted by the transforming language of the poem.

The transforming effect of natural atmosphere on an urban setting is precisely what Turner represents in *Old London Bridge* (plate 19), a watercolor painted circa 1796–97 (TSB XXXIII, U). The ostensible subject here is architecture rather than landscape, and it is worth noting that of the first forty subjects Turner exhibited at the Royal Academy, thirty-one were architectural (Hardie 25). But this particular picture he did not exhibit, and the reason may well have been that in the freedom of its effect, it is much less a record of architectural form than of the natural phenomena touching that form—of the light, shadow, and rippling water that collectively make of it almost an object of landscape.

By the time he painted this picture, Turner had already moved beyond the conventional three-step method of watercoloring wherein objects were first outlined in pencil, then shadowed with monochrome washes, and finally individuated with local color—so that the last step was a matter of filling in outlines.[7] Turner reformed this procedure with the help of Thomas Girtin, whom he met in the early 1790s and with whom he enjoyed the kind of mutually fructifying relationship that Wordsworth had with Coleridge—at almost exactly the same time.[8] What Turner and Girtin did—though Girtin seems to have done it first—was to integrate steps that had been hitherto separate. Instead of proceeding from outline to shade and then color, they applied local color to individual objects and then shadowed them, so that shadow brought unity of tone to the separate objects even as it blended with—and hence was variously modified by—their individual colors. Because the paper was slightly absorbent, the color settled without hard edges, and the wash of shadow went into the color instead of bringing it away. As for outline, it ceased to circumscribe the expressive effects of color and shade. Turner and Girtin were both superb with the pencil, but in the middle of the 1790s they began to draw and invent with the brush, dissolving their outlines in light, color, and shadow to represent the softening influence of atmosphere (Hardie 13–17).

Old London Bridge shows the method at work. Turner does not ignore architectural form in this picture; he transcends it. With a sure hand, he establishes the high horizontal of the bridge, its thick vertical pillars, and its four visible arches; he even individuates certain architectural details, such as the Gothic facing on the pillar at right, and he differentiates the arches not only by varying their height and breadth, but also by minimally pointing three of them—while the fourth, from what we can see of it, seems perfectly unbroken. But all of these architectural elements are in shadow, and our eyes are drawn through the arches to the light beyond, where, anticipating the facades in Turner's late Venetian watercolors, the pale-toned buildings at right merge with their own reflections, and in the center, the slender steeples melt into the sky. These distant objects are not set against the light, as they would be in conventional watercoloring, but rather within it. We therefore see the architec-

7. Hardie 6, 18. In Turner's time, the word *pencil* was often used to mean *paintbrush*. I use it in the modern sense except where indicated.

8. For a period of about three years in the mid-1790s, Turner and Girtin worked together regularly in the evening at the house of Dr. Thomas Monro, who employed them to copy drawings in his possession by established British masters such as J. R. Cozens. According to Farington, "Girtin drew in outlines and Turner washed in the effects" (Wilton, *BW* 30). The most stimulating years in the relationship between Wordsworth and Coleridge were from 1795, when they first met, to 1798, when they jointly produced the first edition of *Lyrical Ballads*.

tural forms in this picture only by looking through the atmosphere that contains them, and the atmosphere tends to consume elaborate outlines. Some, like those of the distant objects, seem to disappear in light, while others seem to disappear in shadow. The finely drawn lines of the tri-faceted central pillar, for example, are in part obliterated by the subtle interplay of light and shade, and the Gothic facing on the pier at left is barely visible through the heavy shadow laid upon it.[9]

Because Turner is ultimately more concerned with the re-creation of atmosphere than with the definition of form, certain things in this picture bear no relation to any possible outline at all. The little figures crossing the bridge, with tiny dots for heads, are made entirely with the brush, as are the railings of the balustrade; the path of light coming through the arch at left widens at the base of the picture, spreading so delicately into the shadow that we cannot say where light ends and shadow begins. In fact, by a series of stippled strokes which no outline could predetermine, light permeates shadow on the surface of the water. Finally, because of the way light comes from the background, we do not see a clear horizon dividing the water from the sky, and the horizontal line of the water level in the foreground, corresponding to the horizontal of the bridge, is merely suggested by the essentially unlinear stipples of light. In *Old London Bridge*, then, Turner's pictorial language enables him to show how atmosphere naturally transforms the world of visible objects.

THE KNOWN AND THE SEEN

At just about the time Turner painted *Old London Bridge*, Wordsworth and Coleridge were discussing the relation between atmospheric trans-formation and poetry. When Wordsworth says in the preface to *Lyrical Ballads* that he has tried to throw over common objects "a certain colour-ing of imagination," he is undoubtedly drawing on conversations that

9. Max Schultz says that in *Old London Bridge*, "the hard angularity of the usual architectural drawing is softened by light" (409). I would simply add the words "and shadow." The hard angularity of the usual architectural drawing is plainly evident in *King's Mews, Charing Cross*, done about 1792 by Thomas Malton the Younger, who taught Turner and definitely influenced Girtin in the early 1790s (Wilton, *BW* 30; and Gage, *CT* 22–23, 227 n. 28). To see how much Turner and Girtin transformed the effect of architectural drawing, we have only to compare the uncompromising linearity of Mal-ton's picture with the atmospheric subtlety of *Old London Bridge* or of Girtin's *West Front of Peterborough Cathedral* (1794), which modestly and yet strikingly anticipates—by a full hundred years—Monet's famous *Rouen Cathedral, West Facade, Sunlight*.

he had with Coleridge in the years 1797 and 1798: conversations that turned, says Coleridge,

on the two cardinal points of poetry, the power of exciting the sympathy of the reader by a faithful adherence to the truth of nature, and the power of giving the interest of novelty by the modifying colors of imagination. The sudden charm, which accidents of light and shade, which moon-light or sun-set diffused over a known and familiar landscape, appeared to represent the practicability of combining both. These are the poetry of nature. (*BL* 2: 5)

It is no accident, I think, that Wordsworth and Coleridge both define the effect of the imagination as a process of coloring. They had noticed how the changing colors of nature could modify the appearance of familiar objects, and they proposed to modify familiar objects in poetry. What they perceived in nature was that color could be changed by light. On the evening of the very first day he met Wordsworth in 1798, Hazlitt tells us that Wordsworth looked out of the window of Coleridge's Bristol cottage and said: "'How beautifully the sun sets on that yellow bank!' I thought within myself," writes Hazlitt, "with what eyes these poets see nature! and ever after, when I saw the sun-set stream upon the objects facing it, conceived I had made a discovery, or thanked Mr. Wordsworth for having made one for me!" (17: 118). Hazlitt does not fully explain the context of Wordsworth's remark, but the reason for his admiring astonishment is—I suspect—that the bank in question was covered with grass. Wordsworth saw it as yellow because the setting sun had suddenly made it appear that way, and his perception was a "discovery," as Hazlitt suggests, because in order to make it he had to suppress the conventional notion that grass is green. To paraphrase what E. H. Gombrich has said of Turner (*AI* 296), he had to suppress what he knew in order to concentrate on what he saw.

Yet while he sees the color of the grass in the spatial context created by a special kind of light, he also sees it in the temporal context generated by his past experience. Only the knowledge gained from this experience allows him to perceive that the yellow thing before him is a bank, for as Gombrich penetratingly observes, "we can never neatly separate what we see from what we know" (*AI* 394). Wordsworth's knowledge is a precondition of his "discovery." In order to perceive the relation of the color to the object it touches and modifies, he must know not only what that object is, but also how it normally appears. He cannot "discover" the yellowness of the bank unless he knows that it is normally green.

What he knows, therefore, is not expelled by what he sees, but is rather transformed by it. He perceives not simply yellow, but the transformation of green into yellow, and it is only by thus integrating what he knows with what he sees that he can experience a consciousness of transformation. Not long after Wordsworth made his remark, he incorporated this perception into "The Tables Turned":

> The sun, above the mountain's head,
> A freshening lustre mellow
> Through all the long green fields has spread
> His first sweet evening yellow.
>
> (Lines 5–8)

Here the complex content of Wordsworth's perception is perfectly explicit. He bears witness not simply to yellow, nor even to yellow grass, but to the yellow*ing* of grass that he knows to be green, to the freshening and even surprising transformation of familiar fields. In the landscape itself, sunlight modifies the appearance of grass; in the perceiver, what is seen modifies what is known. The poet does not discard the learning of manhood for the ignorance of childhood, but seeks rather to combine the two: "to carry on the feelings of childhood into the powers of manhood," as Coleridge said, "to combine the child's sense of wonder and novelty with the appearances, which every day for perhaps forty years had rendered familiar" (*BL* 1: 59, 60).

Fascinated by all of the ways in which light and color could transform a known and familiar landscape, Coleridge himself was acutely sensitive to what Wordsworth describes in "The Tables Turned" and Turner repeatedly depicts: the interaction of colors. A notebook entry of 1800 reads: "Eastdale—the dusky orange upon the yellowing green under the tender gloom of black [?Purple/Poplar]."[10] Coleridge habitually perceived the colors of landscape in this way. In notebook entries dating from 1800 to 1804, he often records the interaction of yellow and green— something he also registers in "Dejection: An Ode" (1802), where not

---

10. Coleridge, *NC* 1: 823. Compare Turner's description of an Italian landscape in 1819: "the olives the light [of sky?] when the sun shone grey green, the ground redish green grey and apt to Purple, the Sea quite Blue. . . . Beautiful dark green yet warm the middle Trees, yet Bluish in parts, [in] the distance the aqueduct reddish, the foreground light grey in shadow" (TSB CLXXVII, inside cover). For further discussion of correspondences such as this, see Heffernan, "The English Romantic Perception of Color," in Kroeber and Walling 133–48. And for full-scale treatment of Turner's theory of color, see Gage, *CT*.

even his stifled grief can keep him from seeing in the western sky a "peculiar tint of yellow green."[11] He found "yellow-red" in one landscape, reddish brown in several others, and during his voyage to Malta in the spring of 1804, he was fascinated by the interplay of green with various shades of blue and purple in the sea.[12] Colors for Coleridge were living things, continually in motion. He could observe the changing colors of a tree and of a sunrise, the subtle turning of a stream from white to blue, the flickering colors of pink rocks seen through white foam, and the silvering of black water beneath ice.[13] It was in these shifting forms that colors most appealed to him. In "Lewti" (1798), he speaks of a pale cloud brightening as it approaches the moon, "with floating colours not a few" (line 18). And on a winter night two years later, he set down a similar effect in his notebook. The hazy light of the moon, he writes, filled up the sky "as if it had been painted & the colors had run" (*NC* 1: 875).

What strikes Coleridge here, of course, is not only the interaction of running colors but the transforming effect of moonlight, which plays such a conspicuous part in his poetry. In "The Nightingale" (1798), he describes its effect on a flock of resting birds:

> On moonlight bushes,
> Whose dewy leaflets are but half-disclosed,
> You may perchance behold them on the twigs,
> Their bright, bright eyes, their eyes both bright and full,
> Glistening, while many of glow-worm in the shade
> Lights up her love-torch.
>
> (64–69)

This passage is studded with lights. Coleridge notices the shade surrounding the glowworms and touching the "half-disclosed" leaflets, but there is nothing simple or predetermined about his chiaroscuro. What we see is rather a cluster of lights: the radiance of many glowworms, the brilliant eyes of the birds, the dewy leaflets catching the light of the moon. At the end of the poem, when the tearful eyes of Coleridge's infant son receive this light, the babe is

11. Line 29. See also Coleridge, *NC* 1: 789, f. 11; 798, f. 38ᵛ; 1319; 1413; 1812, f. 57.

12. Coleridge, *LC* 1: 503; *NC* 1: 549, f. 27ᵛ; 1433, f. 6; 1487, f. 47ᵛ; 2: 2015; 2070, f. 30ᵛ.

13. *NC* 1: 222, f. 34; 581; 753, f. 3ᵛ–4; 1489, f. 55ᵛ; 1800. See also *NC* 1: 925; 1746; 2: 1889, f. 17ᵛ; and *LC* 2: 1004; 3: 304.

> hushed at once,
> Suspends his sobs, and laughs most silently,
> While his fair eyes, that swam with undropped tears,
> Did glitter in the yellow moon-beam!
>
> (102–5)

Turning sorrow into spontaneous joy, the lights permeate the entire range of living things: bushes, birds, glowworms, and infants. As "Nature's play-mate" (97), the infant draws no line between the nightingales and himself; "capable of no articulate sound," he is prompt to catch their inarticulate voices (91–96). Likewise, his eyes catch the moonlight which is also reflected in theirs, and in the all-pervading glitter of this light, the infant and the nightingales become one.

Light plays an equally important role in "The Rime of the Ancient Mariner," where it actually collaborates with color to provoke an unconscious act of love. In part 4, surrounded by "beautiful" men who are dead and "slimy things" that live on, closing his eyes in vain against a sea and a sky that cannot be shut out, the mariner reopens them to see the moon shining on the water:

> Her beams bemocked the sultry main,
> Like April hoar-frost spread;
> But where the ship's huge shadow lay,
> The charmed water burnt alway
> A still and awful red.
>
> (267–71)

At first there is a line implied between the "hoar-frost" of the moonlit sea and the burning red of the shadow. But the color of the ship has already tinted that shadow, and when the water snakes invade it, linear chiaroscuro gives way to the sparkle of light and the spontaneity of running color:

> Beyond the shadow of the ship,
> I watched the water-snakes:
> They moved in tracks of shining white,
> And when they reared, the elvish light
> Fell off in hoary flakes.
>
> Within the shadow of the ship
> I watched their rich attire:

> Blue, glossy green, and velvet black,
> They coiled and swam; and every track
> Was a flash of golden fire.
>
> (272–81)

Beyond the shadow of the ship, the mariner can see only the wakes of the water snakes: the tracks of shining white and the hoary flakes of their spray. Within the reddened shadow of the ship, the colors of the snakes themselves become visible, and the shining white of their tracks is turned to "golden fire." The effect is one of brilliant coalescence. The lights which at first seemed cool, distant, and inaccessibly beyond the burning shadow of the ship have broken up the outline of that shadow, and even as hoar-frost white and burning red come together in flashes of golden fire, the mariner and the water snakes come together in a moment of perception:

> O happy living things! no tongue
> Their beauty might declare:
> A spring of love gushed from my heart,
> And I blessed them unaware:
> Sure my kind saint took pity on me,
> And I blessed them unaware.
>
> (282–87)

The repetition of "unaware" underscores the spontaneity of the mariner's perception. What he suddenly discovers is not only the beauty of the snakes, but the transforming power of color and light.

The transformations wrought by color and light in painting are at once like and unlike this one. Since the impact of the mariner's discovery depends to a considerable extent on its place in a narrative that leads up to it, it has no purely pictorial equivalent. In poetry, the relation between the known and the seen can be established in succession, so that what is first "known" as a slimy snake can then be "seen" as a thing of dazzling beauty. No such succession of percepts can be represented by a single painting. To portray the transformation of natural objects on canvas, the artist must somehow remind us of features we "know" even as he makes us see those features in what is literally as well as figuratively a new light.

This is essentially what Turner does. In *Old London Bridge* (plate 19), the architectural structure of the bridge itself is plainly discernible through the play of light and shadow that consumes some—but not all—of its outlines. In *Buttermere* (plate 1), the valley in the middle distance is made to look like shimmering water, but the barely visible houses and haystacks dotting its surface remind us that it is indeed a valley. In Turner's later work, Gombrich says that "the structure of objects is often quite swallowed up by the modifications of the moment—mist, light, and dazzle" (*AI* 296). But in *Approach to Venice*, exhibited 1844, which Gombrich cites as a case in point (*AI* 295), the structures of at least four gondolas and one small barge (in the foreground at left) are readily discernible. Turner knew those structures perfectly well. Pictures such as *Dort or Dortrecht* and *First Rate Taking in Stores*, both of which he painted in 1818, show that he could render far more complicated craft with a draftsmanlike precision when he chose. In Venice, it was precisely his knowledge of boats that allowed him to see how the atmosphere transformed them, and to represent that transformation so impressively.

The same kind of knowledge underlies the work of Constable. Gombrich says that in *Wivenhoe Park*, painted in 1816, Constable takes the "real shape" of his objects for granted, modifying them "in order to match the here and now of their appearance at a given moment" (*AI* 295). When he represents a boat as little more than a sunlit curve of gunwale on the water, he suppresses most of what he knows about its structure. But there is no question of what he did know; in *Boat Building near Flatford Mill*, painted just the year before *Wivenhoe*, he carefully depicts the anatomy of a boat in the making. In *Wivenhoe* itself, his knowledge of the boat once again enables him to show how light and shadow have transformed it, just as his knowledge of the grassy bank at left allows him to discover—and to reveal—that sunlight makes it look yellow.[14] Combining the known with the seen, pictures like *Wivenhoe* and *Buttermere* represent the kind of transformation that Wordsworth and Coleridge took as a paradigm for poetry, a model for the transforming impact of imagination on the truth of nature. What Coleridge said of genius applies to the process of transformation in romantic poetry and painting alike. Genius, he said, "neither distorts nor false-colours its objects; but on the contrary brings out many a vein and many a tint, which escapes the eye of common observation, thus raising to the rank of gems

14. See also the yellowed grass on the right side of Constable's *Scene on a Navigable River (Flatford Mill)*, exhibited 1817 (National Gallery, London, reproduced in Parris, Fleming-Williams, and Shields, facing 81).

what had been often kicked away by the hurrying foot of the traveller on the dusty high road of custom: (*BL* 2: 121).

THE LANGUAGE OF POWER

The language of transformation is thus a language of revelation, a language that compels us to see what our knowledge has failed to show us. But it is also a language of power, a language that turns a known and familiar landscape into something extraordinary. One of the many things that links romantic painters to romantic poets is precisely their common faith in the power of transformation, their belief in what the language of their respective arts could do with ordinary or even negligible subjects. "It is the honourable characteristic of Poetry," wrote Wordsworth in the advertisement to the *Lyrical Ballads* of 1798, "that its materials are to be found in every subject which can interest the human mind" (*PW* 2: 383). The statement is elaborately deferential, but Wordsworth here is quietly beginning his defense of subjects ranking well below the level of those traditionally required for poetry. As he plainly admits in the preface of 1800, his aim in the *Lyrical Ballads* was to represent incidents from "low and rustic life" (*PW* 2: 386), and his poems in this volume revolve around such unpromising objects as a straggling heap of unhewn stones and a stunted thorn tree. Wordsworth's comment on *The Thorn* itself shows how he set out to transform this particular object. The poem arose, he said, "out of my observing, on the ridge of Quantock Hill, on a stormy day, a thorn which I had often passed in calm and bright weather without noticing it. I said to myself, 'Cannot I by some invention do as much to make this Thorn permanently an impressive object as the storm has made it to my eyes at this moment?'" (*PW* 2: 511). The inconspicuous thorn tree was transfigured by light and shade. In Coleridge's phrase, the "sudden charm" of an arresting metamorphosis had made it "impressive," and Wordsworth wished "by some invention" to imitate this effect in his poem. He does so from the beginning by implicitly connecting the tree to the story of the seduced and abandoned Martha Ray. The woman is not mentioned until stanza six, and the first two stanzas give us nothing but the thorn: an old, grey, knotted, stunted, and "wretched thing forlorn" (lines 1–9), completely overgrown with lichens and tufts of moss that seem determined to drag it down and bury it "for ever" (10–22). By the atmosphere of pathetic desolation with which he surrounds and humanizes the thorn, Wordsworth imitates the "impressive" effect of the storm-whipped tree that caught his eye on Quantock Ridge. Taking as his subject a feature of landscape so inconspicuous that he himself had often failed to notice it, he makes it "impressive" by the atmospheric power of his own language.

Wordsworth and Coleridge both recognized that this transformation of the ordinary into the extraordinary could be achieved in landscape painting as well as in poetry. Writing to George Beaumont in 1811, Wordsworth cited Rubens's *Castle of Steen*—then in Beaumont's collection— as a "noble instance" of what he himself wished to have: "the power of turning to advantage, wherever it is possible, every object of Art and Nature as they appear before me" (2: 506). Some years later, Coleridge spoke at length of what Rubens had done with ordinary materials in *Landscape with a Setting Sun*. Instead of grand subjects, said Coleridge, Rubens gives us

some little ponds, old tumble-down cottages, that ruinous chateau, two or three peasants, a hay-rick, and other such humble images, which looked at in and by themselves convey no pleasure and excite no surprise; but he—and Peter Paul Rubens alone—handles these every-day ingredients of all common landscapes as they are handled in nature; he throws them into a vast and magnificent whole, consisting of heaven and earth and all things therein. He extracts the latent poetry out of these common objects.[15]

Yet expansion of scope was not the only means by which a landscape painter could transform ordinary materials. Constable believed they could be made extraordinary by means of chiaroscuro alone. In defending this point, he had to contend with what not even Rubens had overthrown: the tenacious assumption that paintings should be judged by the predetermined rank of their subjects, not by their "language" of light, shade, and color.[16] Constable aimed to show the reverse. In *English Landscape*, he set out specifically to demonstrate that chiaroscuro was— as he later called it—"the soul and medium of art."[17] Without chiaroscuro, he said, landscape could "never be rendered impressive" (*JCD*

---

15. Coleridge, *TT* 124. Coleridge's description is not entirely accurate (the chateau, for one thing, is depicted in fairly good condition), but his basic point is well taken.

16. As late as 1824, Constable could write: "I have to combat from high quarters . . . the plausible argument that *subject* makes the picture" (Leslie 131).

17. *JCD* 60. In an 1835 prospectus to *English Landscape*, he speaks of chiaroscuro as "a power capable in itself, alone, of imparting Expression, Taste, and Sentiment" (*JCD* 11).

40); with it, any scene or object could become so. Commenting on *East Bergholt*, the frontispiece for *English Landscape*, he wrote:

In this plate the endeavor has been to give, by richness of Light and Shadow, an interest to a subject otherwise by no means attractive. The broad still lights of a Summer evening, with the solemn and far-extended shadows cast round by the intervening objects, small portions of them only and of the landscape gilded by the setting sun, cannot fail to give interest to the most simple or barren subject, or even to mark it with pathos and effect.[18]

Long before Constable published *English Landscape*, Coleridge discovered the power of chiaroscuro in the paintings he saw during his visit to Italy in 1806. "What Tone to colors," he wrote, "chiar-Oscuro [is] to Light & Shade; viz. such a management of them that they form a beautiful whole, *independent of the particular Images colored, lit up, or shaded*" (*NC* 2: 2797; italics added). Yet more than a specific interest in chiaroscuro, what Coleridge and Wordsworth shared with Constable and Turner was a profound conviction that atmospheric effects could make any subject beautiful or impressive, and a profound desire to represent those effects in their respective arts. Wordsworth sought to reenact in poetry the "impressive" effect made by a storm-whipped thorn; Turner likewise thought the duty of the artist was to recreate the "impression" made by an object. With a distant object especially, he wrote, the artist must "give its . . . proper proportion distance by size that the light, shade, and color may unite so as to impress [upon the spectator] that general aura [?] of distant objects [which] even the most uncultivated eyes seem capable of owning."[19]

The words of this undated note (watermarked 1804) are surprisingly close to those of Wordsworth in the final book of *The Prelude*, where we are told that nature often dominates

the outward face of things,
So moulds them and endues, abstracts, combines,

18. *JCD* 12. See also *JCD* 26 and Leslie 280: "*I never saw an ugly thing in my life*: for let the form of an object be what it may,—light, shade, and perspective will always make it beautiful." Compare Emerson: "There is no object so foul that intense light will not make it beautiful" (*Emerson: A Modern Anthology*, ed. Alfred Kazin and Daniel Aaron [Boston: Houghton Mifflin, 1958], 26, quoted in Novak 270).

19. TMS BB, f. 6ʳ. Compare Constable on a seascape by Ruysdael: "The subject is the mouth of a Dutch river, without a single feature of grandeur in the scenery; but the stormy sky, the grouping of the vessels, and the breaking of the sea, make the picture one of the most impressive ever painted" (Leslie 318).

Or by abrupt and unhabitual influence
Doth make one object so impress itself
Upon all others, and pervade them so
That even the grossest minds must see and hear
And cannot chuse but feel.

(A 13. 77–84)

Turner says that even the most uncultivated eyes can have a sense of distance; Wordsworth says that even grossest minds must feel the force of transformation. He goes on to say that poets "send abroad / Like transformation" (93–94), and he himself has just done so. By describing what he saw from the summit of Snowdon on a moonlit night, he has re-created the transforming effect of mist upon the sea and the surrounding hills, and at the same time, he has recreated the sense of distance. In fact, if the painter must make light, shade, and color unite so as to impress on us "the aura of distant objects," as Turner said, Wordsworth uses his elements to the same end:

on the shore
I found myself of a huge sea of mist,
Which, meek and silent, rested at my feet:
A hundred hills their dusky backs upheaved
All over this still Ocean, and beyond,
Far, far beyond, the vapours shot themselves,
In headlands, tongues, and promontory shapes,
Into the Sea, the real Sea, that seem'd
To dwindle, and give up its majesty,
Usurp'd upon as far as sight could reach.

(42–51)

The distance in this picture is composed of three different elements: of mist, sea, and hills. But all of them coalesce to create the kind of unified impression "that even the grossest minds must see and hear / And cannot chuse but feel" (83–84). No clear-cut outline divides the sea of mist from the sea of water, for even as the mist obscures the sea, it becomes a sea itself. At the same time, the hills become creatures of this misty ocean, and the misty ocean paradoxically presents to the "real sea" a vaporous coastline: headlands, tongues, and promontory shapes. It is a coastline, of course, that no cartographer could hope to record. The vapours shoot themselves into various shapes, and the outline of these vapours, like the outline of every other element in this picture, seems to dissolve before our eyes. What results is a magnificent whole: a landscape embodying that spatial infinity in which—as Wordsworth said in a letter of 1824—"things are lost in each other, and limits vanish" (*LY* 1: 134–35).

On one level, Wordsworth's account of what he saw and felt at Snowdon can be read as a poet's apotheosis of nature. The transformations naturally wrought by mist and moonlight provide a model or paradigm for the transformations wrought by the human imagination in poetry. If we take the natural transformation as in some sense the work of God, Wordsworth is saying something very close to what Coleridge says in chapter 13 of the *Biographia Literaria*: that the human imagination is "a repetition in the finite mind of the eternal act of creation in the infinite I AM."[20] But Wordsworth's lines on the spectacle at Snowdon are not simply a tribute to the transforming powers of nature or God; they are also a demonstration of what can be done by the language of transformation in poetry—in short, by words. In the impassioned tribute to the autonomous power of imagination which he makes in book 6 of *The Prelude*, Wordsworth speaks of its sudden emergence from within him as a "usurpation" of the senses: "the light of sense / Goes out in flashes that have shewn to us / The invisible world" (A 6.534–36). In the Snowdon passage, Wordsworth represents at once the visible and the usurpation of the visible. The real sea gives up its majesty, "Usurp'd upon as far as sight could reach." It is hidden by a metaphorical sea of mist, a sea that visually evokes the roaring turbulence of the ocean and yet remains "still" to the ear, "meek and silent" at the poet's feet. Having covered the real sea with a metaphorical one, the poet's language then turns the edge of the metaphorical sea into land: into a plunging coastline that in the virtually infinite distance invades the "real" but invisible sea.

For all his determination to make poetry speak "the real language of men" and to keep his eye upon natural objects in the act of describing them, Wordsworth here fully exploits the transforming power inherent in language itself. That he consciously recognized those powers can be seen in part from the 1802 version of the preface to *Lyrical Ballads*,

20. *BL* 1: 202. In an important recent essay, Leslie Brisman stresses the point that Coleridge defines the human imagination as "the prime Agent of all *human* Perception" (italics added)—by which he distinguishes it from mere animal perception. By "human perception," Brisman shows, Coleridge means "man's capacity to view the world whole, to view the world as the organic creation of the living Power, God." See *BL* 2: 259 and Brisman 126–27.

where his fervent defense of a language faithful to natural appearances and recognizable human passion does not keep him from defending meter on precisely the opposite grounds. Meter tempers the passion excited by a poem, he says, because of its "tendency . . . to divest language, in a certain degree, of its reality, and thus to throw a sort of half-consciousness of unsubstantial existence over the whole composition."[21] If this justification of what could be called a dis-realizing or deconstructive element in poetry sounds uncharacteristic of Wordsworth, we do well to ponder the passage with which he concludes book 5 of *The Prelude*—the book entitled "Books":

> Visionary Power
> Attends the motions of the viewless winds,
> Embodied in the mystery of words:
> There, darkness makes abode, and all the host
> Of shadowy things work endless changes,—there,
> As in a mansion like their proper home,
> Even forms and substances are circumfused
> By that transparent veil with light divine,
> And, through the turnings intricate of verse
> Present themselves as objects recognized
> In flashes, and with glory not their own.[22]

Wordsworth seems at first to derive the power of language from the power of nature—from "the motions of the winds." But essentially, he represents the power of language as independently transformative, and he reveals this power in the very language with which he describes it. In the turnings intricate of verse intricately turned, he deliberately departs from "the real language of men," and notably from the "natural" or prose order of words that he tried to follow in the *Lyrical Ballads* and endorsed in his preface (*PrW* 1: 133). The language that he simultaneously defines and illustrates is one of mysterious regeneration, a language in which shadowy things not only work their changes on forms and substances but

21. *PrW* 1: 147. In the same preface he also says that metrical composition gives delight because it provides "an indistinct perception perpetually renewed of language closely resembling that of real life, and yet, in the circumstance of metre, differing from it so widely" (*PrW* 1: 151).

22. *Prelude* 5. 595–605. In the early version of the *Prelude* these lines are followed by a brief but pedestrian comment on the importance of books to the poet's early life (A 5. 630–37). In the later version, this anticlimactic coda is fortunately cut.

paradoxically radiate a light that transfigures natural objects so that they appear with glory "not their own." Most strikingly, in a phrase that recalls the "bare" and yet garmented city of "Composed upon Westminster Bridge," Wordsworth speaks of poetic language as a "transparent veil." Shelley regularly used the image of the veil to signify a material covering that had to be removed in the process of artistic creation. In his vision of pre-Athenian Greece, for instance, "Art's deathless dreams lay veiled by many a vein / Of Parian stone."[23] But for Wordsworth, the veil signifies precisely what poetic language imposes on natural objects. At once revealing and obscuring, allowing flashes of recognition and yet surrounding objects with an alien light, the transparent veil of language is the verbal counterpart of atmospheric transformation at its most intense.

Nevertheless, the fervor of Wordsworth's tribute to the transforming effect of poetic language is if anything surpassed by the fervor of Turner's tribute to the transforming effect of pictorial language—specifically the language of Rembrandt's *The Mill* (plate 26). Rembrandt impressed both Turner and Constable for the very reason that he disturbed Joshua Reynolds: his all-enveloping chiaroscuro. With his tendency to derogate the "language" of painters, Reynolds treated Rembrandt as a merely mechanical manipulator of light and shade (*D* 147–48). But for Turner and Constable, Rembrandt's chiaroscuro was the clearest sign of his genius. Constable called it the "peculiar language" with which he expressed feeling, and in Constable's lectures on the history of landscape painting, it was the power of Rembrandt's language that led him to present *The Mill* as by itself an "epoch" (*JCD* 62). *The Mill*, said Constable, "is a picture wholly made by chiaroscuro; the last ray of light just gleams on the upper sail of the mill, and all other details are lost in large and simple masses of shade" (*JCD* 62). Turner made this point still more emphatically in his own lectures on landscape. In *The Mill*, said Turner, Rembrandt

depended upon his chiaroscuro, his bursts of light and darkness to be *felt*. He threw a mysterious doubt over the meanest piece of common; nay more, his forms, if they can be called so, are the most objectionable that could be chosen, namely, the three Trees and the Mill, but over each he has thrown that veil of matchless colour, that lucid interval of Morning dawn and dewy light on which

23. "Ode to Liberty," lines 57–58. See also Shelley's lines on the waterfall in his apostrophe to the Ravine of Arve in "Mont Blanc": "Thine earthly rainbows stretched across the sweep / Of the etherial waterfall, whose veil / Robes some unsculptured image" (25–27).

the Eye dwells so completely enthrall'd, and seeks not for its liberty, but as it were, thinks it a sacrilege to pierce the mystic shell of colour in search of form.[24]

Wordsworth saw the language of poetry as a veil surrounding forms and substances; Turner sees the language of Rembrandt's painting as a veil thrown over forms. But this time the veil is more opaque than transparent, palpable enough to arrest the eye. We might even infer that since Turner criticized the French for their severe linearity and since he idolized a Rembrandt who virtually obliterated form, his own aim was to do likewise. But this would be inferring too much. Turner learned how to draw with precision in the 1790s, and he never forgot. The difference between his earlier and later work is that as he grew older, his growing desire to paint what he saw compelled him to suppress much more of what he knew.

The late *Norham Castle, Sunrise* (plate 27), ca. 1835–40, is a particularly revealing case in point. Since Turner painted no fewer than six watercolors of this subject during the years from 1797 to about 1835 (Wilton, *TAL* 172–74), we can compare earlier and later versions to see how forms and substances are gradually consumed by atmosphere in Turner's work. In one of the earliest watercolors, done about 1798 (private collection; reproduced in Gage, *CT*, plate 33), the castle is sharply depicted in the middle distance on a rocky hill overlooking a lake, and we can plainly discern a number of other details: a gentle line of hills in the background, a wooded hill at left with a white cottage on the shore, a rowboat by the cottage, a sailboat drifting under the castle, three cows drinking from the lake in the foreground, and at right a rocky promontory with several more cows on it. If we compare this picture with the oil version of the 1830s, we notice first of all that a number of details have been subtracted or abstracted in the root sense, taken away. We no longer see the hills in the background, the cottage, the sailboat, the rowboat, the rocky banks, or even—with any certainty—the castle, which has now become a virtually indistinguishable part of a blocky blue rise in the middle distance. The cows at right have also disappeared, and the three in the foreground have dwindled to one. What remains are chiefly light

24. Ziff, "Backgrounds" 145. Now in the National Gallery of Washington, D.C., *The Mill* has been cleaned since Turner described it, and its forms may not have been so clear in his time as they are in ours. Many details in it which Constable says are "lost" in shade are in fact definitely visible. Constable himself often observed that masterpieces had been dirtied and discolored by time (*JCD* 86).

and color, which efface or transform everything they touch. Above the blue block of the hill in the middle distance—the darkest spot in the picture—can be seen the yellow light of the sun, and below the hill in the lake can be seen the sun's reflected beams. The predominantly yellow light on the lake distinguishes it from the pale brown banks on either side of it, from the predominantly pale blue shore behind it, and from the still paler sky above it. Yet nothing here is decisively outlined; we are reminded of Wordsworth's dictum that in nature itself, "every thing is distinct, yet nothing defined into absolute independent singleness" (*PrW* 3: 77). Turner removes all definite outlines and a good many details in order to show how atmosphere transforms the natural world. Where he once represented cows, he now represents what light and mist do to a cow, which occupies the foreground precisely so that its attenuated form may signify—in Hazlitt's words—the medium through which it is seen.

To set the late *Norham Castle* beside Turner's analysis of Rembrandt's *Mill* is to realize that in his own work, Turner translates the all-enveloping shadow of Rembrandt into an all-enveloping light. Martin Meisel has recently argued that Turner's work embodies the antithesis of the "material sublime" displayed in the spectacularly infernal canvases of John Martin. "In Turner of the apocalyptic imagination," says Meisel, ". . . the sublime [is] the affective dissolution of material forms in light" (Kroeber and Walling 231, 214). We can find such dissolution not only in the great mythological and apocalyptic works of Turner's last decades, but even in some of his earlier domestic scenes. In *Mortlake Terrace: Early Summer Morning* (plate 28), exhibited 1826, a wall running diagonally across the picture divides the solidity of the terrace from the ethereal world beyond it, where the light of the river so closely resembles the light of the sky that the boats on the river and the buildings ranged along it seem to be floating in space. In his second treatment of this subject, *Mortlake Terrace . . . Summer's Evening* (plate 29), exhibited 1826, the light that envelops all forms on the far side of the wall partially consumes the wall itself, the very edge of the solid world. In the center of the picture, the yellow beam cast by the setting sun stretches across the river and burns its way right through the wall to the terrace in the foreground. Not even Turner's apocalyptic works reveal more strikingly than this one the irresistibly consuming power of light.

Turner's response to Rembrandt's *Mill*, then, tells us at least as much about Turner himself as it does about Rembrandt. When he speaks of Rembrandt's atmosphere as a magnificent veil thrown over mean and "objectionable" forms, he ignores or suppresses the truth about Rembrandt's draftsmanship. The mill is in fact finely drawn, and the striking effect of its sunlit sails is due almost as much to their decisive lines as to their "matchless colour." Dirt may have obscured those lines in Turner's time, or Turner may simply have chosen to take them for granted. Either way, his worship of Rembrandt's atmosphere at the expense of Rembrandt's forms is an act of self-revelation: it simply tells us what mattered most to him. Taking for granted his knowledge of what things are, he spent most of his life in studying the way they appear and in learning to represent their appearance by the language of transformation. His tendency to emphasize or even overemphasize the power of that language is one of the many things that allies him with the romantic poets.

ROMANTIC TRANSFORMATION: THE VISION OF HAZLITT

This alliance becomes even clearer when we consider the terms in which one of Turner's most discerning contemporaries regarded Wordsworth and Turner. I refer to Hazlitt, who stopped short of directly comparing the two but who plainly saw what they had in common when he described the transforming powers displayed in their respective works. More than anyone else in this period, Hazlitt helps us to see what connects a major romantic poet and a major romantic painter.

It is first of all worth noting that Hazlitt greatly admired Rembrandt, Turner's idol, and that he praised him for precisely the qualities that won the admiration of both Turner and Constable. Rembrandt, said Hazlitt, "did not contrive a new story or character, but we nearly owe to him a fifth part of painting, the knowledge of chiaroscuro—a distinct power and element in art and nature" (8: 43). Sometimes Hazlitt saw this element as a separate entity, hanging like a veil between the spectator and the objects in the picture. In Rembrandt's *Salutation of Elizabeth*, he says, "the figures come out straggling, disjointed, quaint, ugly as in a dream, but partake of the mysterious significance of praeternatural communication, and are seen through the visible gloom, or through the dimmer night of antiquity. Light and shade, not form or feeling, were the elements of which Rembrandt composed the finest poetry, and his imagination brooded only over the medium through which we discern objects, leaving the objects themselves uninspired, unhallowed, and untouched" (10: 50). The disjunctions here are curious; Hazlitt sees poetry without feeling, brilliance of atmosphere with "untouched" ugliness of form. But for Hazlitt, as for Turner and Constable, chiaroscuro is Rembrandt's poetic language, and however ugly the figures remain, Hazlitt sees them through the same veil of mystery that Turner eloquently described.

Given his fascination with Rembrandt's chiaroscuro, Hazlitt's response to Turner himself is possibly more remarkable than anything else in his art criticism. Hazlitt's best-known comment on Turner is an observation that he coyly attributes to an anonymous "someone": that Turner's landscapes are *"pictures of nothing and very like"* (4: 76n). Yet the full context of this seemingly derisive remark indicates that Hazlitt was the first to explain what others had merely glimpsed in Turner's work.[25]

Hazlitt admired the exercise of power in the paintings of Rembrandt, the language of light, shade, and atmosphere transforming ugly figures. He was therefore bound to recognize the power of Turner's language, and it is precisely this power that concerns him. In 1814 and 1815, in his reviews of the annual exhibitions at the British Institution, he spoke of it briefly; in 1816, writing on artists who were too pedantic or esoteric, he spoke of it at length. "We here allude," he wrote, "particularly to Turner, the ablest landscape-painter now living, whose pictures are however too much abstractions of aerial perspective, and representations not properly of the objects of nature as of the medium through which they were seen. They are the triumph of the knowledge of the artist and of the power of the pencil [i.e., the paintbrush] over the barrenness of the subject. . . All is without form and void. Someone said of his landscapes that they were *pictures of nothing and very like*."[26]

25. Some of these glimpses were noted by Farington at the Royal Academy exhibition of 1803, which included Turner's *Calais Pier*, *Festival at Macon*, and *Holy Family*: "Opie" Farington records, "thought [*Macon*] very fine, perhaps the finest work in the room—that is in which the Artist had obtained most of what he aimed at. Fuseli commended both 'the Calais Harbour' and the large Landscape, thinking they shewed great power of mind, but perhaps the foregrounds too little attended to,—too undefined.—His Historical Picture 'A Holy Family' He also thought appeared like the embrio, or blot of a great Master of colouring" (FDT 9: 2241).

26. Hazlitt 4: 76n. For Hazlitt's earlier references to Turner, see XVIII, 14, 93. Hazlitt had a habit of plagiarizing from himself, and the earlier comments are incorporated almost verbatim into the later one. The strange thing about the comment of 1816 is that while it aptly describes the effect created by much of Turner's later work, it hardly describes what he had exhibited up to or in the year 1816. The two pictures he exhibited that year—*The Temple of Jupiter Panhellius Restored* (now lost), and *View of the Temple of Jupiter Panellenius with the Greek National Dance of the Romaika*—are both classical landscapes rendered with an almost Claudian clarity in the fore and middle grounds; only the outlines of the distant mountains and the temple are represented as notably softened by distance and intervening light. Still more curious is that in a review of the 1816

It is crucial to see the final remark in the full context of Hazlitt's note. The context takes it beyond the spitefulness that undoubtedly first prompted it, just as Hazlitt's admiration for the power of a painter's language turns a complaint about an esoteric artist into an extraordinary tribute to—he is forced to say—"the ablest landscape-painter now living." Reading the italicized words, we may feel their spitefulness at first; but then we may remember Constable, who said that the business of a landscape painter was "to make something out of nothing, in attempting which, he must almost of necessity become poetical" (Leslie 124). Hazlitt is saying something very similar. When he complains of Turner's preoccupation with atmosphere at the expense of object, when he grudgingly admits that the power of Turner's paintbrush triumphs over the barrenness of his subject, he is talking about the kind of vision that he himself found in great poetry. Only the year before this comment on Turner, he had written of Dante: "The immediate objects he presents to the mind, are not much in themselves;—they generally want grandeur, beauty, and order; but they become every thing by the force of the character which he impresses on them. *His mind lends its own power* to the objects which it contemplates, instead of borrowing it from them. He takes advantage even of the *nakedness and dreary vacuity of his subject*" (16: 41; italics added).

Power of mind and vacuity of subject: the elements Hazlitt sees in the paintings of Turner are essentially the elements he finds in the poetry of Dante. He could also find them in the poetry of his own time. Some eight years after the comment on Turner, he wrote: "Poetry, we grant, creates a world of its own; but it creates out of existing materials. Mr. Shelley is the maker of his own poetry—*out of nothing*" (16: 265; italics added). Hazlitt's words on Turner come back to us, along with the words of Constable. But if Hazlitt seemed to criticize Shelley and Turner for flexing their muscles in a void, he could praise Wordsworth for virtually the same reason. In 1817 Hazlitt wrote of Wordsworth: "He takes the common every-day events and objects of nature, or rather seeks those that are the most simple and *barren* of effect; but he adds to them a weight of interest from the resources of his own mind, which makes the most significant things serious and even formidable. . . . . His mind magnifies the littleness of his subject, and raises its meanness; lends it his strength,

exhibition attributed to Hazlitt, the Jupiter pictures were attacked not for their atmospheric vacuity but for the gaudiness of their coloring; see Butlin and Joll 88.

and clothes it with borrowed grandeur" (4: 120; italics added). Again, the very words recall that Hazlitt saw in Turner's pictures the triumph of power over "barrenness" of subject. Possibly Hazlitt would distinguish between littleness of subject and emptiness of subject, but "vacuity" is his word for Dante's subject above, and in 1825 he wrote of Wordsworth: "He chooses to have his subject a foil to his invention, to owe *nothing* but to himself. He gathers manna in the wilderness, he strikes the *barren* rock for the gushing moisture. He elevates the mean by the strength of his own aspirations" (11: 88; italics added).

With the very words he used to criticize Turner and Shelley, Hazlitt praises Wordsworth. In fact, virtually everything in Hazlitt's comment on Turner makes Turner "poetic" and therefore admirable by Hazlitt's own standards. Turner, he said, put too much atmosphere in his pictures, which represented not the objects of nature but rather "the medium through which they were seen." Yet in concentrating on this medium, Turner was simply isolating—or abstracting, to use Hazlitt's highly significant term—an element that Hazlitt considered essential to both painting and poetry. Speaking of both with the one word "art," he wrote: "The more ethereal, evanescent, more refined and sublime part of art is the seeing nature through the medium of sentiment and passion."[27] This was the very ground on which Hazlitt compared Wordsworth and Rembrandt. "Wordsworth . . . like Rembrandt," he wrote, "has a faculty of making something out of nothing, that is, out of himself, by the medium through which he sees and with which he clothes the barrenest subject."[28]

Hazlitt was fond of comparing Wordsworth to Rembrandt, and in his report of a conversation with the poet, Hazlitt tells us that Wordsworth once

27. 8: 82–83. Elsewhere, citing examples from both poetry and painting, Hazlitt defines *gusto* as "power or passion defining any object" (4: 77). See too 8: 82: "Nature is also a language. Objects, like words, have a meaning; and the true artist [poet or painter] is the interpreter of this language. . . . The eye is too blind a guide of itself to distinguish between the warm or cold tone of a deep blue sky, but mother sense acts as a monitor to it, and does not err. The color of the leaves in autumn would be nothing without the feeling that accompanies it." It is worth noting that in several rough sketches dating from 1807 to 1821, Turner writes the words "Cold" or "Warm" in the sky, marking clouds "Wrm. Yellow" and a river "Warm Blue." See TSB CI, f. 10; CXXVII, f. 32; CXCIX, f. 90ᵛ.

28. 8:43–44. Hazlitt also wrote of Wordsworth: "His poems bear a distinct resemblance to some of Rembrandt's landscapes, who, more than any other painter, created the medium through which he saw nature, and out of the stump of an old tree, a break in the sky, and a bit of water, could produce an effect almost miraculous" (4: 120–21).

made such a comparison himself. "His eye," wrote Hazlitt, ". . . does justice to Rembrandt's fine and masterly effects. In the way in which that artist works something out of nothing, and transforms the stump of a tree, a common figure into an *ideal* object, by the gorgeous light and shade thrown upon it, he perceives an analogy to his own mode of investing the minute details of nature with an atmosphere of sentiment (11: 93). Wordsworth's observation comes to us through the medium of Hazlitt's prose, and it is hard to tell just how much the medium affects the message. Published in 1825, Hazlitt's report includes phrases that he himself had used much earlier. But the conversation with Wordsworth is not dated; he had known Wordsworth personally since 1798; and as early as 1808, in a letter to Beaumont, Wordsworth had mentioned his own "*wonder*" at Rembrandt and his "*high* pleasure" at the management of light in a picture that must be *The Woman Taken in Adultery* (*LW* 2: 208). Indeed, whatever Hazlitt's influence on his perception, it is clear enough that Wordsworth did perceive a resemblance between the chiaroscuro of Rembrandt's painting and the atmospheric effects of his own poetry.

It is hazardous to infer too much from these statements about Rembrandt: to conclude that when they compare Wordsworth to a painter who profoundly impressed both Turner and Constable, Hazlitt and Wordsworth himself implicitly forge a link between the poetry and the landscape painting of their own time. But Hazlitt leads us toward this inference when he defines Rembrandt as an essentially "romantic" painter. The definition appears in an essay of 1817, and it is important to realize that only the year before, Hazlitt had analyzed in print Friedrich Schlegel's distinction between classic and romantic—the same distinction that Coleridge seems to have appropriated as his own. Schlegel, wrote Hazlitt, distinguishes "between the peculiar spirit of the modern or romantic style of art, and the antique or *classical.*" Classic art normally "describes things as they are in themselves" while romantic art describes them "for the sake of the association of ideas connected with them. . . . The one is the poetry of form, the other of effect. . . . . The one seeks to identify the imitation with an external object,—clings to it,—is inseparable from it,—is either that or nothing; the other seeks to identify the original impression with whatever else, within the range of thought or feeling, can strengthen, relieve, adorn or elevate it." The word "art" in this distinction is comprehensive. On the one hand, the poetry of the

Greeks "is exactly what their sculptors might have written. Both are exquisite imitations of nature." On the other hand, the poetry of the "moderns . . . more nearly resembles painting,—where the artist can relieve and throw back his figures at pleasure,—use a greater variety of contrasts,—and where light and shade, like the colours of fancy, are reflected on the different objects. . . . The Muse of classical poetry . . . has the advantage in point of form; [the Muse of modern poetry] in colour and motion" (Hazlitt 16: 60–64).

The word "moderns" here is as slippery and relative as always. Chronologically, it may mean anyone who came after the Renaissance, which takes its name, of course, from the rebirth of classicism in poetry and the arts. But for Hazlitt, the romantic style in painting was epitomized by Rembrandt—the artist whom Constable revered and in whose pictures Turner found the mirror of his own ambitions: forms dissolving in color and chiaroscuro, common objects veiled with "Morning dawn and dewy light." In 1817, the year after he had carefully explained Schlegel's distinction between classic and romantic, Hazlitt wrote of Rembrandt:

> If ever there was a man of genius in art, it was Rembrandt. He might be said to have created a medium of his own, through which he saw all objects. . . . He took any object, he cared not what, how mean soever in form, colour, and expression, and from the light and shade which he threw upon it, it came out gorgeous from his hands. . . . In surrounding different objects with a medium of imagination, solemn or dazzling, he was a true poet. . . . His landscapes we could look at forever, though there is nothing in them. . . . *Rembrandt is the least classical and the most romantic of all painters.* (18: 122–23)

How far can this impassioned account of transformation in a quintessentially "romantic" painter who is also a "true poet" be used to define the whole process of transformation in English romantic poetry and painting? We do well to be skeptical here—even of what is said about Rembrandt himself. Like Turner, Hazlitt exaggerates the gap between form and atmosphere in Rembrandt's work. It is simply not true that Rembrandt's landscapes have "nothing" in them, that they owe everything to chiaroscuro and nothing at all to form, color, or expression. Nor is it true, as Hazlitt seems to imply, that Rembrandtian chiaroscuro is the key to the workings of the romantic imagination in poetry and painting alike. Even if we stay within the world of painting, we must recognize the difference between the rich and textured shadows of Constable's work and the airy radiance of Turner's, which in 1834 was described as "almost dim through an excess of brightness."[29] When we then move to the poets, we must recognize that "accidents of light and shade" constitute not so much an object of poetic imitation as a symbol of what Wordsworth and Coleridge sought to do with ordinary human experience, "the truth of nature." In Coleridge's "Rime," moonlight transforms the water snakes, but just as importantly, the intervention of angelic and demonic spirits transforms a recognizably "natural" story of crime, suffering, and repentance.

Hazlitt's comments on Rembrandt, therefore, cannot by themselves synthesize romantic poetry and romantic painting. What they can do is help us to see that the transformations wrought by atmosphere in the natural world provided poets and painters alike with a model for the transformations they sought to achieve in their respective arts. To re-create landscape, they saw, was to imitate the effect of atmosphere upon it, to represent the known and familiar world through the medium of what Wordsworth called the "transparent veil" of words and what Turner called the "veil of colour." Poets and painters alike perceived that an essential part of the world spread out before them was the medium through which it was seen—whether visual, emotional, or both. What distinguished the poems in *Lyrical Ballads*, said Wordsworth, was that "feeling therein developed gives importance to the action and situation and not the action and situation to the feeling" (*PrW* 1: 128). Turner and Constable put a corresponding emphasis on their own language of feeling—on the color and chiaroscuro which were powerful enough, they thought, to make any subject extraordinary and impressive. If neither they nor the poets could literally make something out of nothing, they nonetheless showed what the language of transformation could do in their respective arts.

29. *Athenaeum*, 10 May 1834, quoted by Meisel in Kroeber and Walling 231n. The critic was describing *The Golden Bough*, exhibited 1834.

CHAPTER 5

THE GEOMETRY OF
THE INFINITE

 THE MOST COMMON way of connecting English romantic poetry and painting is to describe them both—in Wölfflin's terms—as *malerisch* or painterly rather than linear. Much of what I have said in the previous chapter points in this direction, and it is not hard to find further evidence that with the conspicuous exception of Blake, romantic poets and painters alike suppressed linearity for the sake of color, chiaroscuro, and atmospheric suggestion. I have quoted Coleridge's observation that lines belong to law and reason, and colors "to the lively, the free, the spontaneous, and the self-justifying" (*BL* 2: 251). Statements like these invite us to link the spontaneity of romantic poetry with the atmospheric fluidity of romantic art. In "Tintern Abbey," for instance, Wordsworth abandons the end-stopped couplet of his early work for a blank verse in which the lines are frequently enjambed: for a form, that is, which fittingly expresses the unchecked overflow of powerful feeling. Correspondingly, in a watercolor such as *Old London Bridge* (plate 19), painted shortly before the first appearance of "Tintern Abbey," Turner uses light and color with a freedom unconstrained by the predrawn outlines of conventional topography. A tempting way of illustrating the romantic attitude toward linearity, therefore, is to quote what Turner is long supposed to have said about the atmospheric fluidity of his own work: "Indistinctness is my forte."[1]

Awkwardly enough, however, what Turner actually said was "fault" (Holcomb 557–58). To weigh the implications of that small correction is to begin to see the inadequacy of a formula that would reduce the En-

---

1. Gowing 31. Alternatively, one could cite Delacroix's description of a beautiful landscape: "The lark sings, the river sparkles with a thousand diamonds, the foliage murmurs; where are any lines to produce these charming sensations?" (quoted in Mitchell, "Style as Epistemology" 154). This illustrates what Eaves calls "the simplest form of the romantic revolt against academic classicism" (17).

glish romantic vision of landscape to a revolution of atmosphere against line, and specifically against the "firm and determined outline" recommended by Joshua Reynolds, who said that painters should know and precisely express "the exact form which every part of nature ought to have" (*D* 52). The apparently simple antithesis between Augustan form and romantic atmosphere gets complicated as soon as we look at it closely. If Reynolds thought a firm outline indispensable to the portrayal of the human figure, he also thought that "no correctness of form is required" in the rendering of things such as clouds (*D* 223). Only in the romantic period—and specifically in the work of Constable—do we find systematic studies of cloud formations.

Constable's interest in the shapes of clouds is just one manifestation of the way in which a consciousness of line decisively informs the English romantic vision of landscape. Students of Blake have long recognized that his figurally based art is conspicuously linear. What I wish to argue here is that the romantic vision of landscape has a linearity of its own, that romantic poets and painters studied the lines of landscape just as carefully as they studied its atmospheric effects. In fact, precisely because they wished to capture the ever-changing life of a landscape in motion, they had to know more about form than their Augustan predecessors did—not less. To represent the indeterminacy of landscape, and at the same time to externalize their own consciousness of infinity, they had to measure what they felt to be measureless.[2] In essence, they had to formulate a geometry of the infinite.

CROSSING THE LINE

The geometry of the infinite begins on the boundaries of the finite. Wordsworth defined the experience of sublimity as a consciousness of "immeasurable" power, and the kind of poetry that moved him most, he said once, was the poetry of "infinity . . . where things are lost in each other, and limits vanish" (*LY* 1: 134–35). Yet Wordsworth knew only too well that in order to express this feeling of limitlessness, the poet had

2. The word *indeterminacy* requires a comment. In modern physics, the indeterminacy principle—also called the uncertainty principle—states that because the wavelike behavior of particles resists precise definition, "the position and velocity of an object cannot both be measured exactly, at the same time, even in theory" (*Encyclopaedia Britannica*, 15th ed.). In this chapter, I use *indeterminacy* to mean the effect created when an outline is described or depicted as suppressed, broken, or crossed, or when the identity of a particular object or shape is not categorically determinable.

to establish—implicitly or explicitly—the limits he was crossing. In book 1 of *The Prelude*, he tells us that a huge cliff seemed to rise up over him one evening as he rowed a stolen boat across a lake. Towering between him and the stars, the cliff appears to cross the line between earth and sky, animate and inanimate, nature and supernature. The line is crossed, however, only after it has been decisively drawn. Before the cliff emerges at all, the boy has "fix'd" his gaze upon an object equally fixed: the summit of a ridge, which forms "the bound of the horizon." With a painter's sense of spatial definition, Wordsworth thus establishes the most important line in his landscape, and at the very moment when the cliff emerges, we are made to see this line again:

> from behind that craggy Steep, till then
> The bound of the horizon, a huge Cliff,
> As if with voluntary power instinct,
> Uprear'd its head.

(A 1. 405–8)

Till then / The bound of the horizon: the sublime sense of awe and terror communicated by the passage as a whole begins at this moment, when the line that had *till then* been the horizon is crossed, and the new horizon, no longer fixed, rises upward to infinity.[3]

Wordsworth's vision of an uncontrollably rising horizon is paradigmatically romantic. Tolerating neither absolute limit nor absolute division, the romantic poets and painters characteristically tend to unbind or dissolve the most fundamental line in the landscape. Their horizons ascend toward the limitless height of the sky or into the limitless obscurity of its atmosphere. In Wordsworth's description of the Simplon Pass, the height of the decaying woods is "immeasurable" and the torrents seem to shoot down "from the clear blue sky" (*Prelude* 6. 556, 561). On a walking tour of Scotland in 1803, Coleridge saw a waterfall whose summit "appeared to blend with the sky and clouds," and as he later reported, he considered it "in the strictest sense of the word, a sublime object" (*BL* 2: 224–25, 308). This is the kind of sublimity we find not only in the immeasurable height of Alpine woods and torrents or the virtually invisible summit of a Scottish waterfall, but also in the mountaintops of

---

3. Weiskel says that "the determinate horizon is shattered" (101), but that is not quite correct; what actually happens is that a fixed horizon is supplanted by an ascending one. For further commentary on Wordsworth's use of the boundary in this passage, see Arac 34–37.

Turner's *Buttermere* (plate 1), which likewise seem to blend with the clouds that rest upon them. And there are comparable effects in the watercolors of Borrowdale which Constable made in 1806. In particular, the delicately misted mountains of his *View in Borrowdale* perfectly depict an effect that Coleridge described in his notebook three years earlier. "Mountain Forms in the Gorge of Borrodale," he wrote, "consubstantiate with . . . mist & cloud" (*NC* 1: 1603).

For the romantic poets and painters, then, sublimity is a consciousness of *boundaries crossed*. But both words must be italicized. Without consciousness of a boundary, there is no consciousness of crossing, transcendence, or infinity.[4] In Wordsworth's description of the shepherd that he sometimes saw at a distance when he was a boy, the shepherd becomes sublime precisely by crossing a boundary that is—once again—explicitly named:

> as he stepped
> Beyond the boundary line of some hill-shadow,
> His form hath flashed upon me, glorified
> By the deep radiance of the setting sun:
> Or him I have descried in distant sky,
> A solitary object and sublime,
> Above all height! like an aerial cross
> Stationed alone upon a spiry rock
> Of the Chartreuse, for worship.
>
> (*Prelude* 8. 267–75)

Whether emerging from darkness into light or jutting up over the horizon like a cliff of book 1, "above all height," the shepherd becomes a figure of sublime and striking majesty at the moment he crosses a definite line. Without such a line, his appearance "in distant sky" would be merely apparitional.

Yet if all lines seem to fade when the horizon is crossed, it is revealing to find that the romantic poets could see even the boundless immensity of the sky through the framework of a bounded form. Here is Coleridge describing the sky over Malta in 1804:

O that Sky, that soft blue mighty Arch, resting on the mountains or solid Sea-like plain / what an aweful adorable omneity in unity. I know no other perfect

---

4. Paulson aptly notes that Constable's pictures convey a strong sense of boundaries: "a concern for establishing exactly where a property, hill or field ends and another be-

union of the sublime with the beautiful, that is, so that they should both be felt at the same moment tho' by different faculties yet each faculty predisposed by itself to receive the specific modification from the other. To the eye it is an inverted Goblet, the inside of a sapphire Bason; = it is immensity, but even the eye feels as it were to look *thro'* with dim sense of the non resistance / it is not exactly the feeling given to the organ by solid & limited things / the eye itself feels that the limitation is in its own power not in the Object. (*NC* 2: 2346)

Like the vault of paved heaven to which the singer of Blake's "Mad Song" drives his desperate notes, the sky first seems a finite hemispherical enclosure: an arch, an inverted goblet, or an inverted basin. When the doors of perception are cleansed, when the eye of the mind makes the eye of the body see beyond the limits of its purely physical powers, the dome of the universe unresistingly dissolves, and the sky becomes a thing of limitless immensity. But Coleridge does not take the Blakean leap from one kind of perception to the other.[5] Even though his eye may feel that it is gazing on infinity, it continues also to feel the sense of enclosure, for the sky gives him "at the same moment," he says, the beauty of the infinite and the sublimity of the infinite. What Coleridge reveals to us here is that for him, the experience of limitlessness presupposes the consciousness of limit.

He had touched on this paradox two years earlier in "Hymn Before Sunrise," where the night sky is first envisioned as a "substantial" mass of blackness which "thou [Mont Blanc] piercest," and then as the mountain's enclosure: "thy crystal shrine, / Thy habitation from eternity!" (lines 9–12). In Shelley's "Mont Blanc" of 1816, which echoes the *Hymn*, the peak once again "pierc[es] the infinite sky" (line 60), but this time the sky is both explicitly infinite and finite enough to *be* pierced. Shelley's consciousness of finite form in this poem continually participates in

---

gins" (*Literary Landscape*, 114). But as I tried to show in chapter 2 (p. 75), a picture such as *The Leaping Horse* depicts the very moment at which a boundary is crossed.

5. I speak of the leap to infinity as Blakean even though Blake regarded linearity as "the great and golden rule" of life and art; "the more distinct, sharp, and wiry the bounding line," he wrote, "the more perfect the work of art" (*PPB* 540). It is not easy to reconcile this statement with Blake's contempt for precise quantification ("Bring out number weight & Measure in a year of dearth" [*PPB* 35]) and his sublime vision of boundlessness, as in *The Marriage of Heaven and Hell* ("If the doors of perception were cleansed everything would appear to man as it is, infinite" [*PPB* 39]). Eaves's solution is that Blake's "line" is not restricted to literally signifying geometrical entities but is rather a metaphor for the "autographic component in art," or the uncompromising expression of Blake's artistic self. For Blake, says Eaves, "true clarity lies in a vision of life that includes its dark and obscure parts" (41–42).

his vision of infinitude. In section 4, the river of ice that flows from the peak of the mountain descends from "the boundaries of the sky"; in the final section, the sky is oxymoronically called "the infinite dome / Of Heaven" (140–41). Like Coleridge at Malta, Shelley sees the limitlessness of the sky through the limits of a determinate form.

The structures with which Coleridge and Shelley organized the empty skies of the Mediterranean and the Alps were grander, perhaps, but no more complicated than the structures with which Turner and Constable organized and represented the cloud-filled skies of their native land. For Constable in particular, the sky was anything but formless. He could hardly agree with Joshua Reynolds's comment on the formlessness of clouds, and still less could he concur with those who—as he wrote to Fisher—often advised him to consider his sky as "*'a white sheet thrown behind the objects'*" (*JCC* 6: 76–77). Against this view of the sky as an amorphous tabula rasa, a neutral backdrop for the things of the earth, Constable set his own belief in its importance—as well as in the structures of its clouds. Skies, he went on to Fisher, "must and always shall with me make an effectual part of the composition. It will be difficult to name a class of Landscape, in which the sky is not the '*key note,*' the *standard of 'Scale,*' and the chief '*Organ of sentiment.*' You may conceive then what a '*white sheet*' would do for me, impressed as I am with these notions, and they cannot be Erroneous. The sky is the '*source of light*' in nature—and governs every thing" (*JCC* 6: 77).

Constable made this point in 1821. Some ten years earlier, in the bright and vigorous clouds of *Flatford Mill from a Lock on The Stour*, he had already begun to illustrate it. But it was nearer 1821 when he actually began to delineate atmosphere, to represent at once the shape and the fluidity of clouds. In the sky of *A Cottage and Road at East Bergholt* (plate 30), a pencil sketch of about 1817, line informs the very atmosphere that threatens to dissolve it. The shadowy roll of the clouds contrasts with the crisp horizontal edge of the field and the decisive line of the hedge at the bottom of the picture. But the line of the hedge moves diagonally upward to the right, and thus invites us to see a corresponding line in the clouds, which—like the long handle of the reaper's scythe below them—move diagonally downward to the right. Nowhere does the roll of clouds reveal a line. Constable simply implies one by darkening the underedge of the roll, and at right, where the whole sky is darker than it is at left, the underedge grows darker still, approximating but never actually forming a descending line. The explicit line of the hedge and the implicit line of the darkening cloud thus converge toward a point beyond the lower right edge of the picture: the point toward which the hunched and lonely reaper at lower right is walking. With the dark blade and handle of his scythe closing to a point behind him, and the hedge leading up to a darkened point before him, the figure seems caught in a subtle but inexorably contracting diamond of darkness.

About 1821, a few years after this sketch was made, Constable embarked on a series of specialized cloud studies. Possibly prompted by the systematic study of cloud formations in Luke Howard's *Climate of London* (1818–20), the clouds in these studies are decidedly more linear than most of those he had produced before.[6] Paradoxically, however, their outlines help to express the uncontrollable energy of the atmosphere. An oil study of about 1822, for instance, depicts a group of cirrus clouds (plate 31), but in spite of the tight little circles that partially define these clouds, none of them is wholly circumscribed or self-contained. They seem rather to be extensions or explosions of the windstream rushing across the picture and sweeping upward to the right. Defined by outlines but not confined to them, their power springs at once from their distinctive shape and from the stream that sweeps away part of their borders.

A few years before Constable produced his series of cloud studies, Turner produced seventy-nine cloud studies of his own. The striking thing about the sketchbook containing these studies (TSB CLVIII) is that its first few pages include land as well as sky. The horizon starts about one-third up from the bottom of the page, then gradually drops until it disappears from sight, leaving the sky as sole object of Turner's concentration. Turner's studies thus naturally invite comparison with those of Constable. Jack Lindsay argues that the two are different, that Constable focuses on weather while Turner concentrates on "the structure of movement, of complex but unified light sweep" (157). Yet Turner's clouds do resemble Constable's in their combination of structure and fluidity. His skies range from the tranquillity of f. 15, in which wispy streaks of blue form a rough ellipse, to the violence of f. 24 (plate 32), in which storm clouds rush to collision. The stormy sky of the latter sketch has a

6. Though Howard's book may have influenced Constable (see Badt), Louis Hawes has questioned the extent of Constable's dependence on Howard's classifications. Showing that Constable studied clouds directly before the early 1820s and that he knew other treatises on clouds, such as those of De Piles and Gilpin, Hawes finds no evidence that Howard's influence on Constable was "decisive" (344–64).

dark torpedo of blue and gray streaking toward a rectangular cave of white, and the shape of the rectangle is intensified by the knuckles of black and blue along its top. In both pictures, however, Turner uses the technique of the wash to soften or dissolve the outlines of the clouds he depicts. In the tranquil sky, the streaks of blue tend to pale into white; in the stormy sky, the small patch of white is almost engulfed by the streaks of blue and gray. Diagonals run from all corners of the picture toward its center, but they nowhere assume a linear distinctness. In f. 32 (plate 33), Turner uses another diagonal to define the edge of a cloud, but once again, like the shadowy roll in Constable's *Cottage and Road*, the edge is nonlinear. Purple-black with rain and accented by several heavy blots at left, the dark, slanting front of the cloud merges imperceptibly with the lighter part just above it, which is largely done in short pale streaks parallel to the front itself. Beneath this right-to-left slanting front, where the graduation to lighter tone is even subtler, rain slants down from left to right, so that continuity in tone is balanced by contrast in line. Manifesting its structure and yet free of "relentless outline," Turner's cloud embodies the very shape of fluidity.

This combination of structure and fluidity is characteristic of the way Turner saw and represented the natural world. In his third lecture, he staunchly advocated the value of perspective and "the principles of *Lines*."[7] Yet he went on to say in the same lecture that lines were powerless to represent certain effects, that linear perspective had sometimes to be supplanted by "Aerial Perspective," which involved "the aid of shadow, reduced light, and weaker tones of color" (TMS M, f. 22–24). In aerial perspective, lines become zones of gradation, and by these zones, Turner defines what is indefinable by outline.

Consider a painting from his last and most "atmospheric" decade— *Yacht Approaching the Coast* (plate 34), painted ca. 1840–45. In this picture, the setting sun fills the center of the sky with a distinguishable cone of soft white light. As Lawrence Gowing has shown, pictures like this one actually defy the principle of "picturesque" asymmetry, the doctrine that light "should never be placed so as to form a line" (27). Yet it is hardly possible to trace the outline of the cone in Turner's sky. We can apprehend the cone, but we cannot see precisely where it begins and

7. TMS M, f. 22. In his first lecture, Turner says that without "the Geometrical laws of perspective," art "totters at its very foundation" (TMS K, f. 1–6). See also Ziff, "Backgrounds" 127.

ends. Its borders are intangibly aerial, and even as we study its shape, its outline seems to dissolve beneath our eyes.

Correspondingly, the horizon in this picture is at once established and elusive. The left and right sides of the sea in the foreground are decisively darker than the sky, and the short row of buildings in the background at left begins to mark the line between the two elements. But across the rest of the picture no line can be seen. Turning pale in the distance, the sea dissolves into the still paler sky, and the continuity between them is enhanced by the setting sun, which fills the middle of each with corresponding cones of light. Nevertheless, the hourglass of light thus formed is bisected by the implied horizon, and the pale green wave-textured light of the cone in the sea subtly distinguishes it from the whiter, aerial light of the cone in the sky. The very thing that enhances the continuity between the sea and the sky thus helps also to differentiate them, to reinforce the implied horizon, and to create a series of triangles radiating from the center of the picture. The triangles are not outlined, but they are unmistakably there, for the geometrical structure of this picture is as powerful as it is indeterminate.

Significantly, the yacht in this picture seems to be floating in the air as well as on the water. Neither bound to visible masts nor visibly attached to the speckled red blot of a hull beneath them, its crisply defined sails are three white crescents hovering in space—a piece of visual synecdoche. They call to mind the fleet of ships to which Milton compares the flying Satan in *Paradise Lost*: the fleet which, seen from a distance, "Hangs in the clouds" (lines 636–37). Because it thus transcends the horizontal boundary between the sea and sky, Wordsworth found this Miltonic fleet sublime. Its "track, we know and feel, is upon the waters," he wrote, "but, taking advantage of its appearance to the senses, the Poet dares to represent it as *hanging in the clouds*, both for the gratification of the mind in contemplating the image itself, and in reference to the motion and appearance of the sublime object to which it is compared" (*PrW* 3: 31). Wordsworth's comment might well apply to Turner's picture. Like Milton's fleet, Turner's yacht seems to hover in space, at once supported by water and suspended in air. It occupies that indeterminate zone in which the sea virtually *becomes* the sky.

A similar effect is represented at a crucial moment in Coleridge's "Rime." At the beginning of part 3, the spectre bark appears in the distance as "a something *in the sky*" (italics added). Successively described as a little speck, a mist, and then "a certain shape," it is indeterminate

in position as well as in form, for we cannot tell whether it is moving
through the sky or on the sea. When it is near enough to be recognized
and joyously hailed as "a sail! a sail!" (here the synecdoche is verbal), it
is definitely on the sea, cleaving the water "with upright keel." But Coleridge's description of the way the sun descends behind this mysterious
craft at once acknowledges the horizon and transcends it:

> The western wave was all a-flame.
> The day was well night done!
> Almost upon the western wave
> Rested the broad bright Sun;
> When that strange shape drove suddenly
> Betwixt us and the Sun.
>
> (Lines 171–76)

Like the yacht in Turner's picture, the spectre bark appears in the distance with the setting sun behind it. Against a sky that is almost certainly cloudless, the mariner sees the edge of the western wave, for he is
able to tell us precisely that the sun rests "almost" upon it. But he also
sees the western wave as "all a-flame," the distant sea turned into fire by
the sun's reflected light. As it drops, the setting sun burns through the
horizon, and when the spectre bark passes in front of the sun, the mariner sees no horizontal boundary between earth and sky: only the vertical
"bars" and sails of the ship glancing "in the sun." After "the Sun's rim
dips" and "the stars rush out," the horizon is implicitly reestablished,
but when Coleridge tells us that the spectre bark shoots off "o'er the
sea," he is once again describing a craft that may be moving on the sea or
above it, in the sky. Like Turner and like Milton too, Coleridge exploits
the naturally ambiguous appearance of a distant ship. And fittingly, this
ambiguous thing of sea and space makes its appearance in a world where
the horizon is at once acknowledged and transcended, where the sea and
the sky become halves of a continuous whole, where the water burns, as
relentlessly as the sky above it, and where—as the mariner says in part 4
—"the sky and the sea, and the sea and sky / Lay like a load on my
weary eye" (250–51).

Chiastically interchangeable, the sea and the sky of Coleridge's "Rime"
help to reinforce the consciousness of crossing expressed by the poem as
a whole, which takes us no less than four times across the equatorial line
as it moves from the "real" world of the wedding to the fantastic world of
spectres and spirits, from the depths of the sea to the middle and upper

air, from the visible to the invisible, from the stormy South Pole to the becalmed Pacific, from the torture of an incommunicable guilt to the relief of confession, from life to death and back again. Slain by the mariner's crossbow, or—so to speak—crucified on it, the albatross is hung about the mariner's neck "instead of the cross," but the absence of the Christian cross simply reminds us of how many different kinds of crossing are represented in the poem.

Almost equally rich in significant crossing is another great seascape from Turner's last decade: *Slavers Throwing Overboard the Dead and Dying—Typhoon Coming On* (plate 35). Two things about this picture have long been recognized. One is that it evidences Turner's support for a campaign that had already halted British involvement in the slave trade by 1840, when the picture was first exhibited, and that now sought to make the British navy drive all slave ships—of whatever nationality—from international waters.[8] The other is the point first made by Ruskin: that the predominantly crimson and scarlet hues of the picture express a judgment on the guilty vessel, whose "thin masts [are] written upon the sky in lines of blood, [and] girded with condemnation in that fearful hue which signs the sky with horror" (*Works* 3: 572; Landow, *Theories* 438–39). Yet at least as conspicuous as the political theme and the bloody signature is the absence of something we would surely expect to find in any picture of an impending storm painted in Turner's last decade: a vortex. In Thomson's "Summer," commonly thought to be Turner's chief literary source, the storm that sinks the slave ship is explicitly vortical: a "circling typhon, whirled from point to point, / Exhausting all the rage of the sky" ("Summer," lines 984–85). Yet it is precisely this vortical form that Turner resists. What he gives us instead is a burning cross.

The center of the cross coincides with the center of the picture, where the western wave has been set afire by the setting sun. In the lower corners, the jettisoned slaves are being consumed by ravenous fish, the "direful shark[s]" of Thomson's poem (line 1015). But the picture draws our eyes to the burning horizon, which is part of a geometry even more subtle than that of *Yacht Approaching*. Like the spectre bark riding across the horizon in Coleridge's "Rime," the bare-masted slave ship cuts a

---

8. Professor George Landow kindly informs me that this point was first set forth by John McCoubrey in a lecture delivered at the Frick Museum and elsewhere about 1968. On the link between *Slavers* and British involvement in slave trading, see also Lindsay 189, and Butlin and Joll 215.

horizontal line across the middle of the picture. This line is broken by the vertical thrust of the white sunbeam just above it, and the implicit cross thus formed in the center of the picture is reinforced by the explicit crossing of mast and yardarms at left. But the mast is tilted by the swell of the sea, the hull of the ship is engulfed by spray, and where the vertical and horizontal lines of the picture should cross, both of them yield to a spreading inferno of yellow, orange, and red—what Turner elsewhere called the sunset colors of "Fire and Blood" (TSB CI, f. 9). With the sun shedding these hues on the air and water alike, the meeting point of sea and sky becomes at once a fiery intersection and a borderless continuum of burning brilliance. Turner reportedly said on his deathbed that "the Sun is God" (Lindsay 213). Here the sun becomes an infinitely blazing cross on which—in effect—the slaves are crucified. Once again, therefore, Turner establishes linear boundaries in order to cross them.

THE PARADOX OF GEOMETRICAL TRANSCENDENCE

The act of establishing lines in order to cross or suppress them can be seen as a dialectical strategy characteristic of the romantic imagination. What Lorenz Eitner says of political freedom applies to perceptual freedom as well: it "needs the contrast of constraint or captivity to define it and make it vividly apparent" (Kroeber and Walling 14). But a more startling paradox is that the desire to achieve transcendence by crossing boundaries coexisted with a contrary desire to discern geometrical forms in natural objects, and thus to elicit from the fleeting or fragmentary shapes of the natural world a vision of transcendent permanence: what Wordsworth called "the purest bond / Of nature, undisturbed by space or time" (*Prelude* 5. 105–6). In the borderless rainbow of *Buttermere*, Turner defies the Newtonian axiom that light is divisible into precisely definable colors. Yet the interrupted arc made by the bow and its reflection in this picture unmistakably suggest the timeless perfection of the circle.

Wordsworth himself found this perfection suggested by a rainbow he describes in one version of the concluding book of *The Prelude*. Explaining how its seemingly indestructible shape arched over a tunnel-like valley in the midst of a raging storm, he writes:

> A large unmutilate[d] rainbow stood
> Immoveable in heav'n, kept standing there

With a colossal stride bridging the vale,
The substance thin as dreams, lovelier than day,—
Amid the deafening uproar stood unmov'd,
Sustain'd itself through many minutes space;
As if it were pinn'd down by adamant.
                    (*The Prelude*, pp. 623–24, lines 24–30)

Paradoxically, almost miraculously, the stormy violence of the vale assumes an architectural stability. The hills of Coniston form a "tunnel" (10) or inverted arch, and the arch is completed by the bridge-like rainbow, which combines a "substance thin as dreams" with the adamantine durability of circular form. In Wordsworth's lines, as in Turner's *Buttermere*, an evanescent arc of light fleetingly approximates the geometrical permanence of the perfected circle.

"Every thing material," said Turner, "is a portion of the Circle or the Square" (TMS L, f. 19). To reinforce this point and to stress the transcendent immutability of geometrical forms, he quoted a passage from Akenside's *Pleasures of the Imagination* at the end of his first Royal Academy lecture:

Peculiar in the realms of Space or Time
Such is the throne which man for truth amid
The paths of mutability hath built
Secure unshaken, still; and whence he views,
In matters mouldering structures, the pure forms
Of Triangle, or Circle, Cube, or Cone.[9]

Akenside draws on the traditional assumption that thrones and architectural structures—whether mouldering or not—can be seen as embodiments of pure geometrical forms. But when Turner quotes these lines, he is thinking not so much of architecture as of landscape, and of his own life-long struggle to elicit pure geometrical forms from an atmosphere in motion. Fascinated with mist and rainbows, he captures such evanescent things only by perpetuating the outlines that they momentarily assume or imply, by preserving the very moment at which those fleeting shapes approximate permanent geometrical figures, undisturbed by space or time.

If Turner saw portions of circles or squares in "every thing material,"

9. TMS K, f. 23. Taking some freedom with the punctuation, Turner quotes from Akenside, lines 133–38.

the notebooks of Coleridge show again and again his fascination with geometrical forms, his delight in seeing them implied or approximated by natural phenomena. He could see triangles not only in the gabled roofs of houses, but also in crags, in mountain ranges, in a pair of intersecting waterfalls, and especially in the stars. "Doesn't everyone," he asks himself in 1804, "see a triangle in looking at three stars together?"[10] Such a question perfectly illustrates what Coleridge means when he says in the *Biographia Literaria* that the primary imagination is "the prime Agent of all human Perception" (1: 202)—that in every act of perception it works creatively and constructively through the senses. Coleridge could find a geometrical pattern in virtually any object, whether fixed or moving. He could see arches in stones, in trees, and in waterfalls; he noticed circles of light spread on a river bottom by leaping trout; watching birds in flight, he saw circles, ellipses, and even squares.[11] At times, geometrical forms awed him. Writing to Wordsworth in 1815, he said that circles and triangles could excite a sense of "sublimity & even religious Wonder" (*LC* 4: 576).

But as Geoffrey Durrant has noted, Wordsworth himself acclaims the triumph of geometry in the synthesis wrought by Newton, who—as the poet saw—deployed the postulates of Euclid to explain the universe as a whole (21). Recalling in *The Prelude* his study of "geometric science" at Cambridge, Wordsworth tells us:

> With Indian awe and wonder, ignorance pleased
> With its own struggles, did I meditate
> On the relation those abstractions bear
> To Nature's laws, and by what process led,
> Those immaterial agents bowed their heads
> Duly to serve the mind of earth-born man;
> From star to star, from kindred sphere to sphere,
> From system on to system without end.[12]

For Wordsworth, the appeal of geometry lay not only in its power to conduct us to infinity—"from system on to system without end"—but also in its power to relieve us from the "welterings of passion," to exer-

---

10. Coleridge, *NC* 2: 2343. For the references made in the preceding sentence, see *NC* 1: 335, f. 3ᵛ; 1220, f. 19ᵛ; 1496, f. 69; 1477, f. 39; 1899, f. 92ᵛ.

11. *NC* 1: 753; 1220; 582; 1589, f. 56ᵛ; 1851, f. 72ᵛ.

12. *Prelude* 6. 121–28. See also his description of the young Wanderer in *The Excursion:*

cise the reason in a realm set far above "the disturbances of space and time."[13] Yet it is just here that we must wonder—in an interrogative sense—about the kind of permanence Wordsworth found in geometrical forms. If geometry does indeed signify for Wordsworth a world of "dispassionate eternal relations," as Geoffrey Hartman suggests, the cost of admission to this world is the sacrifice of what Hartman finds intimately connected with Wordsworth's concept of poetry—"passionate human relations."[14] Likewise sacrificed is the sense of what might be called linear disturbance—the consciousness of line-crossing which, as I have already noted, plays such a conspicuous part in moments of what seem to be characteristically romantic sublimity. Granted that "pure" geometrical figures seem to embody immutable perfection, how can these necessarily bounded forms be made to constitute a geometry of the infinite? How can geometry be superior "to the boundaries of space and time," as Wordsworth says it is (*Prelude* 6. 135–37)? Wordsworth himself implicitly raises this question in book 2 of *The Prelude*, where he makes the analytical divisiveness of geometry symbolize everything that checks the continuity of his autobiography and threatens the very integrity of his mind. "But who," he asks, "shall parcel out / His intellect by geometric rules, / Split, like a province, into round and square?" (2. 208–10).

Setting that question beside Wordsworth's praise for the transcendent purity of geometrical forms in the later books of the *Prelude*, we can only conclude that he conceived of geometry in two fundamentally different

---

> While yet he lingered in the rudiments
> Of science, and among her simplest laws,
> His triangles—they were the stars of heaven,
> The silent stars!
>
> (1. 270–73)

13. *Prelude* 6. 129–67; 11. 321–33.
14. *Wordsworth's Poetry* 228. At times Wordsworth clearly aspires to a state beyond passionate disturbance, as when he notes how strange it is

> that all
> The terrors, pains, and early miseries,
> Regrets, vexations, lassitudes interfused
> Within my mind, should e'er have borne a
> part,
> And that a needful part, in making up
> The calm existence that is mine when I
> Am worthy of myself!
>
> (*Prelude* 1. 344–50)

But as I have tried to show above in my discussion of "Tintern Abbey" (chapter 2), Wordsworth's desire to get beyond passionate disturbance coexists with a continuing desire to *be* passionately disturbed.

ways: as an analytic science of earthbound measurement (geo-metry) that simply cuts up the terrestrial world into map-maker's segments, and as a coadunative or synthesizing science that enables us to see patterns in the universe as a whole, to link one star with another "from system on to system without end." Those words come from book 6 of *The Prelude*, as quoted above. But Wordsworth's most suggestive treatment of tran-scendent geometry actually appears in book 5, where it plays a central role in his story of the Arab he encountered in a dream.

Though the whole episode of the Arab dream has lately provoked an abundance of commentary, Theresa Kelley has recently noted that for most commentators, the stone and the shell which the Arab bears sym-bolize "the fixed opposition of science or mathematics to poetry" (564). Certainly there are grounds for this interpretation. The dream comes to Wordsworth (or to "a Friend" in the early version of the poem) just after he has been musing on the durability of "poetry and geometric truth" (line 65); the Arab himself calls the stone "Euclid's Elements"; and the shell is called "something of more worth," a prophetic god with "voices more than all the winds, with power / To exhilarate the spirit, and to soothe, / Through every clime, the heart of human kind" (106–9). The openness, delicacy, and articulate resonance of the evidently poetic shell make the stone seem closed and inflexible by comparison, the very embodiment of solid geometry.[15]

Nevertheless, the relation between geometry and poetry in the dream cannot be quite so oppositionally formulated. Lee Johnson has recently argued that in Wordsworth's account of the dream, as in much of his other poetry, he repeatedly uses the geometrical form known as the golden section: a set of unequally divided lines in which the smaller section bears to the larger the same proportion as the larger bears to the whole. Because this "continuous proportion" cannot be measured precisely by numbers, Wordsworth uses it, says Johnson, "to relate the measurable numbers of time"—the metrically numbered lines of his verse—"to the immeasurable geometry of eternity."[16] Whether or not this kind of geo-

15. "The stone," writes Jeffrey Baker, "represents solid geometry, its contours, hard-ness, and tangibility suggesting the logic and verifiable reasoning of mathematics" (72).

16. L. Johnson 12–13, 45, 85. The golden section, says Johnson, can be roughly expressed by the statement that "three is to five as five is to eight," but "the ratio cannot be represented perfectly by any numbers and therefore eludes exact measurement and reproduction in matter—a quality which would suit its transcendental symbolism in [Wordsworth's] verse" (42–43). Johnson finds a "triple golden section" in Wordsworth's

metrical organization can actually be experienced by a reader, it is clear that geometry itself emerges from the story of the dream as something more than a science of solid and measurable objects. If the stone is a book that holds "acquaintance with the stars, / And [weds] man to man by purest bond / Of nature, undisturbed by space or time" (104–6), then it cannot simply represent "solid geometry." It signifies an "immaterial" geometry, as Wordsworth suggests elsewhere (*Prelude* 6. 125). Like its bearer, who is "neither" an Arab nor Don Quixote, and yet "both at once" (6. 125), the stone is indeterminate—at once a stone and a book (6. 111–13). As such, it is not so much the antithesis as the progenitor of the shell, which—as Hillis Miller notes—is "like a stone hollowed out, as if it had been carved, fluted, articulated so that it may speak with voices more than all the winds."[17]

To see the shell as a transformation of the stone is to realize that geometry itself is likewise transformed in the radically destabilizing world of the dream. How else can we explain why the Arab so anxiously seeks to bury a stone-book that encompasses a kind of knowledge "undisturbed by space or time"? If we think of the stone as a fixed and closed form, it represents—as Kelley says—"not science in general but that traditional knowledge which is sustained by rigid logic and resists change" (565). But change and disturbance are precisely what threaten the stone, which in spite of its supremely privileged "acquaintance with the stars" is to be buried in the earth lest it be overwhelmed by the water of a second flood. As the geometry of the earth gives way in the course of *The Prelude* to a

---

account of the dream, which begins with a twenty-eight-line passage contrasting "the desolate landscape [lines 71–80] with objects of eternity [80–98] so that, approximately, 10:18::18:28" (85, 87).

17. Miller 140. Miller nonetheless sees a "binary opposition" between the stone and the shell. "A stone uninscribed, uncarved, unhollowed out," he says, "is just itself. It does not refer beyond itself in any form of displacement" (140). But it is hard to understand how a stone which is also a book can be "just itself," an utterly insignificant thing. Kelley shows that Wordsworth's identification of the stone as "Euclid's Elements" may be indirectly indebted to Josephus's *History of the Jews*, where the Egyptians are said to have prepared for the deluge by raising a column of brick and a column of stone with the "Inventions" inscribed on each: inventions thought by eighteenth-century commentators to be Euclidian geometry (567–69). If the Arab's stone is connected with Josephus's stone column, it is *not* uninscribed. In any case, Jane Worthington Smyser long ago showed that the stone is probably connected with the dictionary of all sciences that Descartes is said to have seen in a dream—along with a *Corpus Poetarum* (269-75). A stone charged with so much textual history cannot be simply a "null sign," as Miller calls it (140), and Miller's own observation about the hollowing out of the stone suggests to me that the stone is the shell *in potentia*.

geometry of the stars, this transcendent but fixed geometry must itself undergo a sea change into something evolutionary and progressive—something perfectly articulated by the shape of the shell.[18]

THE GEOMETRY OF INTERACTION

This vision of a dynamic geometry is what finally enables us to understand how the characteristically romantic desire to cross or suppress boundaries could coexist with the equally powerful desire to discern in matter's mouldering structures the perfection of geometrical forms. The geometry of the infinite involves a dialectical interplay between geometrical abstractions and natural processes, between the confining rigidity of line and the expansive fluidity of atmosphere. The latter embodies the spontaneity of landscape; the former embodies its structure. Both were essential to the re-creation of landscape in English romantic poetry and painting, where the solid arch of architecture gives way to the liquid arch of the waterfall, the aerial arch of the rainbow, the ever-shifting rondure of clouds. Such things cannot simply be frozen into circles. In a world of indeterminacy and irrepressible movement, painters and poets conscious of geometrical figures found shapes that at once suggested those figures and yet defied their control. To represent such forms, they had to portray the vital interaction of angle and curve.

To speak of interaction is of course to summon up the familiar concept of organic unity, and in particular the Coleridgean principle that imagination "reveals itself in the balance or reconciliation of opposite or discordant qualities" (*BL* 2: 12). But two things distinguish the interaction of angle and curve from the kind of unity commonly called organic, or the way this unity is commonly defined. One is that while the concept of organic unity is modelled chiefly on the life cycle of a plant as it grows and decays in time (see Abrams, *Mirror* 218–20), geometrical interaction is temporal only by implication; it is first of all atemporally perceived in space. The other difference is that angularity and curvature are

18. The shell, says Kelley, "embodies a new kind of knowledge which is at once geometric and poetic. Unlike the closed surface of the stone, the shell is an open-ended geometrical spiral whose developing form requires a cooperation between natural processes a 'higher geometry' than that of the stone, whose geometry can describe only static figures" (565). Though she thus interprets the shell as the embodiment of an evolutionary geometry, Kelley tends to overstate the rigidity of the stone, and thus to confirm its opposition to the shell. Her own evolutionary model nonetheless gives us the means to perceive the continuity between the two.

not simply one more pair of opposites to be dialectically reconciled; they are sexually charged qualities, signs of masculinity and femininity. To perceive or represent their interaction is implicitly to witness or re-create a sexual unity.

We have seen this kind of unity in the later work of Constable, specifi-cally in the combination of angle and curve that animates his *Dedham Vale* of 1828 (plate 5) and distinguishes it so sharply from the *Dedham Vale* of 1802 (plate 4). But we have not yet fully considered how antitheti-cal was the interaction of angle and curve to Augustan theories of geo-metrical decorum. The most influential statement of these theories was the *Analysis of Beauty* (1753), in which Hogarth declared that beauty springs from undulation: a line of tempered variety free of any fixed geo-metrical form and uninterrupted by sharp turns (54–55, 76, 158–59, 183). The *Analysis* was shortly followed by Burke's *Enquiry* (1757), which treated straight lines and angles as marks of the sublime, and which therefore made an aesthetic place for angularity. But like Hogarth, Burke thought curvature a mark of beauty, and his distinction between the sublime and the beautiful is based to a considerable extent on the opposition between angles and curves, which for him clearly corre-sponds to the difference between male and female.[19] Joshua Reynolds likewise associated beauty with gentle curves and sublimity with sharp angles, and he argued that with rare exceptions, the repose of the one could not be combined with the energy of the other. In Reynolds's opin-ion, painters had to choose between "sublime" angularity and "elegant" curvature; they could not have both at once.[20]

19. Burke 114–15, 124. While the connection between masculinity and sublime an-gularity is merely implied, Burke explicitly links beauty to feminine curves: "Observe that part of a beautiful woman where she is perhaps the most beautiful, about the neck and breasts; the smoothness; the softness; the easy and insensible swell; the variety of the deceitful maze, through which the unsteady eye slides giddily, without knowing where to fix, or whither it is carried. Is not this a demonstration of that change of surface continual and yet hardly perceptible at any point which forms one of the great constitu-ents of beauty?" (115). In *Iconology*, W. J. T. Mitchell suggests that the sexual orienta-tion of Burke's categories influenced Lessing's attack on the confusion of poetry and painting; Lessing opposed the blurring of genres, Mitchell argues, because for him it was a blurring of genders, the confusion of an intellectual and therefore masculine art with a visual or corporeal and therefore feminine one. The fear of gender confusion, I suspect, likewise underlies Augustan theories of geometrical decorum.

20. See J. Reynolds, *D* 78–79, 237–38. As late as 1813, the dichotomy was re-stated by David Cox (1783–1859), a well-known watercolorist. "Abrupt or irregular lines," wrote Cox, "are productive of a grand or stormy effect; while serenity is the result

Turner refused to make this choice. In his very first lecture, he declared that painting could express motion "only . . . by an appearance of action, *in opposition to that of repose*; this is the necessity of the triangle" (TMS K, f. 7ᵛ; italics added). Turner declares, in effect, that only by the reconciliation of geometrical opposites can the artist capture on canvas the energy of nature. It was the lack of this dynamic opposition that he criticized in Poussin's famous *Deluge*. After studying this picture at the Louvre in 1802, he concluded: "The lines are defective as to the conception of a swamp'd world and the fountains of the deep being broken up." Turner notes that the large boat in the lower right corner is parallel with the base of the picture, as is the edge of the pool at the top of the waterfall and the edge of the water in the background. With the composition of the picture thus suggesting a series of descending terraces, its effect is one of almost static repose, and even the waterfall is "artificially not tearing and desolating, but falling placidly into another poole." [21]

Turner's comment on *The Deluge* is worth close attention. It would be easy to conclude that he was put off only by its rectilinear structure, and that in place of such a structure he would have had the enormous circles or vortices that later appear in his own paintings of the flood. But Turner actually wanted a good deal more. The mere substitution of curves for straight lines would take him back to Hogarth's line of beauty—pure undulation, pure feminine curvature; what he wanted was the line of energy, the phallic line that cuts across a circle or that intersects another line. In a revision of his first lecture dating from about 1818, he notes that even a simple figure formed by two bisecting lines—the schoolboy's rendering of a man—can excite in the mind "the characteristic feeling of Energy of Action" (TMS S, f. 11). With this intervention of male force, Turner's account of geometrical interaction becomes implicitly but unmistakably sexual. When one line intersects another, he says, it suggests the radius of a circle, a line of power centrifugally thrusting outward. "As the laws of $\left[\begin{smallmatrix} \text{motion } commence \\ \text{action proceed} \end{smallmatrix}\right]$ from the *radius* of a *circle*,

---

of even and horizontal lines, where no roughness or intersections appear, to invade the mild harmony of beauty" (7).

21. TSB LXXII, 41–42. Surprisingly enough, Constable commended *The Deluge* for this placidity. "The good sense of Poussin," he said, ". . . taught him that by simplicity of treatment, the most awful subjects may be made far more affecting than by overloading them with imagery. In painting the Deluge, he has not allowed his imagination to wander from the Mosaic account, which tells us of rain only. Human habitation, rocks, and mountains are gradually disappearing, as the water rises undisturbed by earthquakes or

as the periphera of a wheel, so the rotatory power of the joints of the Human Figure, are deductable, and that *action* continues . . . in *straight lines*, as the power of action proceeds, as the blow produced by the arm increases in force and the bone[s] of the forearm and Bracchia approach a straight line." [22]

Turner's own work abundantly illustrates the kind of energy that springs from this implicitly sexual interaction of angle and curve, of circle and radial line. As early as 1798, in a sketch of a leafless tree trunk (TSB LXII, 4), he was beginning to represent the fusion of geometrical opposites that he found in nature. The tree jerks upward in a series of sharply angular zigzags, but the longest of its three upper branches extends to the left, forming a gentle curve with the trunk, which leans slightly in the same direction. The subtle curve of the tree as a whole, then, actually consists of sharply defined angles, of straight lines working against the curve.

On a considerably grander scale, the same opposition appears in *Calais Pier* (plate 36), exhibited 1803. Here the churning white frenzy of the sea is embraced by the long curving arm of the pier: a curve repeated in the clouds overhead, in the outer edge of the white sail at the center, and in the shallow trough of the waves in the foreground. Contraposed to all of these curves are the conspicuously phallic masts of the heaving boats, especially of the two in the middle which lean to the right, radially cutting the curve of the pier as well as the curving masses of cloud. Yet Turner does more than juxtapose curves and straight lines; he integrates them. The diagonal sides of the pier at lower right sharply converge as they recede from the eye, and then become part of a distant curve. Contrastingly, the sails of the boat to the left of center are elegantly curved, but the line of their curves flows into the basically rectilinear mast, and the line of beauty thus becomes a spine of power.

The dynamic cooperation of curves, angles, and straight lines in the external world is something that repeatedly caught the attention of Cole-

---

tornadoes; and the very few figures introduced, interest us the more deeply from the absence of all violence or contortion of gesture" (*JCD* 60–61).

22. TMS S, f. 12. Turner might have illustrated this point with the Renaissance diagram known as Vitruvian man, or with David's *Oath of the Horatii*, which he could have seen on his visit to David's studio in Paris in 1802. (See Gage, *CT* 100.) Both pictures vividly reveal the "rotatory power" of straight limbs radiating from a human figure, and the Vitruvian figure is diagrammatically androgynous—the exhibition of rectilinear masculinity radiating to female circularity.

ridge. His notebooks show that he found geometrical forms almost every-where in nature.[23] But what truly fascinated him was the vital interaction of those forms, the way in which natural objects eluded the control of any one geometrical figure. The perfect symmetry of rectilinear forms struck him as lifeless. In a notebook entry of 1802, he objected to a garden with "tyrannically strait parallelogram enclosures," and later he said that nature herself has no perfectly straight lines, but lines animated by the curve—the emblem of motion, spontaneity, and inner life.[24] The square and the circle, he observed, can be infinitely combined for pleasure (*NC* 2: 2342), and in Coleridge's experience of landscape, such geometrical impossibilities as the squared circle, the angular curve, and the curved straight line become not merely possibilities but facts. He once observed a piece of land "imperceptibly declin[ing] from horizontal into slope": he noted the combination of curve and straight line in a waterfall; and he more than once observed that a mountain could form what he called "a spherical triangle."[25] In "Hymn Before Sunrise," in fact, Mont Blanc ap-pears both angular and spherical, a piercing "wedge" of "sky-pointing peaks" which nonetheless rises "like a vapoury cloud" (lines 9–10, 70–80).

He was equally struck with the geometrical complexity of ships. In a notebook entry of 1804, he observed that the determinate outline of wind-swollen sails makes them a combination of straight edge and curve (*NC* 1: 2012, f. 39). And shortly afterwards, he reflected on the geo-metrical complexity of ships as a whole—in words that might readily apply to the vessels in *Calais Pier*:

Ships, & their Picturesqueness—/ Have I noticed The approximation to Round and Rondure, in the Square & triangular Forms—& that pleasure which de-pends on the subtle Sense of Est quod non est?—Balance: Synthesis of Antithe-sis?—and Secondly . . . the Polyolbiosis of each appearance from the recollec-tion of so many others subtly combining with it / Sails bellying with Sails under

23. Besides the references cited above in notes 10 and 11, see *NC* 1: 227; 418, f. 29; and 1800, f. 92ᵛ.

24. Coleridge, *NC* 1: 1211, f.7ᵛ; 2: 2343. In "Fragment of an Essay on Beauty" (1818), Coleridge writes: "As to lines, the rectilineal are in themselves the lifeless, the determined *ab extra*, but still in immediate union with the cycloidal, which are expres-sive of function. The curve is a modification of the force from without by the force from within, or the spontaneous" (*BL* 2: 251).

25. *NC* 1: 1489, f. 59ᵛ; 1449, f. 6ᵛ; and 1482, f. 40ᵛ. See also *NC* 1: 1457, f. 12ᵛ; 1489, f. 52ᵛ; and 2: 2690, f. 89ᵛ–90.

reef . . . the Ideas of full Sail modifying the impression of the naked Masts, not on the eye but on the Mind, &c &c—. (*NC* 2: 2061, f. 26')

Coleridge nearly teases himself out of thought. Insofar as he registers an impression made "not on the eye but on the Mind," he is of course revealing the difference between words and pictures, for while the writer can say that the present and visible line of a naked mast—again a phallic presence—recalls the absent curve of the full-bellying or pregnant sail, the painter cannot represent an absent form without making it present. Nevertheless, the painter can represent what Coleridge has seen with his eye—"the *approximation* to Round and Rondure" in rectilinear forms.

If we ask whether this approximation can itself be "seen" and depicted or merely "felt" in the mind and evoked by language, we touch a borderline of difference between pictures and words, which are sometimes distinguished by means of the contrast between simulation and evocation. On the one hand, pictures simulate the appearance of visible objects; on the other hand, words signify objects we are asked to remember, imagine, or conceive, and thus they convey to us the Coleridgean "sense of Est quod non est." Yet all "discovery" of geometrical form in natural objects is an act of the mind as well as of the eye. In Turner's *Buttermere* (plate 1), the mind of the artist makes an uncompleted circle from a rainbow and its reflection, and in turn the picture of an uncompleted circle evokes a whole one from the mind of the spectator. In *Calais Pier*, the interaction of angle and curve works like a complex series of allusions in poetry. The angle and the curve evoke the triangle and the circle, and the stability of these geometrical forms in their pure and separate state is at once threatened and energized by their intercourse with each other.

THE ANGLE OF VISION

In romantic poetry and painting alike, geometry is used to express a consciousness of boundaries crossed, of transcendent stability at once evoked and disturbed by the indeterminacy of living forms, and of dynamic interaction. Yet its most important role, I think, is to indicate the observer's relation to the world by the angle from which he sees it. In this light, geometry serves to express at once the subjectivity and the power of the individual consciousness: of consciousness bound to the position of the eye but also bounding through it, using the personal angle of its vision to reconstruct the world.

The most vivid example of this in romantic poetry is the boat-stealing episode in Wordsworth's *Prelude*. I return to this episode by way of Wordsworth's theory of the sublime, which significantly emphasizes the effect of the observer's position on what he sees. Unlike most eighteenth-century theorists of the sublime, Wordsworth did not categorically link sublimity with objective angularity, with the geometrical shape of the objects perceived. Undulating lines, he wrote, may "convey to the mind sensations not less sublime than those which were excited by their opposites, the abrupt and the precipitous" (*PrW* 2: 352). What mattered to Wordsworth was not the geometry of the external world but the state of the observer's mind, which was at least partly determined by the angle of his vision. Wordsworth wrote that to experience sublimity—a feeling of "exaltation or awe"—the observer must get from an object a sense of individuality, a sense of duration, and a sense of power (*PrW* 2: 349, 351). The sense of duration is obviously something felt in the mind rather than seen, and Wordsworth links the sense of power to the "sense of motion" which the mind imputes to the stationary lines of a mountain (*PrW* 2: 352). But the sense of individuality depends on the observer's vantage point. If, writes Wordsworth, a group of mountains

be so distant that, while we look at them, they are only thought of as the crown of a comprehensive Landscape . . . we shall receive from them a grand impression, and nothing more. But if they be looked at from a point which has brought us so near that the mountain is almost the sole object before our eyes, yet not so near but that the whole of it is visible, we shall be impressed with the sensation of sublimity. (*PrW* 2: 351)

The sense of individuality, therefore, depends on the angle and distance from which a particular object is seen. And by thus determining the sense of individuality, the angle of vision helps to determine whether any object will appear sublime. Wordsworth writes in the "Essay" of 1815 that poetry should "treat of things not as they *are*, but as they appear . . . as they *seem* to exist to the *senses*, and to the *passions*" (*PrW* 3: 63). The boat-stealing episode is a study in appearance, for the change in the angles of vision from which the boy sees the cliff is crucial to its impact upon him. As he rows out from beneath the craggy ridge, its summit seems at first "the bound of the horizon" (*Prelude* A 1. 399), and as he looks up at this summit with a "fix'd" and steady gaze, it is clearly "the sole object before [his] eyes." He cannot see any of the cliff that stands behind it until he gets some distance from the shore. Only then does the cliff become visible at all, and when he has rowed as far from the shore as he cares to, he is just approaching the point at which the whole of it would become visible, rising up between him and the stars (*Prelude* 1. 397–410). It "towered" over him—as the 1850 *Prelude* says—precisely because of the angle from which he saw it.

Turner would have understood this perfectly. If Wordsworth believed that poetry should deal with appearances, Turner believed that painting could deal with nothing else. He noted in one lecture that while geometry enables us to perceive solids, painting seeks to represent "not what are solids but what they appear to be" (TMS U, f. 2). And in another lecture, he declared that the laws of perspective tell the artist "how . . . to express the situation of each object, as it appears to the Eye, as well as the relative form breadth and height" (TMS M, f. 1). What Turner saw was that however clear and self-possessed might be the mind behind the human eye, the eye itself—in any given moment—was subjectively bound to a particular vantage point from which the view was limited, and sometimes distorted. One of his examples is strikingly close to Wordsworth's rising cliff. In an undated addition to his third lecture, Turner observed that only when an observer's eye is approximately level with an object can he accurately and geometrically gauge its height. Suppose, he says, we are looking at St. Paul's from the lower part of Fleet Street, which offers the most distant view possible of the front and dome. The angle of our vision would be relatively low, yet even from this angle, we could do no more than guess how far the dome rises above the front. "If thus the Eye is deceived," says Turner, "at that distance, as to its geometric measurements, how much the depression of the dome be expressed were we to approach it—as it would appear rapidly to decrease and at London House yard sinking below the angle of the Front" (TMS M, f. 23ʲ). Essentially, Turner here describes the same set of circumstances that elevated Wordsworth's cliff. Just as the cliff appeared to rise when Wordsworth rowed away from it, the dome of St. Paul's seems to sink as the observer approaches it, and both examples illustrate the subjectivity of perspective.

The subjectivity of perspective was for Turner an inescapable fact of vision. "All things," he wrote, "are limited in a picture to the limited power of the Eye" (TMS BB, f. 64ʲ–65). Throughout his lectures, Turner repeatedly insists that the eye naturally alters the forms of things, and that only by taking stock of this alteration can the painter hope to represent the true appearance of such forms.

Earlier theorists on perspective tried to avoid this problem by advising painters to represent objects at a distance, with the line of sight either level or pitched up at a relatively low angle. Turner would have found such advice, for instance, in Thomas Malton's *Compleat Treatise on Perspective* (1775), which he used in preparing his lectures. On the matter of viewpoint, Malton declares: "If the Optic Angle, under which the whole Picture is seen, exceeds 50, or at the most 60 Degrees, the Distance is not sufficient; as the visual rays will cut the Picture very oblique, near its extremes, and occasion a disagreeable distortion of the Objects on the extreme parts of it."[26] This position seemed to Turner arbitrary and dictatorial. Though he never criticized Malton by name, he sharply attacked Malton's position. Theorists insist, he says, that "the object must not be delineated by a near point which produces distortion." But in the works of great painters, "we have to do with those very distortions, if so they must be called by Theorists" (TMS L, f. 14ᵛ–15). And in nature itself, Turner insisted, objects are seen from every point of view:

in Nature are they not to be look[ed] at in every angle, position, or incidence of vision, comparatively, and are they not to be represented by the Painter because not seen under a certain angle, and are not the powers of the Painter as extensive, or more so, he that may use forms, that would be temerity in [architectural] constructions and impracticable to Sculpture, must he be confined to a certain angle of representation, or of view[?]

Surely not, and those who attempt to forge such fetters to subjugate vision or enslave art rivets but another link of the chain, round the neck of such tyranny. (TMS L, f. 15; see also BB, f. 13)

Tyranny is a strong word, but Turner had some cause to use it. By restricting the range of angles from which a scene might be depicted, parallel perspective riveted painting to the principles of plane geometry: virtually all lines in a picture were to be parallel to the horizontal or vertical lines, and the receding planes that marked the stages of depth in a picture were to be parallel to its surface.[27] Exponents of parallel perspective were dogmatic in its defense. Malton, who called it "an infal-

26. Malton 96–97. Joshua Reynolds makes a similar point in his tenth discourse (*D* 186). On Turner's use of Malton's textbook, see Gage, *CT* 182. I have already noted that Turner studied architectural drawing with Malton's son, Thomas the Younger; see p. 147n.

27. I am drawing here on Kirby 23–24; Malton 47; and Alston 11–15.

lible and most exact science," roundly declared: "I will stake all my knowledge in Perspective . . . that Objects of equal magnitude, and equally distant from the Picture parallel to them, however otherwise situated or elevated will be represented equal" (94, 96). But such a formula took no account of what happened to the appearance of objects when they were seen from certain angles. And if defenders of parallel perspective thought closeup views of tall objects would produce distortion, Turner argued that parallel perspective not only prohibited certain points of view, but actually falsified the way in which things appear at any angle.

Turner's attack on parallel perspective sprang from his conviction that the field of human vision is circular. Strictly speaking, he said, nature presented "only one Horizontal and one perpendicular line" (TMS M, f. 22ᵛ). Since all others became curved as they moved away from the center of focus, they should also curve as they move away from the center of a picture. It was therefore false, he thought, to represent even rectilinear objects as "square in all places to the Eye," or to divide a landscape or a building into "compartments Geometric" (TMS K, f. 15ᵛ–16). The neat and symmetrical structures of geometry simply did not meet the test of vision. From certain angles, as Turner said, "Circles become Ovals Squares lozenges [and] . . . right lines appear to draw or converge together" (TMS I, f. 24). Parallel lines do not meet in geometry, but to the eye they appear to do so; when you approach the towers of Westminster Abbey, said Turner, so that you can just take in their height, "they rapidly decrease upwards and appear to the Eye even to incline towards each other."²⁸ Yet it was not only awkward angles that produced such awkward sights. "The eye," said Turner, "must take in all objects upon a parabolic curve for in looking into space the eye cannot but receive what is within the limits of extended sight, which must form a circle to the eye" (quoted in Lindsay 115).

Turner's theory of curvilinear perspective confirms something in which Wordsworth and Coleridge firmly believed: the creative power of the human eye. The rigid squares and "compartments Geometric" formed by parallel perspective correspond to the universe of "*little* things" which Coleridge found unintelligible and which he longed to convert into something "*one & indivisible*" (*LC* I, 349). The poetry of Coleridge and of Wordsworth too shows not only how the eye itself can begin this work of

---

28. Turner, TMS M, f. 25–25ᵛ. Coleridge likewise noted that a precipice loses its perpendicularity when seen from close range: see *NC* 1: 825, f. 62.

conversion, but also—on occasion—how it uses curvilinear perspective to do so. At the end of "Fears in Solitude" (1798), after climbing up a hill from the quiet dell where he has been meditating, Coleridge is greeted by a splendid view:

> here the shadowy main,
> Dim-tinted, there the mighty majesty
> Of that huge amphitheatre of rich
> And elmy fields, seems like society—
> Conversing with the mind, and giving it
> A livelier impulse and a dance of thought!
> (Lines 215–20)

After solitary and troubled thoughts on the prospect of an armed invasion of England, Coleridge understandably turns to the solaces of landscape, and the trees become his congenial friends. But the geometrical form of this scene is worth noting. Essentially, the prospect as a whole takes its shape from the "amphitheatre" of fields—an amphitheatre suggested by the surrounding stand of elms, but in part created by the curvilinear structure of Coleridge's own vision. Thus formed, the amphitheatre sets his mind in motion, and it too seems to circle about in a "dance of thought."

The link between motion and curvilinear perspective is still more apparent in the boyhood skating incident that Wordsworth recounts in book 1 of *The Prelude*. Racing along a frozen river with his friends, he finds that everything about him seems to be moving in circles:

> and oftentimes
> When we had given our bodies to the wind,
> And all the shadowy banks, on either side,
> Came sweeping through the darkness, spinning still
> The rapid line of motion; then at once
> Have I, reclining back upon my heels,
> Stopp'd short, yet still the solitary Cliffs
> Wheeled by me, even as if the earth had roll'd
> With visible motion her diurnal round;
> Behind me did they stretch in solemn train
> Feebler and feebler, and I stood and watch'd
> Till all was tranquil as a dreamless sleep.
> (A 1. 478–89)

This is a passage of characteristically Wordsworthian daring. Abandoning the fixed "station" from which a topographical poet would typically describe a "prospect," Wordsworth gives his mind's eye to the wind, even as the boy gave his body to it. But the result is not an indistinguishable blur. It is rather a "line of motion," an arc or circle made by banks that are—or rather seem to be—"spinning still." The phrase is subtly oxymoronic; even in their apparent motion the banks are "still" because they seem to move in a constant arc. Conversely, when the boy himself is "still," or more precisely "stopped short," the banks continue to move. "Reclining back," the boy takes up an observer's station, but the very suddenness with which he does so leaves the world still moving around him, the cliffs "still wheeling." What the boy experienced was vertigo; what the poet creates is a vision of circularity stretching infinitely outward, from the spinning banks to the wheeling cliffs to the round and rolling earth. In the words of Turner, the whole world thus forms "a circle to the eye."

But Turner's words apply still more to his own later work, where—as if in reenactment of Genesis—he repeatedly turns elementary energy into circular form. A notable example is the picture I briefly considered in chapter 3—*Snow Storm: Steam-boat off a Harbour's Mouth* (plate 37). By Turner's own account, this was a "record" of what he witnessed from the deck of a ship caught in a snowstorm. Lashed to the mast at his own request so that he might witness the storm, he was a radically destabilized observer. But even as Wordsworth turns the eye of a dizzy skater into the still point of a wheeling earth, Turner projects his own eye into the paddle wheel of the steamboat. Fixed in the very center of the whirling elements, the paddle wheel is an antisun, the dark and steady pupil around which all else revolves.

Unlike Wordsworth's skating scene, however, Turner's *Snow Storm* is not simply organized as a series of concentric circles. Most of its major lines are nearly straight: the steamboat's mast, the diagonal underside of the smoke above it, the slanting horizon that cuts across the middle of the picture, and the intersecting diagonals in the waves at lower left. These lines suggest a vortex because we are made to see them as lines of centrifugal force driving outward from a center of whirling energy. Conspicuous by their absence are the two lines indispensable to parallel perspective: the horizontal and the vertical. Where we look for the vertical, we find a bowed and slanted mast; where we look for a level horizon, we find another slant with a curve at the end: a more emphatic version of the sloping horizontal that Coleridge noted in 1803.[29] The slanting horizon is undoubtedly a "record" of what Turner saw from the tossing vessel, yet more than anything else in the picture, perhaps, it is also his crowning act of defiance toward the doctrines of parallel perspective. Thirteen years earlier, he had exhibited a painting called *Ulysses Deriding Poly-phemus*. This time, lashed to a mast at his own request, he became his own Ulysses, and what he produced might almost be called *Turner De-riding Malton*. Against rectilinear rigidity he sets the curvilinear form of human vision, and against the objective transcript of the way things are, he sets the subjective re-creation of the way they seem.

Turner believed that he could render the power of natural forces only by subjecting himself and his vision to them, only by making a snow-storm—in Wordsworth's terms—"the sole object before his eyes." Yet the act of subjection was also an act of conquest. By the subjective power of his own vision, he made a rounded whole of raging elements, so that for all their turbulence, they nonetheless suggest the transcendent per-fection of the circle. The circle in turn asserts its power not by consum-ing straight lines but by setting them in motion, animating what would otherwise be static parallels and perpendiculars. The abandonment of parallel for curvilinear perspective, therefore, is an abandonment of rigidity for dynamism, and of finitude for infinitude. So long as we can look down on a scene, so long as we can gauge its measurements con-fidently by the laws of parallel perspective, it remains for us fixed and finite. But when a mountain looms up over us, as the huge cliff loomed up over Wordsworth, it is fixed and finite no more. "Parallel lines," wrote Turner, "carry with them no idea of hight while the Oblique one may rise to infinity." In the latter case, altitude is not a product of calculation but "the natural feeling of the mind" (TMS K, f. 14).

The feeling of the mind—the mind's consciousness of infinity—is precisely what the English romantic poetry of the infinite is meant to convey. Essentially, it is a geometry created by a mind working through the eye. Wordsworth wrote about 1798:

> There is creation in the eye
> Nor less in all the other senses; powers
> They are that colour, model, and combine

29. Ruskin is slightly inaccurate when he suggests that Turner obliterates the hori-zon, representing "no distinction . . . between air and sea" (quoted in Butlin and Joll

> The things perceived with such an absolute
> Essential energy that we may say
> That those most godlike faculties of ours
> At one and the same moment are the mind
> And the mind's minister.
>
> *(PW* 5: 343)

When he thus declares the power of the human eye, Wordsworth speaks for Coleridge, Turner, and Constable, too, as well as for himself. In their different and distinctive ways, it was they who created the geometry of the infinite, who saw both limit and limitlessness, who caught from evanescent phenomena the permanence of implied geometrical figures, who found in matter's mouldering structures the pure and yet also vitally disturbed forms of circle, triangle, cube and square. It was they who perceived the dynamic interaction of angle and curve, and who, to represent that interaction in poetry and painting, replaced the line of undulating beauty by a line of complex power. And it was they, finally, who gauged the influence of the eye on natural objects. Instead of receiving the world as a rectilinear grid, they recognized that the energy of the eye could re-create it as a rounded whole. Giving up the superior vantage point from which it may literally look down upon a scene of finite, ordered parallels, the eye submits itself to the immeasurable sublimity of towering cliffs and raging storms. But in the very act of giving up its sovereignty over a geometrically determinate universe, the eye discovers a godlike power to elevate natural forms, to delineate the very structure of their motions, and to perpetuate their evanescent character. Radically transformed in this way by the combined energies of the eye and the external world, geometry became the measure by which the English romantic poets and painters re-created the measureless power of landscape.

---

224). What gives the picture its vortical energy is not the erasure of the horizon, but the tilting of it.

CHAPTER 6

THE REVALUATION OF
REFLECTIONS

 WE HAVE SEEN in the previous two chapters how the act of re-creating landscape led poets and painters alike to focus on the process of perception and on the means of representation itself. To find geometrical forms in landscape is to discover the mind's own aspiration to turn matter's mouldering structures into emblems of permanence and infinity, to perpetuate the sexually dynamic interaction of angle and curve, and to represent its own subjectivity, its own simultaneous consciousness of submission and power. Likewise, to reenact in pictures or words the transformations naturally wrought by atmosphere is to rediscover the languages of painting and poetry. The admiration with which Turner and Constable speak of Rembrandt's chiaroscuro and his "mystic shell of colour" has its counterpart in Wordsworth's veneration for the "mystery of words" which at once veil and unveil what they represent, investing natural objects with a glory "not their own." If Wordsworth's preoccupation with language permeates his poetry as well as his critical essays, the works of Turner and Constable correspondingly reveal a preoccupation with paint, which is no longer a self-effacing medium through which natural forms are transparently conveyed, but a material substance with a polyvalent life and density of its own. What putatively represents water in Turner's *Calais Pier* looked to Beaumont "like the veins in a marble slab" and to others like soap and chalk (Gowing 10). What putatively represents dew in Constable's pictures looked to Turner himself (as well as to others) like whitewash. Such indeterminacy of reference calls reference itself into question.[1] Turner's pictures could

1. The problem of pictorial referentiality has been discussed at some length by Jacques Derrida, who argues that the relation between a picture and what it supposedly represents is no more "natural" or direct than the relation between a written word and a spoken one, or between a spoken word and its signified sense. Even in "pure representation," says Derrida, "the thing most faithfully represented is already no longer pres-

signify the process of representation quite as much as the thing ostensibly represented, the work of the palette knife quite as much as the shape and texture of natural forms. And by 1825 this quality could be seen in Constable's work as well. "It is evident," wrote a critic, "that Mr. Constable's landscapes are like nature; it is still more evident that they are like paint" (quoted in Gowing 10).

Ultimately, this self-referential tendency of romantic poetry and painting is best exemplified by what I have already touched upon in my discussion of Constable's *Cornfield* (plate 20), where the drinking boy— Constable's remembered self—is represented as unconsciously absorbing not the actual scenes around him but the scenes reflected in the water from which he drinks: the scenes that "made [him] a painter." Just as atmospheric transformation can provide a model for the transformations wrought in poetry and painting, reflections in water can symbolize the whole process of re-creating landscape in pictures or words. Yet, "reflection" is an all but dead metaphor for graphic or verbal representation.[2] Speculation about the way in which art "reflects" life hardly ever turns to reflection on the process of reflection itself, or moves beyond the *speculum*, the mirror, which offers only one kind of reflection. In this final chapter, therefore, I would like to consider how another kind of reflection is itself reflected—or represented—in English romantic poetry and painting. The richness of water-borne reflections represented in various ways by Turner, Constable, Wordsworth, Coleridge, and Shelley will compel us to consider anew the very meaning of the word *reflection*.

THE MIRROR AS LAMP

The history of the word *reflection* is complicated. It made its first recorded appearance about 1386, and the *OED* informs us that by 1430 it was being used to mean "the action of a mirror or other polished surface in exhibiting or reproducing the image of an object." By the middle of the sixteenth century, it had come to mean also the reflected image itself, which is what it still means now—in its primary sense. But by

---

ent. . . . The perfect representation is always already other than what it doubles and represents" (44–45, 291–92).

2. Haydon White, for instance, treats it as such even in his suggestively titled essay, "Literature and Social Action: Reflections on the Reflection Theory of Literary Arts." To construe literature as a reflection of social action is, for White, roughly equivalent to construing it as the effect of social action (364).

the end of the seventeenth century, reflection had acquired a secondary sense. In his *Essay Concerning Human Understanding* (1690), Locke defined it as "that notice which the mind takes of its own operations, and the manner of them" (1: 78). Such a "notice" is plainly an analytical activity of the mind, as the *Essay* itself abundantly illustrates, and whatever the object of this analysis, reflection itself came to denote intellectual action. In the very title of Edmund Burke's *Reflections on the Revolution in France*, published one hundred years after Locke's *Essay*, the use of the preposition *on* promises that these reflections will constitute a mental performance. Burke does not offer simply to mirror the events of the revolution, to reproduce its images, to show us unadorned reflections *of* them; he aims rather to set his mind to work *upon* them, to consider their causes and infer their consequences.

We are still using *reflection* in this secondary sense. But the primary sense has persevered, and it is precisely this primary sense that makes *reflection* such a problematic metaphor for artistic representation. In the Renaissance, critics of art and literature alike firmly established the commonplace that both of these arts should reflect reality, and in the eighteenth century, Samuel Johnson intends the highest praise when he says that Shakespeare's plays hold up "a faithful mirrour of manners and of life" (7: 62). Yet ever since Plato, reflection has been a hazardous paradigm for the representation of reality in art. In Plato's analysis of what men see when newly released from the cave of shadowy appearances, the reflection of an object is little better than its shadow, an empty substitute from which men should turn to the thing itself, and thence to the source of all reflected light: from the sun reflected in the moon, in water, or in "any alien medium" to the sun "as it is in itself" (*Republic* 7.516B in Plato 229–30). For Plato, one of the greatest obstacles to our perception of reality is the danger of mistaking a reflected object for a real one, and the danger has been almost universally recognized. It is pointedly dramatized in the enduring myth of Narcissus, who fell in love with his own reflection, and in the autobiography of Milton's Eve, whose very first act was to do the same. As she herself tells Adam in book 4 of *Paradise Lost*, she awakened to find herself

> Under a shade on Flowers, much wond'ring where
> And what I was, whence thither brought, and how.
> Not distant far from thence a murmuring sound
> Of waters issued from a cave and spread

Into a liquid plain, then stood unmoved
Pure as th' expanse of heav'n; I thither went
With unexperienced thought, and laid me down
On the green bank, to look into the clear
Smooth lake, that to me seemed another Sky.[3]

Coming out of the shade "with unexperienced thought," Eve is initially drawn to waters flowing from a cave. Born (like Eve herself) in a
world of shadowy appearances, the waters form a lake that seems "another Sky," a sky that Eve prefers to the real and heavenly one that it
reflects. This first error leads at once to a second. Though created as the
"image" or reflection of Adam, who is himself the image of God, she
immediately becomes entranced with her own reflection. "There," she
says, "I had fixt / Mine eyes till now, and pin'd with vain desire," had she
not been led away by God to Adam. But even then, she is at first repelled
by one "less fair / Less winning soft, less amiably mild, / Than that
smooth watery image," and she must be persuaded that her watery image
is really no match for the "Substantial Life" embodied in Adam (*Paradise Lost* 4. 465–91). In this brief autobiographical narrative, Eve's fascination with reflections is used to reveal her fatal tendency toward self-
infatuation. Shortly after this narrative, in fact, Satan begins to exploit
this tendency by telling her in a dream how beautiful she looks beneath
the moon, which "with more pleasing light / Shadowy sets off the face of
things" (*Paradise Lost* 5. 42–43). The shadowy light of the moon is of
course merely a reflection of the sun, and at sunrise the next day, when
Eve turns to Adam with her story of the dream, she is also turning from
the shadowy light of self-delusion to the bright, clear sun of Adam's reason. Milton would have us do likewise. In his opinion, reflections are
both philosophically insubstantial and morally dangerous.[4]

3. *Paradise Lost* 4. 451–59. Professor Kate Hayles has kindly drawn my attention to
the somewhat different treatment of reflections in Thomas Traherne's "Shadows in the
Water," written at about the same time as *Paradise Lost* (though not published until the
twentieth century). Like Milton's Eve, Traherne's speaker recalls that "In unexperienc'd
Infancy" he saw by the water's edge what he thought was "Another World." But while he
insists throughout the poem on the phantasmal and delusory character of this world, he
finally takes it for a prefiguration of the eternal world "To which I shall, when that thin
Skin / Is broken, be admitted in" (lines 116–18).

4. For further discussion of this point see Bryan Wolf, who compares Milton's treatment of Eve with Jonathan Edwards's rigorously Puritanical interpretation of the Narcissus myth (85–87). "The water," says Edwards, ". . . is a type of sin or the corruption
of man, and of the state of misery that is the consequence of it. It is like sin in its flatter-
ing appearance" (quoted in Wolf 87).

Like beauty, however, moral danger lies in the eyes of the beholder. In the landscapes of English romantic poetry and painting, this moral and philosophical distrust of reflections gives way to outright admiration. Wordsworth was unapologetically fascinated with them, and in his own autobiography, they play a part significantly different from the one they play in Eve's. Coincidentally, his most suggestive treatment of them appears in book 4 of *The Prelude*, where he compares the difficulty of recovering his past with the difficulty of seeing into the depths of a body of water:

> As one who hangs down-bending from the side
> Of a slow-moving boat, upon the breast
> Of a still water, solacing himself
> With such discoveries as his eye can make
> Beneath him in the bottom of the deep,
> Sees many beauteous sights—weeds, fishes, flowers,
> Grots, pebbles, roots of trees, and fancies more,
> Yet often is perplexed and cannot part
> The shadow from the substance, rocks and sky,
> Mountains and clouds, reflected in the depth
> Of the clear flood, from things which there abide
> In their true dwelling; now is crossed by gleam
> Of his own image, by a sun-beam now,
> And wavering motions sent he knows not whence,
> Impediments that make his task more sweet.
> Such pleasant office have we long pursued
> Incumbent o'er the surface of past time
> With like success.
>
> (*Prelude* 4. 256–73)

It is not easy to say just where this simile leads us—or leaves us. To some extent, Wordsworth's attitude toward reflection seems traditional: he implies that he is trying to part the shadow from the substance, even as Plato separates his ideal forms from the transitory objects that reflect them, or even as Milton's God takes the newly created Eve from shadow to substance, from the empty image of her face in the water to the substance of the man whom she herself reflects. Yet if Wordsworth is in fact attempting to part the shadow from the substance, to separate the reflection of clouds and mountains from the reality of underwater pebbles and roots, he is at once distracted and fascinated by the reflections, by the gleam of his own image, by sunbeams, by motions that are sent he knows not whence. The reflections get between his eye and the depths of his past experience, but they are nonetheless "impediments that make his task more sweet," and they are so interesting in themselves that he does not bother to tell us precisely just what element of himself they represent.

The reference to a "gleam / Of his own image" may imply that the reflections correspond to his present feelings, and that Wordsworth is symbolically describing the autobiographer's tendency to confound his present feelings with the past—the tendency he speaks of at the end of "Nutting." The past, he may be saying, is no more readily accessible than the bottom of the lake, for it can be seen only through the medium of the poet's present-tense consciousness. But we cannot be sure about this correspondence. Indeed, looking through the reflected images of this simile, we ourselves have trouble seeing precisely just what its double tenor is, and we find ourselves increasingly perplexed by the task of parting shadow from substance, vehicle from tenor, visible reflection from intellectual reflection. Perhaps just one thing is clear: whatever their significance might be, Wordsworth was captivated by the sheer complexity of reflections in water.

Reflections of this kind were a source of consuming interest to J. M. W. Turner. The fifth of his Royal Academy lectures, which he extensively revised in 1818, is on reflection, and Turner begins by saying that a knowledge of this subject is indispensable to the painter: "Nothing is so difficult and undefined as the Theory of Reflexies and yet they are absolutely necessary to the Painters persuit" (TMS O, f. 1). Turner believed that we live in a world of reflected light, that every color in a scene is modified by reflections from every other color in it, and that so long as there is any light at all in the air, reflections will be everywhere, even in shadows.[5] But what is particularly interesting about Turner's lecture on reflection is that it dwells at length on the reflective properties of water. For purposes of reflection, he says, water cannot simply be regarded as a polished body or a mirror: "It is quite different first from color secondly from motion and thirdly its reflexies which admits of such endless variety incomprehensible contrarieties and phenomena that it imperiously demands more attention than its dismissal it has generally received" (TMS O, f. 6). Taking these three points of difference in reverse order, the

5. TMS O, f. 3v. See also Gowing 21; Turner, TSB CII, f. 15.

"contrarieties" of reflections in water apparently spring from the fact that as Wordsworth also notices (with perplexity), water is both transparent and reflexive, admitting light as well as returning it. Turner himself goes on to say that a mirror "repels the immediate ray while [water] absorbs it the one transparent while mirror is opaque how can they appear the same[?]" Secondly, water and mirrors differ "from motion," for Turner points out that water is subject to breezes and currents which make of its surface an undulating mirror that congregates forms.[6] Finally (or "first"), water and mirrors differ in color:

Water often possesses color but color is not imparted to its reflections or refractions like as a colord glass when every thing seen is viciated by that color even the purest mirrour gives a tone to the sky and as the color is increased it destroys all the color of nature to its own dullness while water often seems to challenge the sky for brightness. (TMS O, f. 6–6ᵛ)

The mirror that Turner here describes is probably the Claude Glass, which was normally not (as is sometimes thought) a tinted lens, but rather a slightly convex blackened mirror (Warner 158–59). Enthusiastically used in the eighteenth century by tourists, artists, and peripatetic poets such as Thomas Gray, it enabled the viewer to see an actual landscape as if it had been already reflected in a somber-toned canvas by Claude Lorrain. The Claude Glass thus at once reflected and beautified nature, and constituted, in fact, an objective correlative for the neoclassical theory that art should reflect not nature as it is, but nature improved, heightened, or refined: what Charles Batteux in 1747 called "la belle nature" (quoted in Abrams, *Mirror* 12). Samuel Johnson himself declared that it would "be as safe to turn the eye immediately upon mankind, as upon a mirrour which shows all that presents itself without discrimination" (quoted in Abrams, *Mirror* 36). Literature, then, was asked to behave like a special kind of mirror: like a Claude Glass, reflecting only what is beautiful and morally edifying. And it was by this theory, as M. H. Abrams observes, that Augustan critics tried to solve the problems arising from the definition of art as reflection (*Mirror* 35).

But Turner's comments on reflection exacerbate these problems. If the Claude Glass symbolized the theory that art should refine what it reflects, this kind of reflection casts a shadow of its own, for as Turner suggests, the Claude Glass eclipses the brilliance of landscape. "It de-

6. TMS O, f. 66; I am also drawing on a separate note made about 1808 in TSB CV, inside cover.

stroys," he says, "all the color of nature to its own dullness while water often seems to challenge the sky for brightness."

The last part of Turner's statement is the most provocative thing in it. Plainly contrasting two different kinds of reflection, Turner makes us realize that a mirror provides only one of them. And the fact that mirrors provide only one kind of reflection calls into question the commonplace equation of reflection with mirrors. Taking this equation for granted, Abrams has argued at length that *mirror* and *lamp* are antithetical metaphors in the history of criticism, that up to the eighteenth century, the mind of the artist is "a reflector of external objects," while in the romantic period it becomes "a radiant projector which makes a contribution to the objects it perceives" (*Mirror* vi). Valuable as this formulation has been, it must be revised to accommodate the differences between kinds of reflective surfaces, specifically between mirrors and bodies of water. In the landscapes of English romantic poetry and painting, reflection is no longer simply a dead or dying metaphor for the representation of nature in the works of literature or art. Instead, reflections themselves become an integral part of what is being represented, and when seen in water, they assume a kind of brilliance that makes them shadows no more. No longer are they morally, philosophically, or even aesthetically inferior to the things they reflect, and no longer do they "refine" the colors of nature by reducing them to monochromatic dullness. In Turner's eyes, the reflected sky is bright enough to challenge the real one, and the watery mirror thus becomes a new kind of lamp.

This is the lamp that repeatedly illuminates Turner's paintings. In *Fishing upon Blythe Sand*, exhibited 1809, the brightest light is not in the sky but on the horizon, where the waves both catch and intensify the light of a sun we cannot directly see. In *Harbour of Dieppe*, exhibited 1825, the yellowed puff of wispy clouds in a pale blue sky encloses a hard white disc, but the hazy glow it lends to the clouds is overpowered by the shimmering white gold of the water beneath it. In *Norham Castle, Sunrise* (plate 27), painted after 1830, the ball of yellow in the clouds is matched if not surpassed by the columns of reflected yellow that radiate across the river. And in *Keelmen Heaving Coals by Moonlight* (plate 38), exhibited 1835, the grimness of an industrial subject is transfigured by reflected moonlight. Ships are densely ranged along both banks of the river Tyne, and within the shadows of the ships at lower right, where darkened figures toil away in a small inferno of red and yellow flame, the water has a cast of red. But a white moon beams down the middle of the river, and the sparkling tints of yellow-green which it reflects unmistakably rival the moonlit sky for brilliance.

An equal sensitivity to the power of reflected light is evident in the work of Constable. In the oil-on-millboard version of *Waterloo Bridge from Whitehall Stairs*, painted about 1819, the light that is diffused and scattered through a cloudy sky is brilliantly condensed on the piece of water near the bridge at right, where the Thames becomes—as in Turner's *Dieppe*—a river of gold. And if Turner makes the horizon shimmer in *Blythe Sand*, Constable does likewise in *Hadleigh Castle*. Successive versions of this picture actually show that he increased the brilliance of the sea as he proceeded. In the full-sized oil sketch made about 1829 (plate 11), the slender and broken streaks of white on the distant waves are barely a match for the intensity of the swirling white clouds above. But in the finished version exhibited in 1829 (Mellon Collection; reproduced in Taylor, plate 121), the clouds have been darkened, and the sea beneath them—which reflects the unseen sun behind them—has become a sheet of shining light.

Watery mirrors could likewise turn into lamps for Wordsworth and Coleridge. In Wordsworth's account of the stolen boat in *The Prelude*, the lake on which he rowed was "shining clear" under the moon, and as he rowed, the drops that fell from the tips of his oars whenever he lifted them out of the water left

> Small circles glittering idly in the moon,
> Until they melted all into one track
> Of sparkling light.
>
> (*Prelude* 1. 365–67)

Later in book 1, the "shining water" of the moonlit sea off Westmoreland appears as a "field of light" (lines 606–7), and in book 5, in the dream of an Arabian desert doomed to inundation, the distant sea advances as "a bed of glittering light" (*Prelude* 5. 129). Comparable sights get into the notebooks of Coleridge. In an entry of September 1803, he speaks of a lake as "a mass of molten silver."[7] In a later entry (from the autumn of

---

7. *NC* 1: 1465, f. 68ᵛ. See also his description of the river Greta in the moonlight: "The moonlight [i.e., moonlit] Greta that in almost direct line from the moon to me is all silver—Motion and Wrinkle & Light—& under the arch of the Bridge a wave ever & anon leaps up in Light . . . silver mirror / gleaming of moonlight [moonlit] Reeds beyond—as the moon sets the water from silver branches becomes a rich yellow" (*NC* 1: 1616, f. 73).

1806), he writes: "—like a lake beneath the Sun seemed to possess in its own right and prodigally give the fiery Light, which by not receiving it flashed forth" (*NC* 2: 2936). In this description, as in Turner's *Dieppe* and Constable's *Waterloo*, the reflected sunlight is so brilliant that it seems to emanate from the water itself.

But it is in his poetry that Coleridge represents most vividly the power of reflected light. In "The Rime of the Ancient Mariner," the moonlit scene that ends part 4 is strikingly similar to what we find in Turner's *Keelmen*. Like the shadows of the ships in the picture, the shadow of the mariner's ship reflects its redness:

> where the ship's huge shadow lay,
> The charmed water burnt alway
> A still and awful red.
>
> (Lines 269–71)

But beyond this reddened shadow, the moon creates a field of reflected light, and even as the reflected light in *Keelmen* transfigures the industrialized and no doubt polluted river Tyne, here it transfigures the water snakes. Hitherto ugly, they now seem beautiful, for they move in tracks of shining white and golden fire (274–81). The mariner's sudden impulse to bless them, therefore, comes not from the moon itself, but from the reflection of its light upon the water.[8] Since the only word applied to moon is "moving" (263), the moonlit sea in this passage clearly exudes a brilliance that the moon itself lacks. Yet the moon itself reflects the light of the sun, and if the moon in this poem reveals to the imagination what the sun paradoxically conceals, as Robert Penn Warren has argued, the whole structure of projected and reflected light has been inverted.

REFLECTION AND IDEALIZATION

The treatment of reflections in English romantic poetry and painting goes well beyond the simple observation of brilliant light upon water. But

8. The brilliance of the snakes in this passage may be partly due to phosphorescence, a light that naturally emanates from them. In *History and Present State of Discoveries Relating to Vision, Light and Colours* (1772), a book known to both Coleridge and Turner, Joseph Priestley discussed this phenomenon at some length, noting particularly the emanation of light from putrescent matter; see Gage, *CT* 129–30. But whether or not Coleridge was thinking of phosphorescence, he was certainly thinking of moonlight. His own marginal gloss tells us that the mariner sees the snakes "by the light of the moon."

what these examples already begin to suggest is that in the romantic period, reflections are more than empty images of real objects, images we are supposed to turn away from. The moon is no longer a weak substitute for the sun, and the reflection is no longer simply inferior to the thing it reflects. Aesthetically, at least, it becomes superior, for its greater brilliance and greater softness make it more ideal. So it seemed to Shelley one day in 1821. Gazing on an Italian scene, he wrote in his notebook: "Why is the reflection in that canal far more beautiful than the objects it reflects? The colours more vivid yet blended with more harmony; the openings from within into the soft and tender colours of the distant wood and the intersection of the mountain lines surpass and misrepresent truth" (quoted in Rogers 149n). The philosopher in Shelley sees truth misrepresented, but the poet in him sees truth surpassed. Two years earlier, in fact, when he wrote "Ode to the West Wind," he envisioned "palaces and towers / Quivering within the wave's intenser day." And in act 3 of *Prometheus Unbound*, written just a few months before the "Ode," he used the beauty of reflections to symbolize the beauty of a renovated earth. After Prometheus is released, the Spirit of the Earth explains to Asia that while he lay within a public fountain, "like the reflex of the moon / Seen in a wave under green leaves," he saw that all things had shed their evil natures (3.4.61–77). What epitomized this regeneration was the beauty of two reflected birds. "I cannot tell my joy," the Spirit says,

> when o'er a lake
> Upon a drooping bough with nightshade twined,
> I saw two azure halcyons clinging downward
> And thinning one bright branch of amber berries,
> With quick long beaks, and in the deep there lay
> Those lovely forms imaged as in a sky.
>
> (3.4. 78–83)

When objects imaged in water are seen as thus transfigured or regenerated, the concept of reflection gains a new significance. Coleridge is thinking specifically about reflections in water when, in the *Biographia Literaria*, he defines the relation between nature and Wordsworth's poetry. Among the "excellences" he finds in this poetry, he says, is "the perfect truth of nature in his images and descriptions, as taken immediately from nature. . . . Like a green field reflected in a calm and per-

fectly transparent lake, the image is distinguished from the reality only
by its greater softness and lustre" (*BL* 2: 121). Coleridge trips on his own
language here, for if the lake were indeed perfectly transparent, it would
reflect nothing at all. But he is clearly enough describing the difference
between a real object and its reflection in terms of gain rather than loss.
The reflected object is not a feeble approximation of the original, but an
intensified and idealized version of it, and the dead or at least moribund
metaphor that art is a reflection of nature gains new life from a new way
of looking—of actually *looking*—at reflected objects.

Wordsworth's poetry shows us this way. It not only reflects nature as a
lake reflects a field; it also bears witness to the "greater softness and
lustre" of reflections themselves. In "Home at Grasmere" (1800) Wordsworth writes of birds flying over a lake:

> They tempt the sun to sport among their plumes;
> Tempt the smooth water, or the gleaming ice,
> To shew them a fair image,—'tis themselves,
> Their own fair forms, upon the glimmering plain,
> Painted more soft and fair as they descend,
> Almost to touch.
>
> (*PW* 5: 321, lines 222–26).

Like Shelley's azure halcyons, the descending birds are beautified in reflection, and significantly, the beauty of their reflections suggests the
heightened radiance of a painting.

Yet Wordsworth did not always view reflections with simple admiration. In "Elegiac Stanzas Suggested by a Picture of Peele Castle, in a
Storm," written five years after "Home at Grasmere," the tranquillity of a
reflection is ruefully remembered as one of the things that locked the
poet into a state of delusion. "Thy Form," he says to the castle

> was sleeping on a glassy sea.
> . . . .
> Whene'er I looked, thy Image still was there;
> It trembled, but it never passed away.
>
> (Lines 4, 7–8)

There was just enough motion to distinguish the surface of the sea from
the surface of a mirror, but hardly enough to prefigure the stormy violence that would later take the life of his brother, who now, of course, *has*
passed away. Nevertheless, the tranquillity of the reflected castle still

has a hold on Wordsworth's memory. Paradoxically, even as he denies the moral permanence of this scene, its very evanescence gives it an aesthetic permanence. It remains as permanent and as ideal as the picture he would have painted of this reflected castle: a reflection of a reflection in which he would have included

> the gleam,
> The light that never was, on sea or land,
> The consecration and the poet's dream.
>
> (14–16)

These lines constitute the crux of the poem. Do they describe an act of self-delusion or an act of imaginative transfiguration? Though he ends the poem by stoically saying "Farewell" to the "blind" happiness with which he beheld the tranquillity of the castle, Wordsworth does not resolve our perplexity here. When the artistic reflection of nature in poetry or painting is brighter than the thing it reflects, or when the visible reflection of light upon water is brighter than the sky it reflects, we have trouble invoking the old Platonic distinction between "substance" and "shadow." And a reflection that "trembled, but never passed away" is at once ephemeral and enduring. The past tense relegates it to the Platonic cave of passing shadows, but what is recalled from the past is precisely an image of indestructibility, of oxymoronically trembling steadfastness. When Shelley later echoes this line in his *Ode to Liberty* (1820), he converts the past tense to an eternal present, and the trembling reflection of Athens becomes an unequivocal sign of permanence:

> Within the surface of Time's fleeting river
> Its wrinkled image lies, as then it lay
> Immovably unquiet, and for ever
> It trembles, but it cannot pass away!
>
> (Lines 76–79)

No longer a passing shadow, the reflection becomes a thing of enduring brilliance. Indeed, five years after "Peele Castle," where he seems to dismiss reflections for their impermanence, Wordsworth himself speaks eloquently of their power to symbolize just the opposite. In the first version of *A Guide through the District of the Lakes*, which appeared as an introduction to Joseph Wilkinson's *Select Views* in 1810, Wordsworth says that a calm lake in the midst of a landscape is the embodiment of perfect tranquility. In it, he says, the heavens are not only brought down into the bosom of the earth, but . . . the earth is mainly looked at, and thought of, through the medium of a purer element. . . . All . . . speaks of tranquillity . . . except the clouds gliding in the depths of the lake, or the traveller passing along, an inverted image, whose motion seems governed by the quiet of a time, to which its archetype, the living person, is, perhaps, insensible:— or it may happen, that the figure of one of the larger birds . . . is crossing silently among the reflected clouds, while the voice of the real bird, from the element aloft, gently awakens in the spectator the recollection of appetites and instincts . . . that deform and agitate the world,—yet have no power to prevent nature from putting on an aspect capable of satisfying the most intense cravings for the tranquil, the lovely, and the perfect, to which man, the noblest of her creatures, is subject. (*PrW* 2: 192)

We are a long way from Plato and from Milton. Here, even as the passing traveller is turned upside down in his reflection, the traditional subordination of reflected object to real object is likewise inverted. The voice of the real bird speaks of fleeting agitation; the silent image of the reflected bird speaks·of tranquillity and permanence. Contemplating the reflection, the spectator finds his imagination carried into a world where clouds pass silently beneath him, where the way up and the way down become one, where actual objects mildly distract him, but the reflection of those objects satisfies his cravings for the tranquil, the lovely, and the perfect. What the spectator sees here is in fact something like what Wordsworth himself sees in a seldom-noticed but singularly remarkable sonnet of 1807—"Composed by the Side of Grasmere Lake":

> Clouds, lingering yet, extend in solid bars
> Through the grey west; and lo! these waters, steeled
> By breezeless air to smoothest polish, yield
> A vivid repetition of the stars;
> Jove, Venus, and the ruddy crest of Mars
> Amid his fellows beauteously revealed
> At happy distance from earth's groaning field,
> Where ruthless mortals wage incessant wars.
> Is it a mirror?—or the nether Sphere
> Opening to view the abyss in which she feeds
> Her own calm fires?—But list! a voice is near;
> Great Pan himself low-whispering through the reeds,
> "Be thankful, thou; for if unholy deeds
> Ravage the world, tranquillity is here!"

> (*PW* 3: 127)

Wordsworth here exploits Petrarchan structure to brilliant effect. Using the sestet to reflect upon the reflection described in the octave, he turns the polished steel of the water's surface into a two-way mirror. What vividly repeats the stars of outer space may be seen as a window that reveals the fires of inner space: the "calm fires" far removed from the turbulence of a warring earth, like ruddy Mars, the unmoved mover. There is a hint of subtle terror in this vision of a Paschalian abyss, and the hint is not entirely dispelled by the tidy contrast of the last two lines. Nevertheless, what this reflection on a reflection finally opens to view is the transcendent "tranquillity" of eternal fire.

A similar pattern is at work in a passage from book 5 of *The Prelude*, but here Wordsworth turns a tranquil reflection into a window on what Eugene Stelzig calls the "inner space of a boy's mind" (162). This is the boy who stood beside the glimmering Lake of Winander and

> Blew mimic hootings to the silent owls
> That they might answer him; and they would shout
> Across the watery vale, and shout again,
> Responsive to his call, with quivering peals,
> And long halloos, and screams, and echoes loud
> Redoubled and redoubled, concourse wild
> Of jocund din; and when a lengthened pause
> Of silence came and baffled his best skill,
> Then sometimes, in that silence while he hung
> Listening, a gentle shock of mild surprise
> Has carried far into his heart the voice
> Of mountain torrents; or the visible scene
> Would enter unawares into his mind,
> With all its solemn imagery, its rocks,
> Its woods, and that uncertain heaven, receiv'd
> Into the bosom of the steady lake.
>
> (*Prelude* 5. 373–88)

I do not know just what "uncertain heaven" means. It may refer to the movement of stars in the actual sky—mentioned in lines 366–67—or to the trembling of the reflected sky on the surface of the water. But even if the surface is lightly rippled, the lake itself is essentially "steady," and the reflections of the solemn imagery around it are carried far into the bosom of its depths, just as the voice of mountain torrents is carried far into the heart of the listening boy. The clamorous echo of sound thus gives way to the silent echo of sight, and the doubling of the "solemn imagery" in the depths of the lake is redoubled in the depths of the boy's mind. Once again, as in the sonnet and the passage from the *Guide*, the fleeting tumult of the actual world is surpassed by the permanence and tranquillity of the reflected one.

What distinguishes the *Prelude* passage, however, is the subtlety with which Wordsworth integrates the literal and figurative meanings of reflection. In the sonnet and the passage from the *Guide*, reflections implicitly symbolize the world of permanence that may be imaginatively constructed by a reflective mind: by a mind reflecting not so much on "its own operations," in Locke's phrase, as on the signs of permanence paradoxically discoverable within the fleeting and clamorous phenomena of the actual world. But in the *Prelude* passage, the mind of the boy is utterly unconscious of its own operations. The visible scene figuratively enters "unawares" into his mind even as it literally appears to enter the lake, penetrating its bosom, reaching far below the reflective surface of the water. Here the illusion of depth that reflections in water literally create explicitly symbolizes the intellectual depth at which the visible scene—including its visible reflections—is registered in the mind of the boy.

In both the 1805 and 1850 versions of the *Prelude*, this whole episode is set within an epitaphic context: the boy is said to have died in childhood, and the poet says he has oftentimes "A long half hour . . . stood / Mute, looking at the grave in which he lies" (lines 396–97). Whether or not Wordsworth is referring to the death and grave of an actual Hawkshead schoolmate, the earliest version of the passage describing the boy's experience is written in the first person; we can therefore safely assume that in the later versions Wordsworth is covertly memorializing his own experience, reflecting on a time when he unreflectingly absorbed the sight of reflections.[9] That time is past, or dead; yet the boy who once

9. The first-person version appears in MS JJ, written 1798–99 (*The Prelude*, pp. xxvi, 639). Wordsworth told Isabella Fenwick that one of his Hawkshead schoolmates excelled all the others in the art of blowing through his fingers, and it is known that another of his schoolmates—John Vickars—died in 1782, when Wordsworth was at Hawkshead (*The Prelude*, p. 547). But to believe that Wordsworth is describing what happened to Vickars or any other of his schoolmates is to presume that an intensely personal and subtly revelatory experience was reported to Wordsworth by a boy of ten or twelve. It is far more likely, I think, that Wordsworth is doing to a largely fictionalized boy what he does to the Wanderer in book 1 of *The Excursion*: projecting onto him the memory of his own childhood.

aroused the silent owls by mimicking their cries and who was made to receive "unawares" the visual mimicry of reflections has now become the poet who knows at once how to mimic in language the sounds of nature—"the voice of mountain torrents"—and to make language an instrument of the profoundest mental reflection.

In the final version of the final book of *The Prelude*, the process of reflection becomes a living metaphor for the mind's idealization of the outer world. After describing the spectacle of mist, moonlight, and roaring waters that he experienced from the summit of Snowdon, Wordsworth writes:

> When into air had partially dissolved
> That vision, given to spirits of the night
> And three chance human wanderers, *in calm thought*
> *Reflected*, it appeared to me the type
> Of a majestic intellect, its acts
> And its possessions, what it has and craves,
> What in itself it is, and would become.
> (14. 63–69; italics added)

The mentally reflected version of the spectacle is ultimately independent of the original, which is partially dissolved even before the act of reflecting it begins. To reflect the vision calmly is to perpetuate in a language of the mind what is already disintegrating before the eye, and to recreate its heaving and clamorous elements in tranquilly ideal terms. The sea of moonlit mist hovering over the roaring streams thus becomes the "emblem of a mind / That feeds upon infinity," a mind intent on voices rising from a dark abyss to "silent light," a mind

> sustained
> By recognitions of transcendent power,
> In sense conducting to ideal form,
> In soul of more than mortal privilege.
> (14. 70–77)

For the infinitely idealizing effect of the mental reflection described here there is no simple equivalent in romantic painting. A poet can use the word *reflected* metaphorically; a painter can only represent the process of reflection itself. Yet in Turner's work, the reflected world—the world represented *as* reflected—is often a conspicuously idealized version of what is represented as original.

We can see this, for instance, in *The Fighting 'Temeraire'* (plate 39), exhibited 1839, which shows a grand old warship being tugged away for demolition. If we compare the actual tugboat at left with the reflection just beneath it, we find something analogous to the contrast between the real bird and the reflected bird in the passage from Wordsworth's *Guide*. The real tugboat throws a plume of smoke and fire from its smokestack, and we can almost hear it chugging away. The reflected boat is more lustrous and more tranquil. With its smokestack quietly dissolving in the water, with its colors heightened and its prow delicately elongated, the boat is quite simply repeated—in a finer tone. And the same can be said of the setting sun at right. The actual sun is sinking, and its descent, as Graham Reynolds suggests, clearly symbolizes the end of the day for the *Temeraire* (*Turner* 178). But like the solemn imagery reflected in the Lake of Winander, the delicately shimmering reflection of the sun is received into the bosom of a steady river. While the actual streaks of red massed just above the sun seem to be almost forcing it down, the reflected reds are spread out on a cloth of liquid gold, and the harshness of time relentlessly passing gives way—in reflection—to something that "speaks of tranquillity."

In representing both the actual ship and its reflection, Turner prompts us to reflect on the power of an art which at once reflects, idealizes, and perpetuates a world of visible objects that is sooner or later bound to dissolve, like the mists around Snowdon, or to be demolished, like the *Temeraire*. In Turner's art as in Wordsworth's poetry, reflection memorializes the all-too-fleeting appearance of natural objects.

REFLECTION AND INTEGRATION

We have seen that romantic poets and painters treat reflections not as inferior but superior to the objects they reflect. Turner says that reflected light on water may rival the sky for brilliance, and both he and Constable demonstrate this effect in their work. Coleridge says that reflections have a greater softness and luster than actual objects; Wordsworth says thay can better satisfy our need for loveliness, tranquillity, and perfection; Shelley says they are far more beautiful, and in the wave's intenser day, he finds emblems of both renovation and permanence. Regarded in this way, water-borne reflections may embody an ideal world. As Coleridge implies, they may actually constitute a model of authentic idealization in poetry and painting, for unlike the Claude Glass, which "refines" the landscape by dulling its light, water-borne reflections intensify the light.

Nevertheless, romantic poets and painters did not always choose to emphasize the difference between reality and reflection. In the oil painting *Willows Beside a Stream* (plate 40), ca. 1807, Turner does quite the reverse. Most of the lines in this picture dissolve in its atmosphere, and it is difficult to see any line between the actual trees and the reflection of them. In the air as in the water, the foliage has a fluid delicacy set off only by the bare and spiky branches of the blasted tree at right, and the visible limbs of the other trees grow down as well as up. In this case, what the reflection conveys is not so much intensification as completion: together with the trees on the bank, the reflected trees create a harmonious, homogeneous—indeed almost rounded—whole. And this particular effect was something repeatedly noticed by both Wordsworth and Coleridge. Here is Coleridge, for instance, in a notebook entry of November 1799: "Monday Morning—sitting on a tree stump at the brink of the Lake by Mr. Clarkson's—perfect serenity / that round fat backside of a Hill with its image in the water made together *one* absolutely undistinguishable Form . . . the road appeared sort of suture" (*NC* 1: 555). And here is Coleridge again, in an entry of 1804:

Images of Calmness of Rydale Lake, Jan. 14. . . . An islet Stone, at the bottom of the Lake, the reflection so bright as to be heaved up out of the water / the Stone & its reflection looked so completely one, that Wordsworth remained for more than 5 minutes trying to explain why that stone had no reflection & at last found it out by me. (*NC* 2: 1844)

Wordsworth should have known better. Some four years before this conversation, he himself had captured a similar effect in "Home at Grasmere," where he describes not only the beauty of reflected birds, but also the harmonious integration of a radiantly wooded hillside with its reflection in a lake:

> Behold the universal imagery
> Inverted, all its sun-bright features touched
> As with the varnish, and the gloss of dreams;
> Dreamlike the blending also of the whole
> Harmonious landscape; all along the shore
> The boundary lost, the line invisible
> That parts the image from reality;

> And the clear hills, as high as they ascend
> Heavenward, so piercing deep the lake below.
>   (*PW* 5: 332, lines 571–79)

Wordsworth is conscious of a line that parts the image from reality: he knows the difference between the sun-bright features of the actual trees and the delicate shimmer of their reflection, touched as with the varnish and the gloss of dreams. And Turner knows the difference too: at the lower right side of his *Willows*, we can barely discern a part of the water-line, a suture between reality and reflection. But in each of these land-scapes, the waterline is virtually erased, and the total effect is one of integration rather than division. Catching both parts of a landscape in a single, comprehensive vision, poet and painter alike transcend the difference between the trees and their reflection. Turner depicts what Words-worth describes: a dreamlike blending of the "whole / Harmonious landscape."

Willows by a Stream is a fair sample of what Turner characteristically did with reflection. Throughout his work, from the Lake District paint-ings of the 1790s to the shimmering Venetian scenes of the 1830s and 40s, he used reflection as a means of integration. In *Buttermere Lake* (plate 1), exhibited in 1798, the arc of a rainbow joins the inverted arc of its reflection to form a ring of light that delicately binds together the lake, the mountains, and the disintegrating clouds. In *The Dogana, San Giorgio, Citella, from the Steps of the Europa* (plate 41), exhibited 1842, reflection turns the water into an extension of the sky. The circular swirling of the clouds at upper left distinguishes them from the horizontal plane of the canal, but sky and water alike are permeated with white and blue. Paradoxically resting on their reflections, on foundations made of airy nothing, the buildings seem suspended in a substance that is neither air nor water, but a perfectly harmonious blending of the two.[10]

10. Two years later, writing to William Miller about the engraving of *Modern Italy—the Pifferari*, exhibited 1838, Turner explicitly advised him to blend a rock with its re-flection in the water (*CCT* 185). The blending of the sky with the water and of buildings with their reflections in Turner's late Venetian paintings makes them notably different from the Venetian paintings of Canaletto (1697–1768), who keeps his reflections mini-mal and whose buildings form a solid, precisely delineated barrier between the water and the sky. (See, for instance, *Venice: The Basin of San Marco, on Ascension Day*.) Even in *Bridge of Sighs, Ducal Palace and Custom-House, Venice: Canaletti Painting*, exhibited 1833, which is nominally an act of homage to the Venetian master, Turner gives far more intensity and importance to reflections than Canaletto does. The art critic for the *Athe-neum* of 11 May 1833, observed that Turner's picture was "more his own than he seems

Turner's blending of reflection and reality provoked some criticism. Commenting on his Venetian scenes at the exhibition of 1842, the *Art Union* declared: "A great error in Mr. Turner's smooth water picture is, that the reflection of colours in the water are painted as strongly as the substance themselves, a treatment which diminishes the value of objects" (quoted in Butlin, Wilton, and Gage 152). This criticism is highly revealing—though not quite in the way intended. On the one hand, it conveys the traditional assumption that reflections are inferior "shadows" of what they reflect and should be represented as such; on the other hand, it recognizes Turner's challenge to that assumption, his deliberate attack on the traditional barrier between reflection and reality. But the critic of the *Art Union* was a little imprecise. By acting on the principle that water could rival the sky for brilliance, by raising the tone of reflected colors to the tone of the colors they reflect, Turner did not diminish the value of objects. He diminished their separateness. He made them collaborate with their reflections to produce an interdependent, integrated, harmonious whole.

Nothing so ethereal as Turner's late Venetian scenes was ever painted by Constable. But Constable was quite capable of using reflections to generate a comprehensive vision of landscape, to integrate earth, sky, and water. In *Malvern Hall, Warwickshire*, which may have been painted about 1809 (Tate Gallery; reproduced in Taylor, plate 9), the hall stands right of center in the distance, with trees clumped at right and stretching out at left. The lake or river crossing the picture in front of the hall mirrors the hall itself, completes the semicircles of the trees, and repeats the bluish white of the sky, contracting its broad expanse to a rough triangle. In *Barges on the Stour*, an oil sketch done about 1811 (Victoria and Albert Museum; reproduced in Taylor, plate 34), the integrative power of reflection is still more evident. The reflection of the sky in the foreground of *Malvern Hall* is cut off by a solid stretch of shore, but in *Barges*, only a slender strip of land at left keeps the river from taking all of the foreground. The river in *Barges*, therefore, not only reflects the barges themselves and the group of trees at right, it also gets most of its colors from the blues and whites of the sky, and Constable underscores the correspondence between river and sky by marking both of them with horizontal streaks.

---

aware of: he imagines he has painted in the Canaletti style: the style is his, and worth Canaletti ten times over: (Butlin and Joll 183).

No such linear rhyme appears in *Water-meadows near Salisbury* (plate 42), which Constable painted much later, in 1829. But this is probably the finest example we have of the way he could use reflection to unify a scene. Here the water occupies all of the foreground, and the top half of the picture is filled with sky. Narrowed in perspective, therefore, the stretch of meadowland that crosses the middle of the picture seems—like Turner's Venice—to be suspended between the two. The sky and the water are not so similar as they are in *Malvern Hall* or *Barges*; the horizontal streaks of a moving stream and the green reflections of the trees distinguish the water from the sky, where rounded white puffs of cloud delicately emerge from a background of pale blue. But the rounded shape of the reflected trees corresponds to the shape of the clouds, and the subtle mixture of white and blue that permeates the water unmistakably shows the influence of the sky.

To make the water re-present the sky, as Constable does here and as Turner does even more vividly in his Venetian pictures, is to suppress the line between reality and reflection and thus to undermine the very notion of reality itself. If, as Derrida says, the most perfect representation "is always already other than what it doubles and re-presents" (291–92), a represented reflection differs only in degree—not in kind—from the representation of what it reflects. This near-identification of the two either diminishes the ontological status of the represented "reality," as the critic of the *Art Union* implied, or elevates the reflection to the point where it participates with the "reality" in a newly created whole. Coleridge saw this kind of relation between an actual sky and its reflection at Malta. Recalling in 1807 what he had seen during his sojourn there in 1804, he wrote in his notebook:

The Sky, o rather say, the Aether, at Malta, with the Sun apparently suspended in it, the Eye seeming to pierce beyond, & as it were, behind it and below the aetherial Sea, so blue, so [a] zerflossenes Eins, the substantial Image, and fixed real Reflection of the Sky—O I could annihilate in a deep moment all possibility of the needlepoint pinshead System of the *Atomists* by one submissive Case! λογος ab *Ente*—at once the existent Reflexion, and the Reflex Act—at once actual and real & therefore, filiation not creation. (*NC* 2: 3159, f. 52ʳ)

As Kathleen Coburn observes, Coleridge goes on to speculate on the process by which thought moves from existence (*Ente*) to λογος, the creative Word (*NC* 2: 3159). But the starting point for this speculation is the memory of what he had seen at Malta: the sea reflecting the sky so perfectly that it became at once "aetherial" and "substantial." No insubstantial image of a real object, it was itself a "real Reflection of the Sky," a "filiation" consubstantial with it, bound up with it in an all-pervading oneness: *zerflossenes Eins*.

The sense of metaphysical oneness that Coleridge felt when he contemplated the sky and its reflection at Malta is altogether comparable to the union of sky and water expressed by the late Venetian paintings of Turner. In Turner's work, however, one of the finest examples of the way in which reflection can fuse contradictory elements is a picture not of Venice but of London: the *Burning of the Houses of Parliament* (plate 43). The effect of this picture is triumphantly visual. Just as the pathetic plight of the drowning men in Turner's *Slavers* is overpowered by the searing brilliance of its sunset, so the magnitude of the destruction wrought by fire in the very seat of British government is overpowered here by the magnificence of the fire itself. At left and right, the blue-green tones of the river Thames reflect the hues of the sky, and at right, the spectral towers of the Abbey and their reflection have the cool delicacy of Turner's Venice. But there is nothing cool about the center of this picture. While a massive tongue of flame takes possession of the sky, its equally massive reflection turns the river into liquid fire, and in this fusion of fire and water, reflection paradoxically becomes the means by which Turner approaches the Platonic "one."

The liquid fire of Turner's Thames, in fact, strikingly recalls a key passage in Shelley's intensely Platonic *Adonais* (1821): the stanza in which Shelley's grief over Keats's death changes to joy because he perceives that Keats's spirit will flow

> Back to the burning fountain whence it came,
> A portion of the Eternal, which must glow
> Through time and change, unquenchably the same.
>
> (Lines 339–41)

Turner's Thames is itself a burning fountain. Challenging the laws of elemental contradiction as it challenges the sky for brightness, the reflected and liquified fire assumes a kind of transcendent radiance which the actual fire churning above it significantly lacks. It is striking to note that in the penultimate stanza of *Adonais*, Shelley speaks of "man and beast and earth and air and sea" as "mirrors of / The fire for which all thirst" (483–85). Had Shelley lived to see this picture, which was painted thirteen years after his death, he might well have seen its mirrored fire as an emblem of that unquenchable fire for which he thirsted.

In the landscapes of Wordsworth, Coleridge, Shelley, Turner, and Constable, reflections in water prompt us to rediscover what *reflection* means. Challenging the sky for brightness, they may visibly embody ideal brilliance. Representing sights but not sounds in a medium that trembles but does not pass away, they may symbolize the tranquillity of ideal permanence. And as agents of integration between earth, air, water, and sky, they enable the poet and painter to represent the life of nature as an indissoluble whole. All of these effects enrich the impact of reflection when it is metaphorically used for the representation of nature in poetry and painting. To understand what reflection really means for the romantic poets and painters is to understand why, in the preface to *Lyrical Ballads* of 1800, Wordsworth defines the mind of man not as a lamp but as a special kind of mirror: "the mirror of the fairest and most interesting properties of nature" (*PW* 1: 40). When reflections are no longer insubstantial copies of real things, when they become instead embodiments of brilliance, symbols of tranquillity, and agents of elemental integration, they paradigmatically express what poets and painters do to "reality" when it is reflected in their own works. The representation of reflections in romantic poetry and painting thus becomes a way of representing the extraordinarily complex process of representation itself.

CONCLUSION

IF IT IS HARD ENOUGH to make reliable generaliza-
tions about the six highly individualistic poets commonly known as "romantic," it is harder still to gener-
alize about romantic poets and painters—even if we
choose to concentrate on just two of each. To consider
romantic poetry and painting synoptically, as I have done, is to discover
anew the irreducible differences between the arts as well as the differences between particular poets and painters. But it is also to see that
romanticism cannot be simply defined as the moment at which the arts
diverged, with poetry declaring its intellectual independence of pictorial
mimesis, its refusal to regard pictures as models of verbal representation. While romanticism challenged the assumptions on which the traditional sisterhood of the arts was based, it also produced a poetry that
reaches out to painting in the intensity with which it re-creates the outer
world and a painting that reaches out to poetry in the subtlety with which
it evokes the inner one. To read Wordsworth and Coleridge in the light
provided by Constable and Turner is to find in their poetry a distinctively
romantic pictorialism: a simultaneous consciousness of enclosure and
expanse, a sense of borders and boundaries that paradoxically helps to
generate a sense of boundlessness, an acute sensitivity to the correspondence between atmospheric effect and the language of transformation,
and a fascination with water-borne reflections as visible representatives
of representation itself. Conversely, to read Turner and Constable in the
light provided by Wordsworth and Coleridge is to see the introspec-
tiveness of their painting: its capacity to represent the private history of
the painter himself, as in the temporalized space of Constable's *Cornfield*, or to symbolize the act of journeying within, as in the blocked prospects and bottomless depths in Turner's pictures of St. Gothard.

The painters and poets I have examined in this book stretched the limits of their respective arts precisely by discovering new ways of making
pictures poetic and poetry pictorial. Coming of age around 1800, they all
inherited landscape as a cultural phenomenon jointly defined by a critical climate in which the correspondence between painting and poetry

was at once affirmed and denied. But in spite of their own part in this ambivalence, in spite of their own resistance to the demands made by the traditional sisterhood of the arts, their works reveal significant affinities. Beneath of the surface of Turner's apparent homage to Thomson and to the sister-arts tradition in *Buttermere* is the resistance embodied in the painting itself, which decisively rejects the lucidly Newtonian world that Thomson verbally depicts. Yet in the very act of rejecting this all-too-easy and enticing commerce with a conspicuously pictorial poetry, Turner creates a picture poetic in its suggestiveness, in its power to elicit the transcendent perfection of the circle by means of a broken arc of evanescent light. Thus, even as Wordsworth's "Tables Turned" represents the picturable transformation of green fields into yellow ones at sunset, *Buttermere* re-creates the world evoked by Wordsworth's poem: a world beyond the analytic control of the "meddling intellect."

It may yet be asked whether romantic poetry and paintings have anything more in common than incidental similarities—an occasional description that seems to resemble a particular depiction, or vice versa. To this question my answer is an unequivocal yes. The four major figures of this study not only re-create landscape; they also redefine the very process of re-creation in their respective arts. In doing so, they make us see both pictures *in* words and pictures *through* words—pictures verbally framed. What Turner and Constable offer us along with their pictures are not only picture titles but also comments in prose and verse on individual pictures as well as notes and lectures on landscape and landscape painting. To compare the pictures and words of these two painters with the poetry, descriptive notes, and critical prose of Wordsworth and Coleridge is to enlarge and enrich a verbal context already provided by the painters themselves, and thus to generate the possibility that English romantic poetry and painting may be seen as a coherent whole.

What kind of shape does the whole assume? Ultimately, I believe, the synoptic study of romantic poetry and painting allows us to see romanticism as the representation of temporalized space. We commonly associate romantic literature with relentless temporality—with process, development, and becoming rather than being, with the fear of stasis that paradoxically accompanies and complicates the desire for timelessness. But the correspondences between romantic poetry and painting force us to recognize that romantic temporality is wedded to space. Neither Wordsworth nor Coleridge can signify time without reference to the remembered or reexperienced places that enable them to register its passage.

Wordsworth must revisit the banks of the Wye to know what five years have done to him, and his "spots of time" are unforgettably bound to spots of place, just as Coleridge is bound to a lime-tree bower while he vicariously travels with his friends and gradually finds his way from melancholy to contentment. The characteristically romantic consciousness of time is born within and inevitably nurtured by the consciousness of place.

This interdependence of space and time in romantic poetry is complemented by the temporalization of space in romantic painting. No longer confined to representing a single "pregnant moment" from a story which the poet alone could supply in full, Turner and Constable temporalize space by making it express a moment of "natural history," the history of their own relation to landscape, or—in Turner's case—the way in which the temporal movement of the elements dominates the would-be epitomizing moment of a great public event. Virtually all the recreations of landscape that we have seen in this book can be understood as versions of temporalized space. A prospect internalized—whether verbally or graphically—is a prospect remembered and therefore subjected to the temporal pressures of meditation. Even when the mind and prospect are suddenly brought together in a moment of reciprocal absorption, as in Turner's *Fall of an Avalanche* or Wordsworth's account of the rising peak, the process of absorption is inescapably temporal, for the movement represented as occurring in the outer world provokes a corresponding movement from within. Equally temporal in their implications are the language of transformation and the geometry of the infinite. The language of transformation represents the effects of atmospheric change on a particular place; the geometry of the infinite represents time as the disruption of space, the crossing or suppression of lines, the simultaneous evocation and disturbance of pure geometrical forms, the dynamically sexual union of angle and curve, the transformation of parallel perspective into a curvilinear perspective that vividly expresses the time-bound instability of the viewer. Finally, to represent reflections is essentially to re-create a process in which an actual landscape is naturally re-created in heightened or idealized form, and is thus presented as a model for graphic or verbal re-creation in a doubling or temporal continuation of the original process.

Looking from poetry to painting and back again, we have seen the romantic imagination hovering between space and time, stasis and movement, tranquil order and violent change. Neither side of these antinomies could by itself satisfy either the poets or the painters of this study.

"The thing to recognize," says Michael Cooke, "is not that the romantics included opposites in their work, as dialectism would suggest, but rather that they proposed acts of inclusion as their ground and goal" (xiii). Cooke is speaking of the romantic poets, but what he says applies to Turner and Constable as well. The ground and goal of the present study has been the act of including painting and poetry within a study of romanticism that seeks at once to bridge the gap between the two arts and to see what the view from the bridge provides. If we think of painting as fundamentally spatial and poetry as fundamentally temporal, these two arts respectively embody the poles of the romantic universe: form and energy, stasis and movement, timelessness and time. But once we recognize that romantic poetry and painting were each engaged in the representation of temporalized space, the synoptic study of the two becomes no longer an exercise in dialectical reconciliation. Instead, each of these two arts enables us more fully to grasp the inclusiveness of the other.

APPENDIX

THE QUESTION OF INFLUENCE

THE QUESTION of influence and personal association clearly demands to be answered in any extended study of four major contemporaries. I have chosen to answer it in an appendix because I have concluded that Wordsworth and Coleridge were the only two of the four who formatively influenced one another, and that the evidence about personal relations between the poets and the painters— or even between Turner and Constable—contributes nothing substantive to an argument about what we can learn from comparing their works.

Turner and Constable, first of all, were two quite different men. Though both of them studied at the Royal Academy in the 1790s, their careers thereafter widely diverged. Turner grappled titanically with the whole tradition of European history painting; Constable focused on rural landscape. Turner became a Royal Academician in 1802, at the age of twenty-seven, and soon acquired wealth and fame; Constable spent most of his life in a pinched obscurity and did not become a full Academician until 1829, when he was fifty-two. For Turner, Constable scarcely existed. On the night Constable was elected, Turner went to congratulate him and the two men talked until 1:00 A.M. (Constable, *JCC* 6: 242), but so far as I know, there is no other record of Turner's interest in Constable or his work, and there is some evidence that Turner did not even want him in the Academy (Constable, *JCC* 3: 19).

On the other side, Constable saw Turner as Jehovah: to be loved, hated, and feared. He was impressed by Turner's "wonderful range of mind" when the two were seated together once at an Academy dinner (*JCC* 2: 110); he called an early Turner "the most complete work of genius I ever saw" (*JCC* 3: 58); and at the Academy exhibition one year he thought Turner's paintings "golden visions—glorious and beautifull" (*JCC* 6: 236). But Turner's paintings could give him pain as well as pleasure (*JCC* 6: 220), and sometimes they simply repelled him. After seeing the exhibition of 1803, which included *Calais Pier* and several other pictures by Turner, he judged the exhibition "in the landscape way most miserable" (*JCC* 2: 34), and Turner, he reportedly said, "becomes more & more extravagant, and less attentive to nature: (Farington, *FD* 2: 99). At the exhibition of 1812, he thought Turner's *Hannibal* "as a whole novel and affecting," but "so ambiguous as to be scarcely intelligible in many parts (and those principal)" (*JCC* 6: 66). Turner was "novel" indeed. He was luminous, clairvoyant, and shockingly original, yet somehow he was part of everything that Constable found objectionable in art. Writing to Leslie in 1823, Constable summed up his views with a grand and damning simplicity. "All that I have ever seen of even the greatest names," he wrote, "are either 'pictures' or nothing," and among his dislikes he specifically mentioned "the stagnate sulphur of Turner" (*JCC* 3: 85). That, of course, was Constable's way of defying a deity—an imagination so powerful that it threatened to consume his own. Two years later, after his paintings had dazzled the French at an exhibition in Paris, he could make the same point with more confidence and less extravagance. To Fisher he wrote: "I deeply feel the honour of having found an original style & independent of him who would be Lord over all—I mean Turner" (*JCC* 6: 191).

Genuine originality is always challenging for those around it—especially when they mean to be original themselves. If Constable was sometimes repelled by Turner's work, it should not surprise us to learn that neither of these painters significantly pleased either Wordsworth or Coleridge. So far as I know, Coleridge never mentioned either of them. Wordsworth had very little to say of Turner, and though we now know that Wordsworth attended at least one of Constable's lectures on landscape painting in 1836 (Reed 481–83), he said nothing recorded about Constable until after the painter's death in 1837. When he was asked that year to subscribe to a fund that would buy one of Constable's works for the National Gallery, he sent one guinea on behalf of what he called this "admirable . . . Artist" (Constable, *JCC* 5: 78). Seven years later, when Constable's daughters sent him a copy of Leslie's *Memoirs of Constable*, Wordsworth dictated a polite letter of thanks. Mentioning the "pleasure" of his meeting with Constable and speaking of *English Landscape* as "a work most honourable to his genius," he concludes: "Pity that he did not prolong his stay in this beautiful country [the Lake District], i.e., that we might have had its features reflected by his pencil" (*JCC* 5: 78). Thus spoke Wordsworth of Constable after his death— and to his daughters. But in the Farington Diary of 4 May 1807 we find a somewhat different reaction to a Royal Academy exhibition which included not only Turner's *Sun Rising through Vapour*, but also two of Constable's Lake District paintings. "Wordsworth & His wife or Sister I met," writes Farington. "He thought it a poor exhibition & she said it was the worst she had ever seen" (*FD* 4: 132). We cannot be certain, of course, that the Wordsworths here were consciously criticizing either Constable or Turner, but much later, Wordsworth is said to have spoken "severely" of Turner "and of all the analogous artists in poetry."[1]

The indifference—or worse—with which Wordsworth and Coleridge regarded the work of Turner and Constable was reciprocated in two quite different

1. Robinson, *CRB* II, 459. Later still, Wordsworth is said to have criticized Ruskin for overpraising Turner in the first two volumes of *Modern Painters* (Shackford 60). On the other hand, Wordsworth was "charmed" with the engravings in Samuel Rogers's *Poems* (1834), some of which were based on pictures by Turner; see Shackford 59–60, and Wordsworth, *LY* 2: 692.

ways. Turner seems to have known nothing of either Wordsworth or Coleridge, but Constable valued the poetry of both. He first met the two during a sketching exhibition to the Lake District in 1806, and sometime between then and 1824 he met Wordsworth at least once more at the London house of George Beaumont.[2] By this time he had come to admire the work of both poets. In 1824 he described "The Rime of the Ancient Mariner" as "the very best modern poem."[3] The year before, during a visit to Beaumont's country estate, Coleorton, he had heard Beaumont read a good deal of Wordsworth's *Excursion*; and though its stories seemed to him maudlin, he found some of its descriptions of landscape "beautifull"—a word he also applied to the Wordsworthian lines inscribed on Beaumont's cenotaph to the memory of Joshua Reynolds.[4] In the 1830s, he twice connected Wordsworth's poetry to his own pictures. As one of the epigraphs for *English Landscape* he used a four-line passage from Wordsworth's *Ode: The Morning of the Day Appointed for a General Thanksgiving* (1816), and on sending a mezzotint of *Weymouth Bay* to a friend, he applied to it a line from "Peele Castle" in order "to give [it] value" (Constable, *JCD* 8; *JCC* 3: 29). Constable's admiration for the poetry of Wordsworth ultimately knew no bounds. In 1835 he actually wrote a sonnet that addresses Wordsworth as "Thou second Milton!" (*JCC* 5: 77).

Moved by this undeniable evidence that Constable met Wordsworth and admired his poetry, Morse Peckham contends that after their first meeting in 1806 Constable was "profoundly affected" by Wordsworth's ideas, and that in 1808 they caused him to redirect his art.[5] This seems to me unlikely. It is certainly true, as Graham Reynolds has observed, that the years immediately following Constable's visit to the Lake District were "decisive" for the liberation and de-

2. See Constable, *JCC* 5: 73–75; and Herrmann and Owen 11–12. Beckett believes that the second meeting occurred in the spring of 1812.

3. *JCC* 6: 186. To be fairly assessed, the phrase must be read in context. When Constable learned how some French critics had criticized the pictures he sent to Paris in 1824, he wrote to Fisher: "They want the objects more formed & defined, &c, and say that [the pictures] are like the rich preludes in musick, and the full harmonious warblings of the Aeolian lyre, which *mean* nothing, and they call them orations—and harangues—and highflown conversations affecting a careless ease—&c &c &c—Is not some of this *blame* the highest *praise*—what is poetry?—What is Coleridge's Ancient Mariner (the very best modern poem) but something like this?" (*JCC* 5: 186). Though Constable clearly admired Coleridge's "Rime," the terms he applies to it scarcely describe the poem itself—let alone explain its resemblance to his own work.

4. Constable, *JCC* 2: 292; Leslie 109. Constable sketched the cenotaph at this time and in 1836 exhibited an oil painting of it at the Royal Academy, quoting Wordsworth's lines in the catalogue (Leslie 253–54).

5. See Peckham, "Constable and Wordsworth" 196–209; *Beyond the Tragic Vision* 140–42; *The Triumph of Romanticism*, chap. 6; and also Noyes 67–68. Karl Kroeber cautiously notes that "it is difficult to estimate Wordsworth's possible influence upon Constable" (*RLV* 45n).

velopment of his style (*CCC* 15). But Reynolds also says that scarcely any of Constable's known pictures can be definitely assigned to these years, and the oil sketch titled *Spring: East Bergholt Common*—which for Peckham exemplifies "the great breakthrough of 1808" (*Beyond the Tragic Vision* 142)—may not have been painted until 1816 (G. Reynolds, *CCC* 15, 91). Whatever he got from his visit to the Lake District, the demonstrably formative periods in his development were the two long summers of 1813 and 1814, when he filled two sketchbooks with vivid, minutely observed drawings of his native Stour Valley and thus laid the groundwork for the great large-scale oils of the Stour that would begin with *The White Horse* in 1819.[6] If the influence of Wordsworth played any significant part in this development, it is hard to explain why Constable's earliest known mention of Wordsworth's poetry did not come until 1823, when he had already achieved the characteristic style of his maturity.[7]

In any case, Constable's own report on his first meeting with Wordsworth scarcely indicates that he had met a man who had changed his life. On 12 December 1807, about a year after his visit to the Lake District, Constable reportedly "remarked upon the high opinion Wordsworth entertains of himself. He told Constable that while He was a Boy going to Hawkeshead School, His mind was often so possessed with images, so long in extraordinary conceptions, that He was held by a wall not knowing but He was part of it" (Farington, FDT 13: 3888). In connection with his "Ode: Intimations of Immortality," Wordsworth much later told the same story to Isabella Fenwick (*PW* 4: 463), but the tone in which Constable tells it here—if we can trust this report—is less than sympathetic. What Constable remembers from his meeting with Wordsworth is not so much a visionary prophet as a self-absorbed egotist, and this impression was evidently reinforced by what he had heard of Wordsworth's comments to another artist, David Wilkie. According to Farington, Constable said that Wilkie "was offended with Wordsworth who offered to propose subjects to Him to paint, &

6. "Not until he spent a long summer at East Berghold in 1813," says Graham Reynolds, "did Constable show in his drawings the freedom and novelty now apparent in his oil paintings." But he "emerged from his summers of seclusion at East Bergholt fully certain in his own mind of the way to compose into large-scale paintings the unemphatic features of the Suffolk countryside" (*CCC* 16–17).

7. Though *The Excursion* was published in 1814, Constable's reaction to Beaumont's reading of it in 1823 strongly suggests that this was his first experience of the poem. On the basis of a newly discovered letter sent from Constable to Wordsworth on 15 June 1836, Mark Reed concludes that Constable "almost certainly" read Wordsworth first in *Lyrical Ballads* about 1801 or early 1802. But the letter simply says "it was from [Beaumont's] hands that I first saw a Volume of Your poems" (Reed 481–83). Though Constable had met Beaumont in 1795 and though Beaumont himself would have learned about *Lyrical Ballads* in 1801 (Reed 483), there is no particular reason why the "Volume" to which Constable refers should have been the two-volume *Lyrical Ballads* of 1800 rather than the one-volume *Excursion* of 1814. In any case, we have no definite evidence that Constable knew any of Wordsworth's poetry before 1823.

gave him to understand that when He could not think of subjects as well as paint them He wd. come to him."[8] If this report is accurate, Wordsworth was plainly revealing his conviction that poetry was superior to painting, that poetry—or the poet himself—was the source from which the painter should take his inspiration. I suspect that Constable was just about as offended by this notion as Wilkie was. He admired many poets, but he took his subjects from his own observation of landscape, and to my knowledge, not one of his paintings, drawings, or sketches was ever based on anything written by Wordsworth. If in 1833 he applied a Wordsworthian line to a mezzotint of *Weymouth Bay*, we cannot safely infer that he was thinking of Wordsworth in 1816, when the picture was painted. What we can infer is something rather different. The pleasure with which Constable heard Beaumont read *The Excursion* in 1823, and the enthusiasm that he thereafter expressed for Wordsworth's poetry, sprang from his somewhat belated discovery that Wordsworth was a great and original poet of landscape, and hence a valuable ally in Constable's struggle to establish the respectability of landscape painting.

It is nonetheless clear that neither Wordsworth nor Coleridge took any significant interest in either Constable or Turner, and it is not easy to understand why. Both of the poets appreciated painting. Hazlitt tells us that Coleridge "had no idea of pictures" in 1798, but after his visit to Germany the following year and to Italy in 1805–6, he impressed even Hazlitt with his knowledge of the old masters (Hazlitt 11: 33). In England he knew the work of Hogarth, Reynolds, Blake, and Wilson; he learned a great deal about painting from Beaumont, whom he met in 1803 (Coleridge, *LC* 2: 1063); and he ardently defended the work of Washington Alston, the American painter whom he met in Rome and whose exhibition at Bristol in 1814 moved him to write a series of essays on the fine arts.[9] As for Wordsworth, Martha Shackford has shown that he was familiar with the work of about one hundred painters, and that twelve of his poems were prompted by pictures (73). In addition, he was a good friend of the painter and sculptor Benjamin Robert Haydon, who thought his knowledge of art "extraordinary" (*AMH* 2: 730–31), and an intimate friend of Beaumont, whose painting of Peele Castle prompted his "Elegiac Stanzas" in 1805.

Beaumont is in fact the one man who might have helped Wordsworth and Coleridge to appreciate the works of Turner and Constable. Generous and en-

8. Farington, FDT 13: 3888. See also Wordsworth's letter to George Beaumont of February 1808: "In the Poem I have just written [*The White Doe of Rylstone*] you will find one situation which, if the work should ever become familiarly known, would furnish as fine a subject for a Picture as anything I remember in Poetry ancient or modern." Beaumont dutifully painted the picture, which was engraved as a frontispiece to the poem in 1815 (Wordsworth, *LW* 2: 196, 196n).

9. Coleridge, *LC* 3: 534. For a good comprehensive discussion of Coleridge's interest in painting, see Carl Woodring, "What Coleridge Thought of Pictures" (in Kroeber and Walling 91–106).

couraging patron of poets and painters alike, he had come to know Wordsworth, Coleridge, and Constable by 1803, and he had probably been at least aware of Turner from as early as 1793, when he bought a drawing from Turner's close friend and co-worker Thomas Girtin (Herrmann and Owen 11). Yet if Beaumont was ideally situated to know all of these poets and painters well, to bring them together under one or more of his commodious roofs, and to nurture communication among them, his own tastes were calculated to keep them apart. For one thing, Beaumont did not like the work of Turner. As a disciple of Reynolds and a man of distinctly conservative taste, he was unable to appreciate a radically original style, and Luke Herrmann observes that from abut 1802 onwards, he "must have seen in Turner's work . . . a real and dangerous challenge to the traditions of landscape painting which he held so dear" (16). Beaumont never bought a work by Turner nor entertained him in his house (Herrmann and Owen 16), and it is safe to assume, I think, that if Wordsworth or Coleridge ever heard him speak of Turner, what they heard was negative. With Constable the case is only superficially different. Beaumont often entertained him, and it was at Beaumont's house that he met Wordsworth at least once. But for essentially the same reason that Beaumont could not appreciate Turner, he was the very last person to explain and defend the work of Constable—to poets or to anyone else. The decorously embrowned style in which Beaumont painted and which he earnestly recommended to Constable himself was decidedly not the style in which Constable chose to paint. Between Wordsworth and Coleridge on the one hand, then, and the radically original styles of Turner and Constable on the other, Beaumont could only erect a wall.

The one man best equipped to put a window in that wall was William Hazlitt. As Haydon said of him, he "practised painting long enough to know it," and he brought to the study of literature "a stock which no literary man ever did before him" (*DH* 2: 65). At the age of twenty in 1798, the same year in which he first met Wordsworth and Coleridge, Hazlitt began to study painting, and until he was thirty-four he worked at portraits—with mediocre results. Only in his thirties did he truly discover and begin to display his talent as an essayist, and by then his experience with painting had fully prepared him to be a circumspect critic of art—as well as of drama and poetry. Hazlitt was one of the very few literary men of his time who perceptively appreciated both Turner and Constable. I have discussed his comments on Turner in chapter 4. His opinion of Constable emerges from a dialogue between a Frenchman and an Englishman which he published in 1826. Admitting that Constable's "affectation of dashing lights and broken tints and straggly lumps of paint" may distress the French, the Englishman nevertheless asks his French companion: "Why do not your artists try to give something of the same green, fresh, and healthy look of living to nature?" (Hazlitt 10: 127). With insights such as these, Hazlitt provides an important link between the worlds of painting and poetry in the English romantic period. But unfortunately, in the very year that he published his perceptive comments on Turner—1816—he also began to publish a series of malicious attacks on Wordsworth and Coleridge, whom he saw as apostates to the cause of the French Revolution. From then on, he was hardly in a position to help the poets see what Turner and Constable had achieved.

All of this evidence leads me to conclude that no significant influence flowed either way between the two major poets and painters of this study.

REFERENCE LIST

Abrams, M. H., ed. *English Romantic Poets: Modern Essays in Criticism*. 2d ed. London, Oxford, and New York: Oxford University Press, 1975.

————. *The Mirror and the Lamp: Romantic Theory and the Critical Tradition*. 1953. Reprint. New York: W. W. Norton & Co., 1958.

————. *Natural Supernaturalism: Tradition and Revolution in Romantic Literature*. New York: W. W. Norton & Co., 1971.

Akenside, Mark. *The Pleasures of Imagination*. London, 1765. First edition 1744.

Alston, J. W. *Hints to Young Practitioners in the Study of Landscape*. 3d ed. London, 1804.

Annals of the Fine Arts. London, 1817–20. This periodical, ed. James Elmes, was issued annually in four successive volumes.

Appleton, Jay. *The Experience of Landscape*. New York, 1975.

Arac, Jonathan. "Bounding Lines: *The Prelude* and Critical Revision." *Boundary 2*, 7 (Spring 1979): 31–48.

Bachelard, Gaston. *The Poetics of Space*. Trans. Maria Jolas. New York: Orion Press, 1964.

Badt, Kurt. *John Constable's Clouds*. Trans. Stanley Goodman. London: Routledge and Kegan Paul, 1950.

Baker, Jeffrey. *Time and Mind in Wordsworth's Poetry*. Detroit: Wayne State University Press, 1980.

Ball, Patricia M. *The Science of Aspects: The Changing Role of Fact in the Work of Coleridge, Ruskin, and Hopkins*. London: Athlone Press, 1971.

Barbier, Carl Paul. *William Gilpin: His Drawings, Teaching, and Theory of the Picturesque*. Oxford: Clarendon Press, 1963.

Barrell, John. *The Dark Side of the Landscape: The Rural Poor in English Painting, 1730–1840*. Cambridge: Cambridge University Press, 1980.

————. *The Idea of Landscape and the Sense of Place, 1730–1840: An Approach to the Poetry of John Clare*. London: Cambridge University Press, 1972.

Blake, William. *The Poetry and Prose of William Blake* [*PPB*]. Ed. David V. Erdman with commentary by Harold Bloom. New York: Doubleday, 1965.

Bloom, Harold. *The Anxiety of Influence: A Theory of Poetry*. 1973. Reprint. New York: Oxford University Press, 1975.

————. "The Internalization of Quest-Romance." In *Romanticism and Consciousness: Essays in Criticism*, 3–24. New York: W. W. Norton & Co., 1970.

Brisman, Leslie. "Coleridge and the Supernatural." *Studies in Romanticism* 21 (Summer 1982): 123–59.

Burke, Edmund. *A Philosophical Enquiry into the Origin of our Ideas of the Sublime and Beautiful.* Ed. James T. Boulton. 1958. Reprint. Notre Dame, Ind.: University of Notre Dame Press, 1968.

Butlin, Martin, Andrew Wilton, and John Gage. *Turner, 1775–1851.* London: Tate Gallery Publications, 1974. Catalogue for the Royal Academy exhibition of 16 November 1974–2 March 1975.

Butlin, Martin, and Evelyn Joll, eds. *The Paintings of J.M.W. Turner.* 2 vols., plates and text. New Haven and London: Yale University Press, 1977. All citations refer to text volume unless indicated by plate number.

Byron, Lord. *Childe Harold's Pilgrimage and Other Romantic Poems.* Ed. Samuel Chew. New York: Odyssey Press, 1936.

————. *Letters and Journals.* Ed. Rowland E. Prothero. 8 vols. London: John Murray; New York: Charles Scribner's Sons, 1898.

Clark, Kenneth. *The Romantic Rebellion: Romantic versus Classic Art.* New York: Harper & Row, 1973.

Cohen, Ralph. *The Art of Discrimination.* Berkeley and Los Angeles: University of California Press, 1964.

————. *The Unfolding of the Seasons.* Baltimore: Johns Hopkins University Press, 1970.

Coleridge, S. T. *Biographia Literaria [BL].* Ed. J. T. Shawcross. 2 vols. London: Oxford University Press, 1907.

————. *Coleridge's Shakespearean Criticism.* Ed. T. M. Raysor. 2 vols. London: Constable & Co., 1930.

————. *Collected Letters of Samuel Taylor Coleridge [LC].* Ed. Earl Leslie Griggs. 6 vols. Oxford: Clarendon Press, 1956–71.

————. *The Complete Poetical Works of Samuel Taylor Coleridge.* Ed. Ernest Hartley Coleridge. 2 vols. Oxford, 1912. All of Coleridge's poems are quoted from this edition.

————. *The Notebooks of Samuel Taylor Coleridge [NC].* Ed. Kathleen Coburn. 3 vols. to date. London: Routledge and Kegan Paul; Princeton: Princeton University Press, 1957–73. Numbers following the volume number refer to notebook entry numbers.

————. *The Table Talk and Omniana of Samuel Taylor Coleridge [TT].* Ed. T. Ashe. London, 1888.

Constable, John. *John Constable's Correspondence [JCC].* Ed. R. S. Beckett. 6 vols. London: Her Majesty's Stationery Office; Ipswich: Suffolk Records Society, 1962–68.

————. *John Constable's Discourses [JCD].* Ed. R. B. Beckett. Ipswich: Suffolk Records Society, 1970.

————. *John Constable: Further Documents and Correspondence [JC: FDC].*

Ed. Leslie Parris, Coral Shields, and Ian Fleming-Williams. London: Tate Gallery; Ipswich: Suffolk Records Society, 1975.

Constable, W. G. *Richard Wilson*. London: Routledge and Kegan Paul, 1953.

Cooke, Michael. *Acts of Inclusion: Studies Bearing on an Elementary Theory of Romanticism*. New Haven and London: Yale University Press, 1979.

Cowper, William. *The Poetical Works of William Cowper*, 4th ed., ed. H. S. Milford. 1934. Reprint. London, New York, and Toronto: Oxford University Press, 1959.

Cox, David. *A Treatise on Landscape Painting and Effect in Watercolor*. London, 1813. Reprinted in *The Studio: Special Number*. London, 1922.

Crane, Ronald, ed. *A Collection of English Poems*. New York and London: Harper & Brothers, 1932.

Cummings, Frederick, Allen Staley, and Robert Rosenblum. *Romantic Art in Britain: Paintings and Drawings, 1760–1860*. Philadelphia: Philadelphia Museum of Art, 1968. Catalogue of the 1968 exhibition at Detroit and Philadelphia.

Darwin, Erasmus. *The Botanic Garden*. Part 2. London, 1789 (actually 1791).

De Quincey, Thomas. *The Collected Writings of Thomas De Quincey*. Ed. David Masson. 14 vols. London: A. & C. Black, 1896–97.

Derrida, Jacques. *Of Grammatology*. Trans. Gayatri Spivak. Baltimore: Johns Hopkins University Press, 1976.

Dryden, John. *The Poems of John Dryden*. Ed. James Kingsley. 2 vols. Oxford: Clarendon Press, 1958.

Durrant, Geoffrey. *Wordsworth and the Great System: A Study of Wordsworth's Poetic Universe*. Cambridge: Cambridge University Press, 1970.

Eastlake, Charles. *Contributions to the Literature of the Fine Arts with a Memoir Compiled by Lady Eastlake*. 2d ser. London, 1870.

Eaves, Morris. *William Blake's Theory of Art*. Princeton: Princeton University Press, 1982.

Eitner, Lorenz. *Neoclassicism and Romanticism, 1750–1859*. Englewood Cliffs, N.J.: Prentice-Hall, 1970.

Essick, Robert. *William Blake, Printmaker*. Princeton: Princeton University Press, 1980.

Farington, Joseph. *The Farington Diary [FD]*. Ed. James Grieg. 8 vols. London: Hutchinson, 1923–28.

———. Farington Diary Typescript [FDT]. British Museum, Department of Prints and Drawings.

Field, Barron. "Memoirs of the Life and Poetry of William Wordsworth." Begun 1836. British Museum, Add. MSS 41325.

Finberg, A. J. *The Life of J.M.W. Turner, R.A.* 2d ed., rev. by Hilda F. Finberg. Oxford: Clarendon Press, 1961.

Fink, Z. S. *The Early Wordsworthian Milieu*. Oxford: Clarendon Press, 1958.

Frank, Joseph. "Spatial Form in Modern Literature." In *The Widening Gyre.* New Brunswick, N.J.: Rutgers University Press, 1963. This is a revised edition of the essay that first appeared in three parts in *Sewanee Review* 53 (Spring, Summer, and Autumn 1945).

Free, William. *William Cowper.* New York: Twayne Publishers, 1970.

Freud, Sigmund. *The Interpretation of Dreams.* Ed. and trans. James Strachey. New York: Basic Books, 1972.

Fried, Michael. "Representing Representation: On the Central Group in Courbet's *Studio.*" In *Allegory and Representation: Selected Papers from the English Institute, 1979–80,* ed. Stephen Greenblatt, 94–127. Baltimore: Johns Hopkins University Press, 1981.

Frye, Northrop. *A Study of English Romanticism.* New York: Random House, 1968.

Fuseli, Henry. *Lectures on Painting Delivered at the Royal Academy.* Part I, London, 1801. Part II, London, 1820.

Gage, John. *Color in Turner: Poetry and Truth [CT].* New York and Washington: Frederick A. Praeger, 1969.

————. "Turner and the Picturesque—I." *The Burlington Magazine* 57 (January 1965): 16–25.

Gessner, Solomon. "Letter . . . to . . . M. Fuslin . . . on Landscape Painting." In *New Idylls by Gessner,* trans. W. Hooper. London, 1776.

Gilpin, William. *An Essay upon Prints.* 2d ed. London, 1768.

————. *Observations . . . on . . . the Mountains, and Lakes of Cumberland, and Westmoreland.* 2 vols. London, 1786.

————. *Observations on the River Wye.* 2d ed. London, 1789. First edition published 1782.

————. *Observations on the Western Parts of England.* 2d ed. London, 1808.

————. *Three Essays: On Picturesque Beauty; on Picturesque Travel; and on Sketching Landscape.* London, 1792.

Girard, René. *Deceit, Desire, and the Novel: Self and Other in Literary Structures.* Baltimore: Johns Hopkins University Press, 1965.

Gluck, Gustav. *Die Landschaft von Peter Paul Rubens.* Vienna: Anton Schroll & Co., 1945.

Gombrich, E. H. *Art and Illusion [AI].* Princeton: Princeton University Press, 1969.

————. "Moment and Movement in Art." *Journal of the Warburg and Courtauld Institute* 27 (1964): 293–306.

Goodman, Nelson. *Languages of Art: An Approach to a Theory of Symbols.* 2d ed. Indianapolis: Hackett Publishing Co., 1976.

Gowing, Lawrence. *Turner: Imagination and Reality.* New York: Museum of Modern Art, 1966.

Hagstrum, Jean. *The Sister Arts: The Tradition of Literary Pictorialism from Dryden to Gray*. Chicago: University of Chicago Press, 1958.

Hardie, Martin. *Water-colour Painting in Britain*. Ed. Dudley Snelgrove, Jonathan Mayne, and Basil Taylor. Vol. 2. London, 1967.

Harris, James. *Three Treatises: The First Concerning Art, The Second Concerning Music and Poetry, The Third Concerning Happiness*. 5th ed. London: F. Wingrave, 1792.

Hartman, Geoffrey. *Beyond Formalism*. New Haven and London: Yale University Press, 1970.

————. *Wordsworth's Poetry, 1787–1814*. 1964. Reprint. New Haven: Yale University Press, 1971.

Hawes, Louis, "Constable's Sky Sketches." *Journal of the Warburg and Courtauld Institute* 32 (1969): 344–64.

Haydon, Benjamin Robert. *The Autobiography and Memoirs of Benjamin Robert Haydon [AMH]*. Ed. Tom Taylor and Aldous Huxley. 2 vols. New York, 1927. The pagination is continuous.

————. *The Diary of Benjamin Robert Haydon [DH]*. Ed. Willard Bissell Pope. 5 vols. Cambridge: Harvard University Press, 1960–63.

————. *Lectures on Poetry and Design [LPD]*. Vol. 1, London, 1844. Vol. 2, London, 1846.

Hayes, John. *The Drawings of Thomas Gainsborough*. 2 vols. New Haven and London: Yale University Press, 1971.

Hazlitt, William. *Complete Works of William Hazlitt*. Ed. P. P. Howe. 21 vols. London and Toronto: J. M. Dent and Sons, 1930–34.

Heffernan, James A. W. Review of *The Prose Works of William Wordsworth*, ed. W.J.B. Owen and Jane Northington Smyser. *English Studies* 56 (December 1975): 558–60.

————. *Wordsworth's Theory of Poetry [WTP]*. Ithaca and London: Cornell University Press, 1969.

Heidegger, Martin. "The Origin of the Work of Art." In *Basic Writings*, ed. David Farrell Krell. New York: Harper & Row, 1977.

Herrmann, Luke, and Felicity Owen. *Sir George Beaumont of Coleorton, Leicestershire: A Catalogue of Works by Sir George Beaumont at Leicester Museum and Art Gallery*. No date or place of publication given.

Hilles, Frederick W., and Harold Bloom, eds. *From Sensibility to Romanticism: Essays Presented to Frederick A. Pottle*. New York: Oxford University Press, 1965.

Hirsch, Diana, and the Editors of Time-Life Books. *The World of Turner, 1775–1851*. New York: Time-Life Books, 1969.

Hogarth, William. *The Analysis of Beauty*. Ed. J. Burke. Oxford: Clarendon Press, 1955.

Holcomb, Adele. "'Indistinctness is my fault.' A Letter about Turner from C. R. Leslie to James Lenox." *Burlington Magazine* 114 (1972): 557–58.

Honour, Hugh. *Romanticism*. New York and London: Harper & Row, 1979.

Hunt, John Dixon, ed. *Encounters: Essays on Literature and the Visual Arts*. London: Studio Vista, 1971.

————. *The Figure in the Landscape: Poetry, Painting, and Gardening during the Eighteenth Century*. Baltimore and London: Johns Hopkins University Press, 1976.

————. "Wondrous Deep and Dark: Turner and the Sublime." *The Georgia Review* 30 (Spring 1976): 139–54.

Ingarden, Roman. *The Literary Work of Art: An Investigation on the Borderlines of Ontology, Logic, and Theory of Literature*. Trans. George G. Grabowicz. Evanston, Ill.: Northwestern University Press, 1973.

Johnson, Lee M. *Wordsworth's Metaphysical Verse: Geometry, Nature, and Form*. Toronto: University of Toronto Press, 1982.

Johnson, Samuel. *The Yale Edition of the Works of Samuel Johnson*. 8 vols. to date. New Haven and London: Yale University Press, 1958–69.

Kant, Immanuel. *The Critique of Judgement*. Trans. James Creed Meredith. 1952. Reprint. Oxford: Clarendon Press, 1961.

Kelley, Theresa. "Spirit and Geometric Form: The Stone and the Shell in Wordsworth's Arab Dream." *Studies in English Literature* 22 (Autumn 1982): 563–82.

Kirby, John Joshua. *Dr. Brook Taylor's Method of Perspective Made Easy Both in Theory and Practice*. London, 1754.

Knight, Payne. *An Analytical Inquiry into the Principles of Taste*. 3d ed. London, 1806.

Kroeber, Karl. "Experience as History: Shelley's Venice, Turner's Carthage." *ELH* 41 (1974): 321–39.

————. *Romantic Landscape Vision: Constable and Wordsworth [RLV]*. Wisconsin: University of Wisconsin Press, 1975.

Kroeber, Karl, and William Walling, eds. *Images of Romanticism: Verbal and Visual Affinities*. New Haven and London: Yale University Press, 1978.

Landow, George. *The Aesthetic and Critical Theories of John Ruskin*. Princeton: Princeton University Press, 1971.

————. "The Rainbow: A Problematic Image." In *Nature and the Victorian Imagination*, ed. U. C. Knoepfelmacher and G. B. Tennyson, 341–69. Berkeley and Los Angeles: University of California Press, 1977.

Lea, Sidney. "Wordsworth and His 'Michael': The Pastor Passes." *ELH* 45 (1978): 55–68.

Lee, Rensselaer. *Ut Pictura Poesis: The Humanistic Theory of Painting*. 1942. Reprint. New York: W. W. Norton, 1967.

Leslie, C. R. *Memoirs of the Life of John Constable.* Ed. Johnathan Mayne. London: Phaidon Press, 1951.

Lessing, Gotthold Ephraim. *Laocoön, Nathan the Wise, Minna von Barnhelm.* Trans. W. A. Steel and Anthony Dent; ed. W. A. Steel. 1930. Reprint. London: J. M. Dent & Sons; New York: E. P. Dutton & Co., 1949.

Lindenberger, Herbert. *On Wordsworth's "Prelude."* Princeton: Princeton University Press, 1963.

Lindsay, Jack. *J.M.W. Turner: His Life and Work.* New York, 1966. London: Cory, Adams & Mackay; Greenwich, Conn.: New York Graphic Society, 1966.

Lipking, Lawrence. *The Ordering of the Arts in Eighteenth-Century England.* Princeton: Princeton University Press, 1970.

Locke, John. *An Essay Concerning Human Understanding.* 19th ed. 2 vols. London: T. Longman, 1793.

Malek, James. *The Arts Compared: An Aspect of Eighteenth-Century British Aesthetics.* Detroit: Wayne State University Press, 1974.

Malins, Edward. *English Landscaping and Literature, 1660–1840.* London, New York, and Toronto: Oxford University Press, 1966.

Malton, Thomas. *A Compleat Treatise on Perspective in Theory and Practice: On the True Principles of Dr. Brook Taylor.* 2d ed. London, 1778.

Manwaring, Elizabeth. *Italian Landscape in Eighteenth-Century England.* New York, 1925.

Marin, Louis, "Toward a Theory of Reading in the Visual Arts: Poussin's *The Arcadian Shepherds.*" In *The Reader in the Text*, ed. Susan Suleiman and Inge Crossman, 293–324. Princeton: Princeton University Press, 1980.

Matteson, Lynn R. "The Poetics and Politics of Alpine Passage: Turner's *Snowstorm: Hannibal and his Army Crossing the Alps.*" *Art Bulletin* 42 (September 1980): 385–98.

McFarland, Thomas. *Romanticism and the Forms of Ruin: Wordsworth, Coleridge, and the Modalities of Fragmentation.* Princeton: Princeton University Press, 1981.

Miller, Hillis. "The Stone and the Shell: The Problem of Poetic Form in Wordsworth's Dream of the Arab." In *Mouvements premiers: Etudes critiques offertes à George Poulet*, 125–47. Paris: Librairie Jose Corti, 1972.

Milton, John. *The Complete Poetical Works of John Milton.* Ed. Douglas Bush. Boston: Houghton Mifflin Co., 1965.

Mitchell, W.J.T. *Blake's Composite Art: A Study of the Illuminated Poetry.* Princeton: Princeton University Press, 1978.

———. *Iconology: Image, Text, Ideology.* Chicago: University of Chicago Press, forthcoming 1985.

———, ed. *The Language of Images.* Chicago and London: University of Chicago Press, 1980.

————. "Style as Epistemology: Blake and the Movement Toward Abstraction in Romantic Art." *Studies in Romanticism* 16 (Spring 1977): 145–64.

Monk, Samuel H. *The Sublime: A Study of Critical Theories in Eighteenth-Century England*. 1935. Reprint. Ann Arbor: University of Michigan, 1960.

Moorman, Mary. *William Wordsworth: A Biography. The Early Years, 1770–1803*. Oxford: Clarendon Press, 1957.

New York Graphic Society. *Fine Art Reproductions of Old & Modern Masters*. Greenwich, Conn.: New York Graphic Society, 1968.

Nicolson, Marjorie. *Mountain Gloom and Mountain Glory: The Development of the Aesthetics of the Infinite*. Ithaca, N.Y.: Cornell University Press, 1959.

————. *Newton Demands the Muse: Newton's Opticks and the Eighteenth-Century Poets*. Princeton: Princeton University Press, 1946.

Novak, Barbara. *Nature and Culture: American Landscape and Painting, 1825–1875*. New York: Oxford University Press, 1980.

Noyes, Russell. *Wordsworth and the Art of Landscape*. Bloomington and London: Indiana University Press, 1968.

Onorato, Richard J. *The Character of the Poet: Wordsworth in "The Prelude."* Princeton: Princeton University Press, 1971.

Owen, W.J.B. "The Sublime and the Beautiful in *The Prelude*." *Wordsworth Circle* 4 (Spring 1973): 67–86.

Palmer, Samuel. *Life and Letters of Samuel Palmer*. Ed. A. H. Palmer. London, 1892.

Park, Roy. *Hazlitt and the Spirit of the Age: Abstraction and Critical Theory*. Oxford: Clarendon Press, 1971.

————. "'Ut Pictura Poesis': The Nineteenth-Century Aftermath." *Journal of Aesthetics and Art Criticism* 28 (Winter 1969): 155–76.

Parris, Leslie. *Landscape in Britain c. 1750–1850*. London: Tate Gallery Publications Department, 1973. Catalogue of the Tate Gallery exhibition of 1973–74.

Parris, Leslie, Ian Fleming-Williams, and Conal Shields. *Constable: Paintings, Watercolours & Drawings*. 2d ed. London: Tate Gallery Publications, 1976. Catalogue of the Tate Gallery exhibition of 18 February–25 April 1977.

Paulson, Ronald. *Emblem and Expression: Meaning in English Art of the Eighteenth Century*. Cambridge: Harvard University Press, 1975.

————. "Gainsborough's Landscape Drawings." *Eighteenth Century Studies* 6 (Fall 1972): 106–17.

————. *Literary Landscape: Turner and Constable*. New Haven and London: Yale University Press, 1982.

Peacock, M. L., Jr., ed. *Critical Opinions of William Wordsworth*. Baltimore: Johns Hopkins University Press, 1950.

Peckham, Morse. *Beyond the Tragic Vision: The Quest for Identity in the Nineteenth Century*. New York: George Braziller, 1962.

————. "Constable and Wordsworth." *College Art Journal* 12 (Spring 1953): 196–209.

————. *The Triumph of Romanticism*. Columbia: University of South Carolina Press, 1970.

Plato. *The Republic of Plato*. Trans. Francis MacDonald Cornford. New York and London: Oxford University Press, 1945.

Pope, Alexander. *The Poems of Alexander Pope*. Ed. John Butt. 11 vols. Twickenhom Edition. London: Methuen & Co.; New Haven: Yale University Press, 1951.

Pott, Joseph Holden. *An Essay on Landscape Painting*. London, 1783.

Prest, John. *The Garden of Eden and the Re-Creation of Paradise*. New Haven: Yale University Press, 1981.

Price, Uvedale. *An Essay on the Picturesque*. 1794. Reprinted in *Sir Uvedale Price on the Picturesque*, ed. Sir Thomas Dick Lauder. London, 1842.

Randel, Fred. "Coleridge and the Consciousness of Romantic Nightingales." *Studies in Romanticism* 21 (Spring 1984): 33–55.

Reed, Mark. "Constable, Wordsworth, and Beaumont: A New Constable Letter in Evidence." *Art Bulletin* 64 (September 1982): 481–83.

Reynolds, Graham. *Catalogue of the Constable Collection [CCC]*. Victoria and Albert Museum. London: Her Majesty's Stationary Office, 1973.

————. *Constable's England [CE]*. New York: Metropolitan Museum of Art, 1983. Catalogue of the Metropolitan exhibition of 16 April–4 September 1983.

————. *Turner*. London: Thames and Hudson, 1969.

Reynolds, Sir Joshua. *Discourses on Art [D]*. Ed. Robert Wark. San Marino, Cal.: Huntington Library, 1959.

————. *The Literary Works of Sir Joshua Reynolds*. Ed. Edmund Malone. 3 vols. London, 1819.

Richardson, Jonathan. *The Works of Mr. Jonathan Richardson* [the Elder]. Ed. J. Richardson [the Younger]. London, 1773.

Robinson, Henry Crabb. *Diary, Reminiscences, and Correspondence of Henry Crabb Robinson*. Ed. Thomas Sadler. 3 vols. London, 1869.

————. *Henry Crabb Robinson on Books and their Writers [CRB]*. Ed. Edith J. Morley. 3 vols. London: J. M. Dent and Sons, 1938.

Rogers, Neville. *Shelley at Work: A Critical Inquiry*. Oxford: Clarendon Press, 1956.

Rosenblum, Robert. *Transformations in Late Eighteenth Century Art*. Princeton: Princeton University Press, 1974.

Rossiter, Stuart, ed. *The Blue Guides: England*. 8th ed. London: Ernest Benn Ltd.; Chicago: Rand McNally & Co., 1972.

Rothenstein, John. *An Introduction to English Painting*. New York: W. W. Norton & Co., 1965.

Rousseau, Jean-Jacques. *The Confessions*. Trans. J. M. Cohen. 1954. Reprint. Baltimore: Penguin Books, 1975.

Ruskin, John. *The Diaries of John Ruskin*. Ed. J. Evans and J. H. Waterhouse. 3 vols. Oxford: Clarendon Press, 1956–59.

———. *The Works of John Ruskin*. Ed. E. T. Cook and Alexander Wedderburn. 39 vols. London, 1903–12.

Schultz, Max. "Turner's Fabled Atlantis: Venice, Carthage, and London as Paradisal Cityscape." *Studies in Romanticism* 19 (Fall 1980): 395–417.

Schweizer, Paul. "Constable, Rainbow Science, and English Color Theory." *Art Bulletin* 54 (September 1982): 424–45.

Scott, John. *Critical Essays*. London, 1785.

Shackford, Martha Hale. *Wordsworth's Interest in Painters and Pictures*. Wellesley, Mass.: Wellesley Press, 1945.

Shaftesbury, Earl of [Anthony Ashley Cooper]. *The Moralists*. 2 vols. London, 1732. First published in 1711.

Sheats, Paul. *The Making of Wordsworth's Poetry, 1785–1798*. Cambridge: Harvard University Press, 1973.

Shelley, Percy Bysshe. *Complete Works*. Ed. R. Ingpen and W. E. Peck. 10 vols. London: Ernest Benn, 1926–30.

———. *The Letters of Percy Bysshe Shelley*. Ed. Frederick L. Jones. 2 vols. Oxford: Clarendon Press, 1964.

———. *Shelley's Literary and Philosophical Criticism*. Ed. John Shawcross. London, 1909.

———. *Shelley's Poetry and Prose*. Ed. Donald Reiman and Sharon B. Powers. New York: W. W. Norton, 1977. All Shelley's poems are quoted from this edition.

Sherwin, Paul. *Precious Bane: Collins and the Miltonic Legacy*. Austin and London: University of Texas Press, 1977.

Smyser, Jane Worthington. "Wordsworth's Dream of Poetry and Science: *The Prelude V*." *PMLA* 71 (March 1956): 269–75.

Steiner, Wendy. *The Colors of Rhetoric: Problems in the Relation between Modern Literature and Painting*. Chicago and London: University of Chicago Press, 1982.

Stelzig, Eugene. *All Shades of Consciousness: Wordsworth's Poetry of the Self in Time*. The Hague and Paris: Mouton, 1975.

Summers, David. "Conventions in the History of Art." *New Literary History* 13 (Autumn 1981); 103–25.

Taylor, Basil. *Constable: Paintings, Drawings, and Watercolours*. London: Phaidon Press, 1973.

Thomson, James. *The Complete Poetical Works*. Ed. J. Logie Robertson. London, New York, Toronto, and Melbourne: Oxford University Press, 1908.

Traherne, Thomas. *Poems, Centuries, and Three Thanksgivings*. Ed. Anne
    Ridler. London, New York, and Toronto: Oxford University Press, 1966.
Turner, J. M. W. British Museum Add. Ms. 46151 [TMS]. The manuscripts cov-
    ered by this number are designated alphabetically.
————. *Collected Correspondence of J.M.W. Turner [CCT]*. Ed. John Gage. Ox-
    ford: Clarendon Press, 1980.
————. Sketchbooks of Turner in the British Museum [TSB]. Designated by
    roman numerals. Many of these books contain notes by Turner.
————. *The Sunset Ship: The Poems of J.M.W. Turner*. Ed. Jack Lindsay. Lon-
    don: Evelyn, 1966.
Walpole, Horace. *Anecdotes of Painting*. 4 vols. London, 1771.
Warner, Deborah Jean. "The Landscape Mirror and Glass." *Antiques* 105 (Janu-
    ary 1974): 158–59.
Warren, Robert Penn, ed. *The Rime of the Ancient Mariner, with an Essay*. New
    York: Random House, 1946.
Wasserman, Earl. *Shelley: A Critical Reading*. Baltimore and London: Johns
    Hopkins University Press, 1971.
Waterhouse, Ellis. *Gainsborough*. London: Edward Hulton, 1958.
Watson, J. R. *Picturesque Landscape and English Romantic Poetry*. London:
    Hutchinson Educational, Ltd., 1970.
Watson, Ross. *Joseph Wright of Derby: A Selection of Paintings from the Collec-
    tion of Mr. and Mrs. Paul Mellon*. Washington, D.C.: National Gallery of Art,
    1969. Catalogue of the exhibition 22 November 1969–1 May 1970.
Weiskel, Thomas. *The Romantic Sublime: Studies in the Structure and Psychol-
    ogy of Transcendence*. Baltimore and London: Johns Hopkins University
    Press, 1976.
White, Haydon. "Literature and Social Action: Reflections on the Reflection
    Theory of Literary Art." *New Literary History* 11 (Winter 1980): 363–80.
Wilkinson, Gerald, ed. *Turner's Early Sketchbooks [TES]*. New York: Watson-
    Guptill Publications; London: Barrie & Jenkins, 1972.
————, ed. *Turner's Sketches, 1802–1820 [TS 1802–20]*. New York: Watson-
    Guptill Publications; London: Barrie & Jenkins, 1974.
Wilton, Andrew. *British Watercolours, 1750 to 1850 [BW]*. Oxford: Phaidon
    Press, 1977.
————. *J.M.W. Turner: His Art and Life [TAL]*. New York: Rizzoli International
    Publications, 1979.
————. *Turner and the Sublime [TS]*. London: British Museum Publications,
    1980.
Wittgenstein, Ludwig. *Philosophical Investigation*. Trans. G.E.M. Anscomb.
    Oxford: Basil Blackwell, 1967.
Wlecke, Albert O. *Wordsworth and the Sublime*. Berkeley, Los Angeles, and
    London: University of California Press, 1973.

Wolf, Bryan Jay. *Romantic Re-Vision: Culture and Consciousness in Nineteenth Century American Painting and Literature*. Chicago and London: University of Chicago Press, 1982.

Wordsworth, Dorothy. *Journals of Dorothy Wordsworth*. Ed. Mary Moorman. 2d ed. London and New York: Oxford University Press, 1976.

Wordsworth, William. *The Poetrical Works of William Wordsworth [PW]*. Ed. Ernest De Selincourt and Helen Darbishire. 5 vols. Oxford: Clarendon Press, 1940–49. 2d ed. of vol. 2 rev. by Helen Darbishire, 1952. Except for *The Prelude*, all of Wordsworth's poems are quoted from this edition.

———. *The Prelude: Or, Growth of a Poet's Mind*. Ed. Ernest De Selincourt. 2d ed. rev. by Helen Darbishire. Oxford: Clarendon Press, 1959. The letter A before a book number of *The Prelude* designates the 1805–6 version; when no letter A is used, I am citing the 1850 text. P. or pp. are used to cite material from the introduction, notes, or appendix to this edition.

———. *The Prose Works of William Wordsworth [PrW]*. Ed. W.J.B. Owen and Jane Worthington Smyser. 3 vols. Oxford: Clarendon Press, 1974.

Wordsworth, William, and Dorothy Wordsworth. *The Letters of William and Dorothy Wordsworth [LW]*. Ed. Ernest De Selincourt. 2d ed. rev. by Chester L. Shaver, Mary Moorman, and Alan G. Hill. 6 vols. to date. Oxford: Clarendon Press, 1967–1982.

———. *The Letters of William and Dorothy Wordsworth: The Later Years [LY]*. Ed. Ernest de Selincourt. 3 vols. Oxford: Clarendon Press, 1939. The pagination is continuous.

Ziff, Jerrold. "'Backgrounds, Introduction of Architecture, and Landscape': A Lecture by J.M.W. Turner." *Journal of the Warburg and Courtauld Institute* 26 (1963): 124–47.

———. "J.M.W. Turner on Poetry and Painting." *Studies in Romanticism* 3 (Summer 1964): 193–215.

INDEX

Abrams, M. H., 35, 42n58, 92n38, 104, 140, 187, 207, 208

Absorption. *See* Theatricality and absorption

Addison, Joseph, 3, 14n14, 37, 40n50

Akenside, Mark, 34, 182

Alps, 17–21, 66–67, 122, 128. *See also* Sublimity, Turner, Wordsworth

Alston, Washington, 233

Angle and curve, 28, 187–92, 201–2. *See also* Geometry, Line and color

Angle of vision, 192–200

Apollo, 88

Appleton, Jay, 105, 106

Atmosphere, 201–2, 225; Coleridge on, 143; in Turner, 161–63, 164–66; Turner on, 155–57; Wordsworth on, 156–58. *See also* Line, Sister arts

Augustine, Saint, 65

Autobiography, 104–5, 107, 225; in Constable, 73–75, 77–78, 98–102, 105; mind and nature in, 108, 115; prospect vs. refuge in, 105–7; and self-consciousness, 103, 111–15, 117–20, 135; in Turner, 104; in Wordsworth, 57–61, 64–69, 93, 95, 96, 99–102, 205–6

Bachelard, Gaston, 59n6

Baker, Jeffrey, 101, 185n15

Barrell, John, 3n1, 100, 134n15

Barry, James, 71n16

Batteux, Charles, 207

Beaumont, George, 95, 121, 234; and Constable, 142, 232, 233–34; and Turner, 201, 232–34; and Wordsworth, 13, 155, 167, 233–34

Beckett, R. B., 50, 231n2

Bicknell, Maria, 105, 116–17

Blair, Hugh, 37

Blake, William, xvi, 38n45, 40n50, 49, 75, 134; *French Revolution*, 55; and linearity, 170–71, 174n; "Mad Song," 174; *Marriage of Heaven and Hell*, 54, 88

Bloom, Harold, 16, 104

Boileau, Nicholas, 6n7

Boundaries. *See* Line and color and individual artists

Boydell, John, 47

Breughel, Pieter, 5

Bridgeman, Charles, 7n9

Brisman, Leslie, 158n20

Brown, John "Capability," 8, 12, 13n13, 14, 106

Bryan, Michael, 71

Burges, Thomas, 83n29

Burke, Edmund, on darkness, 106–7, 117; on the French revolution, 203; on painting and poetry, 40–41, 43, 105; on sublimity, 4, 117, 122–23, 188

Burns, Robert, 39

Butlin, Martin, 84n32, 86, 104, 124

Byron, Lord (George Gordon), xvi, 55–56, 65–66, 78

Camera obscura, 45, 46

Canaletto, Antonio, 220n10

Chiaroscuro. *See* Light and shade

Christ, 180

Church, Frederick Edwin, 116

Clark, Kenneth, 75, 85, 89

Claude. *See* Lorrain

Cobham, Lord, 7

Coburn, Kathleen, 222–23

Cohen, Ralph, 9, 11n12

Cole, Thomas, 87, 121, 123n14

Coleorton Hall, 13

Coleridge, Hartley, 112

Coleridge, Samuel Taylor, xiv, xv, xvi,